Public Relations and Neoliberalism

Public Relations and Neoliberalism

The Language Practices of Knowledge Formation

KRISTIN DEMETRIOUS

Oxford University Press is a department of the University of Oxford. It furthers
the University's objective of excellence in research, scholarship, and education
by publishing worldwide. Oxford is a registered trade mark of Oxford University
Press in the UK and certain other countries.

Published in the United States of America by Oxford University Press
198 Madison Avenue, New York, NY 10016, United States of America.

© Oxford University Press 2022

All rights reserved. No part of this publication may be reproduced, stored in
a retrieval system, or transmitted, in any form or by any means, without the
prior permission in writing of Oxford University Press, or as expressly permitted
by law, by license, or under terms agreed with the appropriate reproduction
rights organization. Inquiries concerning reproduction outside the scope of the
above should be sent to the Rights Department, Oxford University Press, at the
address above.

You must not circulate this work in any other form
and you must impose this same condition on any acquirer.

Library of Congress Cataloging-in-Publication Data
Names: Demetrious, Kristin, author.
Title: Public relations and neoliberalism : the language practices of
knowledge formation / Kristin Demetrious.
Description: New York : Oxford University Press, 2022. |
Includes bibliographical references and index.
Identifiers: LCCN 2022021191 (print) | LCCN 2022021192 (ebook) |
ISBN 9780190678395 (hardback) | ISBN 9780190678401 (paperback) |
ISBN 9780190678425 (epub)
Subjects: LCSH: Public relations. | Neoliberalism. | Persuasion (Rhetoric) |
Communication in politics. | Environmentalism. | Mont Pèlerin
Society—History. | Free enterprise—Societies, etc.—History. |
Liberalism—Societies, etc.—History.
Classification: LCC HM1221.R44 D46 2022 (print) | LCC HM1221.R44 (ebook) |
DDC 659.2—dc23/eng/20220707
LC record available at https://lccn.loc.gov/2022021191
LC ebook record available at https://lccn.loc.gov/2022021192

DOI: 10.1093/oso/9780190678395.001.0001

9 8 7 6 5 4 3 2 1

Paperback printed by Marquis, Canada
Hardback printed by Bridgeport National Bindery, Inc., United States of America

CONTENTS

Acknowledgments vii

Introduction: *The Words to Say It* 1

1. The Promise of Prosperity: Transplanting the "New Realities" 11

2. Communicating the "Practical Faith": The Historical Neoliberal and Public Relations Nexus 46

3. "We Need a New Narrative": Neoliberalism and Public Relations Language Practice 75

4. Happiness, Plastic Truth, and the Story of Climate 109

5. "Borderlands": Public Relations and the Broken Moorings of Language 148

6. Airborne: Public Relations, Plasticity, and Pandemic Politics 177

References 205
Index 227

ACKNOWLEDGMENTS

There are many people that help to bring about a book. In this, I am grateful to colleagues at Deakin University for the valuable support that was offered in many different ways: in particular to Geoff Boucher, Janine Little, Lisa Waller, and Andrew Singleton. Lending her expertise in climate change, Alexis Demetrious reviewed the chapter dealing with this, which was much appreciated. I would like to acknowledge Christine Daymon, a friend and colleague who has long been a source of stamina and courage. I am also grateful to Linda Hon at the University of Florida for her interest in my research and her commitment to reform in the field. In nurturing the ideas that are explored in this book, my PhD supervisor and colleague at Deakin University over the early 2000s, Dr Patrick Hughes, was especially significant. Patrick and I shared a view that the production of "theory" in public relations served to valorise the field and divert attention from its real-world impacts, and its critics. Moreover, that there was a great deal more to say about PR's relationship to society, language and the construction of "knowledge." In preparing the manuscript for publication, my editor Meredith Keffer from OUP provided valuable advice, and I thank her for that. Thanks, too, go to the anonymous reviewers for their helpful comments and engagement with the ideas. For personal support, deep appreciation is offered to my family and friends. I thank Jim, Jannes, Alexis and Eugene, Georgia, Viv and Jim, and my siblings, as well as Dorinda Talbot and Caroline Madin who kept me going over what turned out to be a longer journey than anticipated.

Introduction

The Words to Say It

Today, voices raising the ideas of renewal, or an ambivalent social critique in public debate, may become objects caught up in conflict and language games, and fail to make any mark at all. And sometimes there are no voices to be heard; perhaps because there are no words to say. Public debate determines politics, and all too often, politics fails. Public relations has a hand in making this reality. Organized around an all-encompassing, market-based view of the world, a public relations campaign or plan is designed to enclose or eliminate debate. Implementing it may spotlight an array of public fears, problems, and concerns, and develop a tightly controlled message in response, releasing it at strategic points of public debate so that it can control any opposition coming from groups or individuals. From the outset, the intent is to reduce or deactivate resisting ideas, and to lock in thinking and set expectations. In negotiating this approach, public relations conceives of "communication" as a programmatic, instrumental, and ethically neutral process.

In this practice, public language, or the language of political participation, may be emptied of meaning and brutalized, while at the same time being towed into a powerful slipstream of market-based ideas. With sensibilities dulled by the persistent and pervasive messaging in public debate, or crumpling from its barbs and poisonous stings, the public starts to turn away, and in one way or another accepts this reality as inevitable. And within online conditions there are many other patterns and effects, which we are only just beginning to understand. For Graeme Turner, the digital conditions that promised so much, and that produced "communication giants" like Amazon, Facebook, and Google, instead have fallen short:

> Ironically, the much vaunted capacity of the digital world to enable us all to share more effortlessly than ever before has turned out instead to multiply the number of tribalised points of concentration. Furthermore, in relation to the nature and conditions of contemporary democracies, and as the tech giants establish their oligopolies in large part through the marketing of hate, anger, and misinformation as forms of entertainment, there are serious concerns about the future of a democracy that depends upon the existence of an informed and engaged public.[1]

These cultural conditions not only determine what or whose voices are heard, but also form an iron grip on the public imagination, deafening them to the cries of those marginalized individuals and groups entrapped by circumstance and subject to fear, vulnerability, and hardship, or to the science that is critical to the planet's survival. This book is about public relations. But it is also about how we have learned to think, to speak, and to live using the language of public relations, as its practices and ideas are absorbed, and have become inseparable to, contemporary conditions. In this uncoupling, I show how the relationships that joined money, power, and an ideological agenda to the public relations industry impelled a partnership that led to its wider propagation and proliferation in society.

The idea of this book was seeded in my investigations of the public relations industry, and its disproportionate, but sometimes unrecognizable, discursive power and political practices in contemporary society, and their effects and implications. These investigations are seen through a prism that business, government, and any others subscribing to simple

---

1. Turner (2021, 1033).

notions of "public relations" have political purpose, and in pursuit of this, link organizational goals to economic priorities that in turn generate practices with a train of associated "moral considerations, apparently on the assumption that what is warranted is also ethically acceptable."[2] However, arguably, this position could be regarded as somewhat narrow, as there are multiple interpretations of public relations, with no single "correct" approach.[3] While I agree that there are variations in viewpoints in research and practice within the field, public relations belongs to the family of market-based society, and overwhelmingly the underlying assumption of public relations is to respond (quash, silence, discredit) any or all of the public's resistance to the organization's self-interested goal, such as building support for a business-expansion activity. Augmenting this, the dominant discursive power of the public relations industry and its practices have thrived, particularly in the American context, where there has been an uncritical focus on practice, reiterated and reinforced through theory building[4] and an educational approach "that functions as a mechanism for self-perpetuation."[5] For Jacquie L'Etang, "One of the major difficulties of the dominant paradigm is its failure to account adequately for the role of power, but there are other weaknesses too, including the existence of a limited and somewhat prescriptive research agenda."[6] Therefore, despite some pockets of criticality and difference within the field of public relations, its concepts and categories cohere around the magnet of market-based society and work to enclose ideas around these themes.

2. Pieczka (1996, 149).

3. Curtin (2012, 35–36).

4. Magda Pieczka (1996, 144–153) discusses the far-reaching influence of US academic James Grunig's work by citing his role in the "Excellence" study funded by the International Association of Business Communicators in 1985. She argues that this study put "the answers before the questions" and defined public relations in terms of systems theory based on a predominantly functionalist approach that has organizational self-interest at its core.

5. Pieczka (1996, 143).

6. L'Etang (2009, 14).

A central claim of my 2013 book, *Public Relations, Activism and Social Change: Speaking Up*, which informs this work, is that the ethical breaches of the public relations industry are systemic, and not accidental or unplanned.[7] Rather, a powerful communication template propelled by the public relations industry served the neoliberal agenda to create political diversion, division, and hegemony at the same time. This idea was developed from, and depends on, the theoretical foundations of "intrinsic public relations" and "extrinsic public relations" practices, to understand its relational and ethical implications. Apropos of that, public relations, an instrument of early market neoliberalism, has been used continuously into the twenty-first century, and produces, assembles, and polices a discursive monoculture to both keep the subject in and to keep out new statements that might lead them to alternative views.[8] The idea of extrinsic and intrinsic public relations practices to understand public relations language, commonly understood as "spin," has a heuristic value to show how it may not just create, but maintain complex cultures of control through which people consent to these conditions, or hegemony.

The analysis of unethical public language practices as "extrinsic and intrinsic public relations" draws on a Foucauldian archaeological analysis of discourse in the hope that it will yield deeper and more rigorous knowledge. This stands in contrast to some public relations research that is based on what Foucault refers to as the conventional history of ideas. Limiting to such an approach within the field would concentrate, for example, on lists of facts, and chronologies of public relations campaigns, planning, tactics, events, and sectors, and would be interested in establishing continuities or "beginnings and ends" that might inform explanatory theories.[9] So while there is considerable value in detailed historical work that seeks to understand and undermine the scourge of "spin," for example Margot Opdycke Lamme and Karen Miller Russell's (2010) historical analysis of

---

7. Demetrious (2013, 73).

8. Demetrious (2013, 30).

9. Foucault (1972, 137).

public relations, which explicitly rejects ideas of progress or evolutionism to avoid "the patterning, or colligation, of history," nonetheless, this approach remains incomplete because it is concerned with the variations of the dominant systems.[10]

In the same way, there are weaknesses in taking a solely Foucauldian approach which, by looking for general rules of discourse, could overlook the significance of temporal phenomena or specific conditions that affect the speaking subject.

To address the limitations in both these approaches, this book furthers that 2013 project by opening the argument in several important ways: first, by redescribing historical ideas about public relations and its relationship to society, and second, by looking for discursive rules which run through bodies of discourse. This provides a rich, complex understanding of power and addresses the limitations of both an archaeological and a conventional approach.

As such, I focus on a key temporal moment that occurred in 1947 in Switzerland, at the first meeting of a small organization championing free enterprise, the Mont Pèlerin Society. The Mont Pèlerin Society set in motion the movement of neoliberal meaning that promoted the idea of free enterprise as indispensable to human freedom, a powerful convergence at "the level of *sense* and the level of *reference*" that formed an ordering of ideas, that served to move together history and fiction.[11] The Mont Pèlerin Society's founder and president, noted Austrian economist Friedrich Hayek, imagined a select but diverse transnational group, who would work in concert to elevate these seemingly outdated ideas, in an intellectual climate that favored socialism and collectivism. In this, I argue that the extent to which public relations language practices are entwined with and rely on this relationship is only just being understood, especially in the development of a powerfully but largely invisible language structure that was used extensively to describe and to redescribe the extrinsic and intrinsic contradictions of market society for the public. The

---

10. Lamme and Russell (2010, 282).

11. Ricoeur (2009, 274).

extraordinary doctrines developed within this crucible offer not just a cultural phenomenon and marker, but a way to interpret many articulations in mainstream public relations and to understand their larger significance for public language and debate.

In attempting to develop a new approach to "why" and "how" this has come to be, my research has been richly informed by the thesis that a modular form of market-based language is colonizing public discourse and is having a profoundly stifling effect. Uwe Poerksen's *Plastic Words* puts forward the idea that zombie plastic words—innocuous, empty, or hollow-sounding, like "communication," "development," and "identity,"— are neatly transported into different discursive settings, but when this relocation involves the occupation of a higher sphere, like science for example, they assume "the semblance of generally applicable truths."[12] While the interior truth of plastic words may not be apparent, nonetheless they are busily at work, like a corporate takeover of language, acquiring new assets in fields and association, and from there building new synergies. Poerksen's work shows that the proliferation of plastic words—seemingly mundane or benevolent—threatens public debate as a nourishing communicative and social space. But while Poerksen provides an important set of ideas around mobile, imprecise, pliant plastic words, he does not focus on the reason for their rapid global proliferation in late modern society. In fact, he states, "[i]t is as though there were a place somewhere in the world where these words were being released at intervals, as though at an unknown place there existed a factory releasing them complete from its assembly line, or as if they were coming into being simultaneously in many different places."[13] It is precisely on this point that this work builds. I contend that Poerksen's ideas regarding the assemblage and impetus for plastic words is the thick entwinement between public relations and neoliberalism. In taking up this line of argument, I explore the significance of the communicative relationship between the two, and the consequences, which I argue are largely underestimated. While significant gestures have

---

12. Poerksen (1995, 4).

13. Poerksen (1995, 1).

been made in understanding neoliberalism as an unwieldy, transnational, free-market collective, centrally united by a fierce opposition to collectivism, the theorization around how language is harnessed in this support of their complex obstructive agenda—especially in different social and political contexts—and in relation to the public relations industry, is incomplete. As such, this work attempts to rethink and provide ideas that reinterpret and respond to this phenomenon. Informed and shaped by public relations modes and practices, neoliberalism's grip as a "common sense" way of being in the world has been naturalized in everyday life. More specifically then, the focus is on the ways in which neoliberalism's motivating ideas and precepts have infiltrated and radically transformed culture and practice, and what the effects of this may be. These are important, ambitious, and urgent questions. For as Turner argues: "as evidence mounts of the political fragility of the democratic state in the present, a public-facing cultural studies has much to contribute to the urgent task of investigating the function of populism, its relation to the power and influence of the communication platforms, and their transformation of the content and practice of formal and informal politics."[14] Therefore my arguments go beyond the concept of singular plastic words to understand how they assemble into narratives which construct irreducible public relations realities, an explanation which I argue has been largely overlooked in many evaluations of public relations.

This book focuses on the impasses of public debate, not only to analyze why this is happening, but to show how this repeated problem—this scourge—can be thought about in new ways. This is important because dissent and a variety of styles of debate and public language define a layered participatory democracy that is interested in fairness and justice, and marks it as distinct from a narrow market-based model focused on competition and growth. Despite there being many theories and strands to the argument, I believe they cohere strongly around the central thesis, which is that the combined forces of neoliberalism and public relations have become absorbed in public language and imagination, to the extent

---

14. Turner (2021, 1034).

that they have impoverished public debate in ways that threaten our humanity and the planet's survival. I attempt to offer a complex and nuanced picture highlighting the ways in which public relations, not only as an industry, but also as a mode and style of being and relating in the world, seeps into and affects all areas of life: professional, corporate, domestic, political, activist, and technological. And the metastasis of neoliberal meaning into so many realms has vastly different ramifications for society and individuals. I hope that this adjusted focus, looking at the confluences and contradictions, opens potential for critical work in the communicative field. Quite apart from this book, I hope others will be stimulated to seek out *Plastic Words*, to gain insights into the ways that the "said" and "unsaid," the benign, and the ordinary implant public discourse and insinuate meaning toward a market-based view of the world in many expected and unexpected settings.[15]

The first three chapters in this book lay the communicative, historical, and cultural ground for the argument. In Chapter 1, I discuss the combined forces of public relations and neoliberalism, and the communicative conditions that have led to a stalemate in public debate, delimiting the possibility of inclusive and informed dialogue and deliberation in contemporary democracies. In tackling this, I unpack what I mean by both neoliberalism and public relations, and discuss the significance of this critical nexus for the structuring of language practices that control and shape subjectivities. In Chapter 2, I map the historical connections in public relations and neoliberalism and canvass the powerful network of relationships between the free market proselytizers and the public relations industry, as it emerged in the 1930s, 1940s, and 1950s. Central is how key figures, like Friedrich Hayek and Ludwig von Mises, emerged from the neoliberal hothouse of the Mont Pèlerin Society to intersect with US businessmen in the burgeoning public relations industry, and what effects this may have had for language practice. Chapter 3 establishes the argument that neoliberalizing ways are now found in all areas of communicative life through language structures and practices. It discusses

15. Poerksen (1995).

specific discursive constructs, like narrative, that have been harnessed to kindle the flame of neoliberal meaning in a long-term gradual process. Implanted with plastic words, these "neonarratives" are used in a range of public relations settings and deployed in the language games used to secure a share of the public's mind, memory, and imagination. But as I have discussed, their impact is much more extensive than this.

The following two chapters focus on two of the most pressing global issues and public debates of present time: human-induced climate change and the human rights of people seeking to become members of a nation-state through refugee status, political asylum, and immigration. In Chapter 4, I examine the public relations industry's significant role in a long-standing campaign to entrench and enable the practice of climate change denial, with a focus on the communicative practices that legitimize the ongoing and widespread disavowal of the reality of human-induced climate change. Arguing that climate change denial has entailed a relentless and muscular campaign, the chapter shows how public relations and neoliberal forces have actively contributed to the shaping of a public relations–inflected narrative: one that takes in plastic words such as "information" and "environment," whose ambiguous meanings are rendered apparently innocuous, and even benign or positive. The chapter reflects on how the elasticity of such plastic words is exploited to serve the aim of discrediting evidence-based climate science. Climate change denial as a knowledge formation has successfully undermined reasoned debate about mitigating anthropogenic climate change, by creating a semblance of discursive coherence around the idea. This, in turn, encourages an optimistic understanding of a world whose changing climate is no cause for alarm, and whose market-driven creativity is imperative for celebrating, while also privatizing and profiting from "the environment." The chapter thereby highlights the ways in which neoliberal reason, interwoven with public relations language practices, is systematically embedded in the public imagination, in ways that enable cultures of misinformation to proliferate, as well as to suppress and misdirect public debate.

Chapter 5 discusses the ways in which human rights matters on the edges of the nation-state are shaped by language, meaning-making, and neoliberalism in relation to the idea of "borderlands." "Borderlands," as a space, straddles and intersects with two meanings. The first is a harsh, real, physical space, subject to law and regulation. The second is a liminal conceptual space, or a third space which refugees, asylum seekers, people seeking to immigrate, and stateless people occupy as "outsiders within."[16] It is a place of exclusion, transition, and dislocation, where two different realities juxtapose on the edges of the nation-state. I argue that, in public debates, these realities are submerged as interpretations of the world increasingly intersect with neoliberalism and public relations practices to narrow cultural dispositions. One of the characteristics of this debate is its nebulousness and lack of form as a unity. This chapter takes a different stance, by probing the spaces in which public relations, detached from institutional sites, is working more broadly in metastatic ways which affect the cultural flows in human rights and social justice matters. Specifically, I am interested, not just in this mono-thinking and its effects, but also in how things might change to awaken interest and the anticipation of change and possibility.

Finally, in Chapter 6, I discuss how the pandemic has focused a bright light on the failures in public language, while simultaneously providing impetus for changes in contemporary communicative conditions that suggest ways forward. Public debate, now subject to oversimplification and debasement by populist antagonism and jeering incivility passed off as political struggle, has proliferated since the global health crisis, but is being challenged within unexpected political settings. This is not a solution-based book, but in this chapter, I offer a stance that acknowledges the complexity and fragility of the communicative space, and the nuanced ways in which language can be used to shape social and cultural formation, to prise open possibility and provide a way of speaking about language that may assist in countering its deadening effects. As such, it looks at how public language is remaking itself, and how individuals and groups are interpreting positions from this new stance.

---

16. Norma Elia Cantu and Aida Hurtado describe the layered knowledge for people living between borders as an "outsider within" (2012, 7).

1

The Promise of Prosperity

Transplanting the "New Realities"

In hindsight, the communicative conditions of the late twentieth century supporting public deliberation and debate precipitated some pivotal action.[1] Giving rise to the politics of race, gender, and sexuality, as well as civil, green, and peace movements, the 1960s and 1970s opened new spaces for critique and set the groundwork for important reform. The economic sphere also succumbed to these dynamics. In 1986, for example, a moratorium on commercial whaling came into effect that changed the course of marine conservation for this species, some on the verge of extinction.[2] In 1987, heeding urgent scientific advice, global action[3] mobilized decisively

---

1. "New realities": see Drucker (1989, 3).

2. It was not, however, a universal ban. Today, "Iceland, Norway and Japan continue to partake in commercial whaling, in spite of the International Whaling Commission 1986 ban on this practice, citing cultural or scientific reasons for this continuation" (Cunningham et al. 2012, 5).

3. Prather et al. (1996, 551) describes the coalition of action that formed to slow the ozone-depleting chemicals stemming from rapid free-market growth: "The threat to the global ozone layer posed by CFCs and related halocarbons has been dispelled because, since the early 1970s, the global community has followed a path of scientific understanding, public awareness, environmental activism and boycotts, national regulations, industry studies of CFC substitutes and, finally, an international agreement—the 1987 Montreal Protocol on Substances that Deplete the Ozone Layer. Without this sequence of events, which culminated first in restricted use of CFCs and later in a complete phase-out of these chemicals, ozone depletion would be worse than it is today and the global atmosphere would have been committed to a very different future over most of the next century."

to avert the catastrophic depletion of the ozone layer brought about by the reckless use of chemicals, such as chlorofluorocarbons (CFCs), used in mundane consumer goods like aerosol spray cans, foam, air conditioners, and refrigerators.[4] This was accomplished despite the chemical industry's challenge of the phase-out of the potent substances.[5] And in 1998, protection for the Antarctic came into force.[6] Rich with minerals, including coal and iron ore, and oil and gas, the pristine continent was under threat from a pact that would have opened up mining and drilling, but it is now protected by an international agreement.[7]

From today's standpoint, such momentous shifts in global policy settings may seem remarkable, as some of the most important discussions society needs to have about our place as human beings and as a planet appear to have reached a stalemate. Indeed, the mediated spheres in democratic society designated to lift ideas and public views seem evermore distanced from the voiceless and the neglected, and evermore coveted as fertile ground for political and commercial purposes. These calculated interventions have complex implications. They serve as a vehicle, not just for shaping the public's political opinions and setting the tenor of debate, but for cultivating allegiances. Once the public is subdivided into fixed categories, complex issues that affect us all can be condensed into simplified messages, stripped of nuance, and released strategically to unflold as a new reality. And this referential process may support an intensifying intolerance and incivility. Inflammatory, mocking, and obstructive styles of public debate contribute to feelings of powerlessness and disappointment with deliberative processes in democracy to work for

---

4. Australian Government (2021).

5. A "vicious" industry response to this aerosol boycott and ban included: "personal attacks, blacklisting, and disparagement. CFC manufacturers paid for full-page newspaper advertisements questioning scientific findings, and many newspapers and trade journals covered the story" (Andersen et al. 2018, 411).

6. Australian Government (2021a).

7. The Convention for the Regulation of Antarctic Mineral Resource Activites was replaced by the Madrid Protcol, 1991 (Australian Government 2021b).

the common good.[8] This may be compounded when public censure fails to moderate, reign in, or condemn extreme incivility, as might be expected.[9] Once these unruly conditions are normalized, journalists, politicians, and media commentators tend to present complex ideas as reductive and to ignore the chain of interacting social and ethical effects they might generate, and instead provide unwitting consent for this division and, sometimes, rage. In doing so, they make this simplified world seemingly new, and more real, while distracting us from other ways in which life can be rich and meaningful, so it seems less real. The hardening of political positions into divides may serve to stifle not only the imagination, but ways of exploring language together to work through humanity's shared predicament and struggle. Of course, that is the point. But how did it happen and why did society let it happen? And is it possible to break the deadlock and respond to this failure in public debate in more than sporadic, isolated, and fragmented ways?

Public relations language practices and texts embed neoliberal values in everyday vernacular to achieve these conditions. From the personal to the political, and in fields as diverse as education, social work, and religion,[10]

---

8. Thomas Christiano (1997, 243), discusses deliberative democracy as a process "grounded in substantial public deliberations" where arguments for and against, that are calibrated to an understanding of the common good, are ventilated. He says this conception contrasts to that of interests groups jostling on their own behalf or for elitist forces (Christiano 1997, 243).

9. In Donald J. Trump's candidacy for the US presidency, there was an unexpected tolerance for his provocative and seemingly deliberate strategy to propagate, sow, and broadcast division with his public statements. This receptivity was attributed to Trump's presidential aura and his market-inflected populist style of messaging. See Demetrious (2020).

10. See Stephen J. Ball's (2016, 1046–1047) discussion of the reworking of caring professions like education. He points out that, rather than discussing neoliberalism in narrow economic or political terms, "I will discuss interpersonal relations, identity and subjectivity, how we value ourselves and value others, how we think about what we do, and why we do it."

In a similar way, Nathan Schneider (2007, 8), discusses religion and neoliberalism and remarks that it is "much more than an economic theory. Once in place, it becomes a totalizing system that brings more and more aspects of society under the umbrella of markets, with the markets as the only remaining ends in themselves." While for Christian Stark (2011, 59) the colonization of non-market fields like social work by neoliberal thought has enormous consequences for the way in which it is conceptualized and implemented, by placing emphasis on the "amelioration of negative social and economic consequences [. . .] [whereas] a central aim of social work

together, these forces produce a closed discourse focused on the economy, competition, growth, and progress.[11] And the overwhelmingly instrumental force of neoliberalism, interacting with public relations modes and styles, disables or obstructs the possibility of engaging with language in its arguably most significant purpose as a social, relational activity, in which meanings are negotiated and struggled over by interlocutors. Effects of such practices undermine the communicative role of language in democratic society, by limiting or bypassing opportunities for critical intervention and questioning.[12]

Failures in public debates, such as those that are drawn out, divisive, confused, and that only arrive at a stalemate, may occur when neoliberalism combines as an ideology and as language practice to intervene in meaning-making. In this case its modes of discourse are mobilized to create categories of social control, known as "publics."[13] However, identifying and managing "publics" is not just a convenient way of grouping individuals

must be the capacity to resist any further worsening of the basic social conditions in the form of cuts in social service."

11. The ubiquity of networked communication in society has counterintuitive impacts for Jodi Dean (2008, 102): "The proliferation, distribution, acceleration, and intensification of communicative access and opportunity, far from enhancing democratic governance or resistance, results in precisely the opposite, the postpolitical formation of communicative capitalism."

12. Jodi Dean (2008, 104) coins the term "communicative capitalism," referring to this collective depoliticization: "Communicative capitalism designates that form of late capitalism in which values heralded as central to democracy take material form in networked communications technologies. Ideals of access, inclusion, discussion, and participation come to be realized in and through expansions, intensifications, and interconnections of global telecommunications. But instead of leading to more equitable distributions of wealth and influence, instead of enabling the emergence of a richer variety in modes of living and practices of freedom, the deluge of screens and spectacles undermines political opportunity and efficacy for most of the world's peoples."

13. US public relations theorists Denis L. Wilcox and Glen T. Cameron reveal how an opportunistic leveraging of "triggering events" can help build support from "publics" and unleash desired behaviors (2012, 171). "Public relations practitioners should spend more time thinking about what behaviours they are trying to motivate in target publics than about what information they are communicating to those publics. Professionals should build triggering events into their planning to cause people to act on their latent willingness to behave in a certain way." See also Hughes and Demetrious (2006, 99), who argue that there are essentialist assumptions brought to bear in the composite of "publics," which are likely to include the problems with which they are associated, and the ways in which they are likely to react.

for benign purposes. These practices not only cultivate, but privilege, in a long-term preparatory mode, certain ways of thinking, working, relating, being, and even imagining the world. Instilling such passivity in the public is highly political. It persuades that some people matter more than others, and ensures that certain ideas, events, and agendas enjoy high visibility, while others are actively marginalized or pass quietly from view. While resistance or advocating for change in its many forms is a dynamic response in a democratic political system, public relations language strategies and practices informed by the discourses of neoliberalism aim to dominate communication. This is because their broadly monolithic and monologic modes and styles, and their distinctive lexicon, which are so resolutely rehearsed, replicated, and reviewed, pervade all aspects of an individual's life. The result is that opportunities for discursive struggle, for questioning or interrogating those forms of communicating, are rendered confused, weak, and ineffective.[14]

The study of public relations and neoliberalism opens a rich seam of new material to understand and piece together this nexus. From this standpoint, I seek to show how neoliberalism was discursively made, beyond the narrow lens of an economic theory, to understand and explore the symbiosis with public relations, and how it has worked to propel and transform wider social and cultural conditions into the all-encompassing reality that citizens feel powerless or disinclined to confront. The long-term advocacy of the neoliberal project by the public relations industry is embedded within institutions and networks of power in business, politics, and media. In promoting an economic growth agenda, systematic public relations language practices are ready and primed to manage the intrinsic contradictions that reveal small openings in neoliberal logic, to quietly maneuver the subject back to a desirable, problem-free, and apparently inevitable account of how things are and how they will or should be. These

---

14. PR Watch exposes the misdeeds and "hidden activities of secretive, little-known mega-firms such as Hill & Knowlton, Burson-Marsteller and Ketchum PR—the 'invisible men' who control our political debates and public opinion, twisting reality and protecting the powerful from scrutiny" (2021).

globally dominant language practices, and their hallmark vocabulary of soothing, idealized words, work in the current cultural conditions to maximize their impact via prevailing media platforms. In tandem, other more extreme forms of the PR repertoire work to extinguish opposition or dissent that threatens to expose the deeper contradictions running through neoliberal logic.[15]

In this chapter, I argue that public relations language strategies and practices are inescapably entangled with neoliberalism, with troubling and urgent implications. Current conditions have led to neoliberalism's spread, its seepage, into many unexpected discursive realms that prop up the dominance of market-based ideas and undercut individual and collective appetite and capacity for reform, or interest in debating the pressing issues of today. In untangling this cultural lassistude, I trace the provenance of these language practices and strategies to the twentieth century, examining the ways in which highly influential public relations, intellectual, business, and political networks have helped to propel and embed them in the vernacular. Mapping out key neoliberal ideas and reason, I also reflect on the authorization of public relations as a discourse to understand what gave these ideas extraordinary mobility and reach. But importantly, I consider how communication activities and the industries that produce this language work as both a self-referencing structure and as a product. In this, the Habermasian idea of the public sphere, as a communicative realm of action central to the meaning making and political process in society, is a crucial site to examine. These strands of inquiry may go some way to show how the public relations and neoliberal nexus maintains its powerful thrall to dominate society in the twenty-first century and contribute to the failures of public debate.

---

15. The notions of intrinsic and extrinsic public relations practices are drawn from Foucault's discussion of the contradictions contained within a single discourse, and the opposition to a discourse posed by different discursive formations, respectively (Foucault 1972, 149–156). They are further developed in my (2013) book-length exploration of the specific practices harnessed by the public relations industry in its attempts to secure discursive coherence for its communicative practices, and in fending off alternative or oppositional voices and coalitions.

For US management theorist Peter F. Drucker, by 1989, the new century and the future had already arrived,[16] one in which there were sharp divides. On the one hand, the new world was complicated by economic, social, and political paradoxes, disappearances, and confrontations, but on the other hand, there was enormous opportunity, growth, and expansion.[17] His book, *The New Realities*, makes the point that, at the time, these shifting contours in the terrain may seem quite unremarkable and slip into place unannounced:

> History too knows such divides. They also tend to be unspectacular and are rarely much noticed at the time. But once these divides have been crossed, the social and political landscape changes. Social and political climate is different and so is social and political language. *There are new realities.*[18]

A key occupation of this book is to understand why some debates are heard or not heard, and why some voices are louder than others. Why is there disenchantment in contemporary communicative conditions,

---

16. In his book, Drucker (1989) provides a sweeping analysis of the changing transnational dynamics to affect business, politics, and society, including the knowledge industries and rise of data-based technology and information-based businesses, such as public relations. While Drucker identifies a critical disjuncture in the economic development leading to the degradation of the environment, he nonetheless is deeply wedded to the idea of world economy and the primacy of market maximization and does not reflect much on these contradictions as such. Drucker writes: (1989, 3–5): "Some time between 1965 and 1973 we passed over such a divide and entered the 'next century.' We passed out of creeds, commitments, and alignments that had shaped politics for a century or two. We are in political *terra incognita* with few familiar lands to guide us." In the future "the educated person" would be the product that shapes society and fuels the economy (Drucker 1989, 236). Hence a "knowledge society," for Drucker sees education as capital investment; "a specific type of mass education, which can increase productivity and competitivness of a given national economy" (Krašovec 2013, 75).

17. In 1989, the idea of the state with indissoluble borders abated somewhat when "the Berlin Wall collapsed unexpectedly, followed by the socialist Soviet Union, and the cold war bipolar global order" (Beck 2009, n.p.). As a corollary, in the late 1980s, the collapse "created the conditions for reforms developed in accordance with the economic doctrine of the Chicago School, for all of Eastern Europe" (Piotr and Toporowski 2020, 4).

18. Drucker (1989, 3).

and with what? And how can citizens and academics puncture "the new realties" to imagine an alternative way to imagine, speak, and live?

THE NEOLIBERAL PROJECT

Neoliberalism is a set of beliefs in the liberal tradition[19] that is grounded in the centrality of free markets, government in a reductive role as an administrator, and economic calculation as the basis of determining or judging the value of all human, social, and political activities.[20] The roots of neoliberalism, and its various inflections as the first wave,[21] can be traced to the period between the world wars, that includes the stock market crash of 1929 that led to the Great Depression.[22] These specific events contextualized the establishment, in 1947, of the Mont Pèlerin Society, a transnational intellectual hub that gave rise to a distinctive partnership with US public relations, both as an industry and language practice. Initiated by Austrian economist and thinker Friedrich August von Hayek, the founders of the Mont Pèlerin Society were interested in advancing the neoliberal project as a catalyst in "constructing and deploying elaborate social machinery designed to collect, create, debate, disseminate, and mobilize neoliberal ideas."[23] A hot house, the Society built strong links to

---

19. For Philip Mirowski, neoliberalism works as a "thought collective" and is everywhere, so for most people it is invisible (2015); Brown (2015); Davies (2014).

20. Jamie Peck suggests that neoliberalism as a free-market "project" is porous and absorbed into a myriad of social and cutlral settings, intersecting with "many authors, many birthplaces" (2010, 39, 39–81). Public debate is a crucial site to propel the political ideas of neoliberalism: see Demetrious and Surma (2019).

21. Rowe et al. aruge neoliberalism comes in "three waves": "ordo-liberalism, radical liberalism, and post-neoliberalism" (2019, 150–155). They locate the first wave in 1920s–1930s in which two distinct strands competed in ideas; the second in the 1970s and 1980s when the theories of Friedrich Hayek and Milton Friedman were influential; and the third wave in the global financial crisis of 2007–2008 "and the following decade which ushered in a particular form of alt-right politics in the United States, Australia, parts of Europe and Britain."

22. "Public relations grew in fits and starts" from this point, according to Tedlow (1976, 26).

23. Mirowski (2015, 432). The Society included a range of charismatic individuals, including those involved in or closely connected to the institutional practices of public relations, who

powerful business, academic, and political networks, as well as focusing on the spread, uptake, and popularization of neoliberal ideas. Supporters of the neoliberal project—including moneyed and influential individuals, economists, academics, public relations practitioners, journalists, and media commentators—while not unified in their views, did share an antipathy for social orders guided by government interventionist economic policies and social welfare programs. These were regarded as suppressing both the freedom and creativity of the individual, and the energy and impersonal force of the all-knowing market, defined primarily as an "engine for epistemic truth."[24] Many of them, as I will show, also understood the powerful role of public language in building the realities they envisioned.

In the following decades, the second wave of neoliberalism broadly secured discursive and ideological dominance as a radicalized economic theory at work in global political settings.[25] In tandem, it attached to university departments of economics in Europe, the United States, and the United Kingdom.[26] Augmenting this was the rise of powerful private research-focused institutes or think tanks that represented and promoted neoliberal ideas within political and social networks.[27] With economic instability characterizing the 1970s, neoliberal politics gained increasing visibility and appeared to offer ready "solutions" to what became regarded as

---

exercised extraordinary reach and influence in the insinuation of neoliberalism into daily life during this period and in the decades that followed. See Chapter 2 for an exploration of this partnership in further detail.

24. Mirowski (2019, 7).

25. Rowe et al. (2019, 154) argue that second-wave neoliberalism was pushed into non-economic settings.

26. According to Mirowski (2018), these included University of Chicago Economics, the London School of Economics, l'Institut universitaire des hautes études internationales at Geneva, St. Andres, Scotland, University of Freiburg, the Virginia School, and George Mason University. See also Stedman Jones (2012, 87).

27. A surge of think tanks was established in the 1940s and 1950s, including the American Enterprise Institute and the Foundation for Economic Education in the United States and the Institute of Economic Affairs in the United Kingdom; and the second wave in the 1970s, including the Centre for Policy Studies and the Adam Smith Institute in the United Kingdom, and the Heritage Foundation and the Cato Institute in the United States (Stedman Jones 2012, 134; see also 134–179). See also Chapter 2 and Chapter 4.

the failures of welfare economics, or Keynesianism.[28] By the early 1980s, and with articulate and committed championing of free-market policies by global political leaders, including Margaret Thatcher in the United Kingdom, Ronald Reagan in the United States,[29] and Hawke and Keating governments in Australia,[30] neoliberal ideas began to direct and shape economic and social policies. In the early 1990s, the increasing shift of economic activity away from labor and wages to capital and the financial sector saw corporate profits grow and executive salaries rise.[31] During this period, Rowe et al. argue that neoliberalism acquired "pejorative radical connotations" with "authoritarianism, class warfare and entrenched inequality."[32] Since then, governments have acted to restructure government and public services according to an economized model—settings that served to entrench and embolden the neoliberal project.

A third wave of neoliberalism can be traced to the global financial crisis of 2007–2008, which dramatically exposed the inherent weaknesses of financialization and the idea that markets know best, and work best, unfettered and unaccountable.[33] This catastrophe should have sounded the

---

28. Harvey (2005, 22–24). Policies of monetarism and industry deregulation were implemented by the Labour government (under Prime Minister James Callaghan) in the United Kingdom, and by the Democrats (under President Jimmy Carter) in the United States, respectively (Stedman Jones 2012, 216–217). To understand its historical continuities and ruptures, Elizabeth Humphrys periodizes neoliberalism in Australia in four key stages: "1. A proto-neoliberal stage from 1973–1983. 2. A vanguard neoliberal stage from 1983–1993. 3. A piecemeal neoliberalisation stage from 1993–2008. 4. A neoliberal crisis stage from 2008 onwards". (Humphrys 2019, 76–77). The "proto-neoliberal" stage in Australia saw the newly elected Labor government undertake significant "economic structural adjustment" to respond to a "prolonged economic slump" with "widespread consensus" across its own party and with support of "the union movement" (Humphrys 2019, 99).

29. Stedman (2012, 254–269); neolibralism was associated with "Reaganomics, Thatcherism, monetarism, and a rollback of the post-war welfare state" (Rowe et al. 2019, 154).

30. Humphrys (2019, 100) posits that some of the "vanguard neoliberal stage" reforms implemented in Australia by the Hawke and Keating governments are considered "paradigmatic of neoliberalism," such as floating the dollar, providing foreign banks entry, the corporatization and privatization of public assets and agencies, and welfare targeting, among others.

31. Peetz (2018, 34).

32. Rowe et al. (2019, 154).

33. In Stedman Jones's words: "These policy failures [to control the irresponsible practices of bankers; to encourage excessive borrowing; to regulate the financial markets] illustrate beyond doubt that the faith in markets had become divorced from reality" (2012, 341).

death knell for neoliberalism. But instead it "bounced back with increased vigour, albeit with greater contradictions."[34] These conditions further entrenched neoliberal reason in public discourse, as governments told instructive "stories" about how the imposition of austerity measures would lead to the restoration of the authority of the market.[35] This remarkable turnaround highlights the power of the neoliberal project's constitutive language strategies and practices to delimit the public imaginary. However, this was not the only distinctive characteristic of the third wave. Rowe et al. argue "the following decade . . . ushered in a particular form of alt-right politics[36] in the United States, Australia, [and] parts of Europe and Britain." The rise of far-right politics intersected, not only with turbo-charged conditions of neoliberalism, but also digital anominity and the rise of authoritarian subcultures "masquerading as libertarianism."[37]

NEOLIBERALISM: A CONTESTED TERM

Is "neoliberalism" a robust idea to understand the world, or little more than a rubric covering a range of disconnected and disgruntled analyses? While some scholars have derided the elasticity of the term and disputed its adequacy, others[38] grapple productively with such objections and yet defend its usefulness. Their defense is on the grounds that, although the term is contingent and provisional, it identifies a hegemonic process, and serves as a useful "prompt to find, specify, and learn from adaptive processes,

---

34. Holborow (2015, 34).

35. Kelsey, Mueller, Whittle, and KhosraviNik (2016, 4).

36. "Alt-right" is a loose reference to far-right politics, but for Andrew Jones, "leading up to the 2016 American election [it] specifically referred to an alt-right American political movement that drew upon racial supremacy, anti-feminism and right-wing populism connected with the Republican party" (2017, 3).

37. Means and Slater (2019, 9).

38. For example, Peck (2010); Peck and Theodore (2019); Brown (2015, 2019); Mirowski and Plehwe (2015); Davies (2014); Harvey (2005); Stedman Jones (2012); Burgin (2012).

recurring patterns, constitutive connections—across sites, domains, and registers, including those made in resistance."[39]

Nonetheless, Jamie Peck and Nik Theodore warn against any essentializing of the term. They argue that its formation is best interpreted as a combination of interacting dynamics: "a somewhat improvised, often experimental, and shape-shifting repertoire of procorporate, promarket programs, projects, and power play."[40] Highlighting the importance of interpreting neoliberalism as "partial, polycentric, and plural," Peck and Theodore draw attention to "the conjunctural, cohabitative, and combinatorial forms that variegated neoliberalism (must) take."[41] Cumulatively embedded, neoliberalism is thus understood as incomplete, irregular, and constantly moving in ways where "it defines the rules of the game" even though it is "never acting alone."[42]

HAND IN HAND: PUBLIC RELATIONS AND NEOLIBERALISM

The intimate relationship between public relations and neoliberalism offers considerable scope to understand how political language strategies and practices, which silence or discourage opportunities for deliberative argument, shape "new realities." Shedding light on this, Wendy Brown argues that the constructivist project of neoliberalism[43] is made by a "distinctive form of reason,"[44] which has "a radically extended reach of the private, mistrust of the political and disavowal of the social, which together normalize inequality and disembowel democracy."[45] This governing

39. Peck and Theodore (2019, 255).
40. Peck and Theodore (2019, 260).
41. Peck and Theodore (2019, 251).
42. Peck and Theodore (2019, 246).
43. Brown (2003); Mirowski (2015, 434–435).
44. Brown (2015, 35).
45. Brown (2018, 61).

rationality, both diffused and variegated,[46] which thoroughly transforms notions of common sense and the real, entails the marketization of all areas of life. Today this political, yet anti-political, style of reason informs and modulates (and is informed and modulated by) the public relations language strategies, discursive practices, and vocabulary constituting disparate domains—including science, education, health, welfare, work, government, politics, and the media—in diverse geographical, cultural, social, and temporal contexts. A corolloy is that human subjects are narrowly identified (or struggle not to identify) as atomized, self-interested individuals, entrepreneurs, and market actors. Thus, neoliberal reason seeks to reconfigure the meaning and value of all areas of life in the idiom of the market, so that their purpose becomes to serve the market through a thoroughgoing competitive focus and orientation: a focus on the production of inequality.[47]

Neoliberal reason is woven through diverse discourses, which are thereby transformed, and which in turn may modify knowledge, practices, and regimes of truth. A good example is university education, partly because its raison d'être is to promote open styles of learning which involve critical thinking, questioning, in an autonomous, yet reflective relationship with society.[48] In concept at least, universities are places of (unconstrained) truth and independence. However, for Jeannie Rea, university education today is principally understood in instrumental terms: as an increasingly private economic investment in an individual's future prosperity. She discusses the privitization of the sector where "the process and consequence of marketization" reassigns vice chancellors as "CEOs answering to university councils as corporate boards of management," at the same time commodifing students "at best as clients, and at worst as

---

46. Brenner, Peck, and Theodore (2010).

47. There are many definitions of neoliberalism, but William Davies points out that there are some shared understandings, including a view that its: "ethical and political vision is dominated by an idea of competitive activity, that is, the production of inequality" (2014, 310).

48. Derrida (1983).

customers."[49] Consequently, the objective of education changes, too, and becomes, in its dominant designation, a "capital investment." This style of depoliticized education was anticipated by second-wave neoliberalist Peter F. Drucker.[50] Hence flexibility, job readiness, earnings, vocational research, student loans, and private sponsoring are emphasized. For Stephen Ball,[51] what becomes clear through the infusion of neoliberal reason is that not only do the strategies and practices of education change, but the very vocabulary that now legitimizes it changes, too. The practices and purposes that define the educational endeavor are thereby discursively transformed. Ball emphasizes that these small moves incrementally join up, so that they are pulled "within a unifying discourse of standards, quality, skills, competences and improvement. Ultimately, they are linked to a set of economic necessities. They contribute to a steady overall increase in visibility, measurement and standardization, and they represent a change in the relations of power between teachers and the state. And they make further changes thinkable!"[52]

BEYOND SURVIVAL: NEOLIBERALISM AND PUBLIC RELATIONS

In the now vast body of literature tracing the rise and the practices of neoliberalism, few scholars specifically reference the central role and relationship of public relations either as an institution or as a language practice.[53] However, public relations' direct and indirect influence in propagating the reach and impact of neoliberalism, through the shaping and disseminating

---

49. Rea (2016, 9).

50. Krašovec, (2013, 76–78).

51. Ball (2016).

52. Ball (2016, 1052).

53. See, for example, Holborow (2015); Martín Rojo and Del Percio, eds. (2019); Mirowski and Plehwe (2015); Dean (2009); Davies (2014); Brown (2015); Peck (2010); Phelan (2014), and Steger and Roy (2010).

of now ubiquitous language strategies and practices—in diverse public, organizational, institutional, community, and private realms—has yet to be thoroughly investigated.

From the early twentieth century, public relations practices were mobilized in support of an emergent neoliberal agenda, a partnership that has increasingly limited the potential of a social imaginary to bring people together in a common or democratic collective purpose. The focus on public relations simply as the deployment of corporate publicity or promotion, or as "spin," designed to block the potential for open and informed debate, serves as a first step. But confining analysis thus can lead to rather simplistic interpretations that do not sufficiently capture the significant meanings and effects of the powerful nexus. One result is that analysis of the partnership tends to focus on the poor reputation of public relations. To limit inquiry to this aspect is to regard both its industry-based activity and its influence in communicative practice as an inevitable, and even indispensable, byproduct of market societies,[54] functioning in tandem with and enabled by commercial media imperatives.[55] By contrast, I aim to pay particular attention to the burgeoning of this complex partnership, and—in the spirit of resistance—interrogate its combined forces and effects in transforming corporate, political, and public communicative contexts, and the cultural vernacular itself.[56]

Historically, public relations-inspired language practices have been used successfully on behalf of powerful corporate sponsors to disseminate apparently coherent and positive accounts of the benign nature of all manner of practices that cause social and individual harm—including

---

54. McKie and Munshi (2007); Moloney (2006); Macnamara and Crawford (2010).

55. However, see Sean Phelan for a critical discussion of the neoliberal colonization of media institutions and spaces, and the consequential need for the disciplinary fields of communication and media to interrogate both the concept, and its practices (2018, 539-552). Phelan refers to "Sensationalized PR-driven and celebrified" media, "emblematic of a dumbed-down public culture," and as one oriented to the entertainment of "consumers." He also details the ways in which, in the interests of "consumer choice, media pluralism and individual freedom," neoliberal policies have built a media landscape hostile to non-market forces (2018, 542). See also Phelan (2014).

56. See Anne Cronin's book-length study of the impact of public relations and capitalism on contemporary culture. Cronin (2018, 4) is also interested in its political effects arguing that, "Commercial democracy is a new vernacular form of democracy that speaks the language of

smoking, the use of asbestos, deforestation, the dumping of toxic waste—as well as to stifle, or even silence, efforts to speak out against such accounts.[57] This ruthlessly instrumental and market-driven approach to communication was established in the early decades of the twentieth century, and would lay the foundations of an enduring and mutually profitable relationship between public relations and the neoliberal project. The authoritative status of public relations pioneer, Edward L. Bernays, was secured following his several publications relating to the management of the mass public. However, it was the influence of writer and reporter Walter Lippmann's landmark work, *Public Opinion*, in 1922, which shaped Bernays's own thinking, and whose ideas Bernays popularized in his book *Crystallizing Public Opinion*, published the following year.[58] Indeed, Bernays latched on to Lippmann's ideas of the limits and contradictions of democracy, and used these to justify a covert and persuasive approach to manage their effects in the age of mass communication.[59] And as Liz Franczak observes, Bernays's "elegant, expert-driven solution to the quandaries of liberal governance in mass democracy became all but official political writ."[60] In other words, Bernays's establishment of the new

representation and agency but is disconnected from the practices and formal legitimacy of conventional representative democracy". As such, public relations has come to displace, in part, the social contract, "with alternative promises of representation, voice, and agency" (2018, 4–23).

57. See Demetrious (2013, 55–77) for examples of such corporate public relations campaigns in the late 1970s and 1980s. These include James Hardie Industries' promotion of asbestos as a safe product and attempts to discredit authoritative research that showed a strong correlation between exposure to asbestos and disease; and Waste Technologies Industries' various efforts to distract public attention from the potential health risks associated with the construction of a waste disposal facility in East Liverpool, Ohio.

58. See Ewen (1996, 147–173) for a detailed account of the ways in which Lippmann's thinking informed Bernays's practice and theorizing of public relations' role "within the modern architecture of power" (1996, 166).

59. Curry Jansen (2009). Lippmann was a complex thinker who grasped the implications of the interplay between politics, democracy, and the interpretative processes in large-scale societies that depend on remote media representations for decision-making. His motivations are sound. However, according to Sue Curry Jansen (2013), Bernays was a shallow-thinking self-promoter who distorted key aspects of Lippmann's work.

60. Franczak (2019).

occupation of "public relations counsel"[61] capitalized on the thinking gaining cultural currency that the democratic ideal of political participation on the part of the citizenry was largely, according to Lippmann, an "unworkable fiction."[62] Integral to this position was, first, the absolute right of select individuals and groups who were considered to have superior powers of reasoning to direct and shape the "collective mind" of the crowd;[63] second was the complementary notion of citizens as "publics," which, as I have discussed, were akin to a commodity that, with the right direction or management, would yield to the overtures generated by these elite groups, and act in response to appropriate guidance and media cues.[64] Thus, the appeal to powerful elites of the promise of this new "technology"

---

61. Public relations counsel was described by Bernays in his 1928 book *Propaganda*. It refers to a relatively small number of communicators who formed what Bernays termed the "invisible government" (1928, 9). Publics were not just described but also understood as herds, who did as they were told. According to Bernays, these herds followed their assigned leaders, and the herds' thinking was formed "by means of clichés, pat words or images which stand for a whole group of ideas and experiences" (Bernays 1928, 50). The compatibility between public relations and neoliberal thinking is unmistakable here.

62. Lippmann ([1922] 1991, 31).

63. Ideas from social psychology emerged in the late nineteenth century and the early decades of the twentieth, focused on understanding crowd behavior as primitive and irrational. Of particular note is the work of Gustave Le Bon, who coined the term "collective mind" in his book *The Crowd: A Study of the Popular Mind* ([1895] 1960). This is achieved "by simplifying ideas, substituting affirmation and exaggeration for proof, and by repeating points over and again" (Reicher 2001, 186). Le Bon's work, according to Stephen Reicher (drawing on the work of Serge Moscovici), was highly significant, and "has not simply served as an explanation of crowd phenomena but has served to create the mass politics of the twentieth century" (2001, 185–186). This view fit squarely with public relations' conviction that the democratic "experiment" was flawed, while techniques like repetition, exaggeration, and simplification were useful tools to predict and control the "masses." This point illustrates the critical social contradiction upon which public relations language practices for knowledge formation are founded.

64. See Hughes and Demetrious (2006) and Demetrious (2016). This understanding of "publics" gathered force over subsequent decades, as public relations theorists designed systematic goal-oriented programs of action to classify, target, and shape "public opinion." This is evident in Grunig and Hunt's theory of managing publics (1984). Such approaches and practices not only continue to prevail in the industry, but are ubiquitous in mainstream culture. See also Cronin's problematizing "the public." She examines how, in the shift from state to corporate power, in which the latter is not accountable to the populace, terms such as "stakeholders" and practices such as "stakeholder engagement" are used to validate practices in diverse domains, including government, higher education, and environmental policy (Cronin 2018, 17–22).

of public relations ensured that, as Franczak puts it, "Bernays's new discipline would [. . .] come to decisively shape the political and cultural machinations atop the American social order for the next century."[65] Broadly speaking, from the 1920s onward, the emerging public relations industry promoted these ideas, and over subsequent decades, worked in tandem with corporate and private interests and government to exert influence through attempts to manage "publics," and by extension, "public opinion."[66] Moreover, the public relations industry, and its sponsors and supporters, expected these interventions to be exercised unseen and to go unquestioned in the broader culture.

An instructive illustration of how public relations' policing of public debate has been legitimized and normalized from the later decades of the twentieth century to the present day, and of how it has thus effectively served the expansion of the neoliberal project itself, is found in the concept and the activities of so-called boundary riders.[67] Coined by public relations theorists in the 1980s,[68] this occupational term is used to describe the ways in which public relations practitioners work deliberately to shape and smooth over the intrinsic contradictions of, and to ward off extrinsic opposition to, the privileged discourses favored by their clients. Such discourses and, by extension, the language strategies and practices they inform by garnering sufficient authority, constitute a form of knowledge, a "regime of truth," which is "linked in a circular relation with systems of power which produce and sustain it, and to effects of power which it induces and which extend it."[69] Boundary riders in public relations are on the lookout for tears in the borders, or fault lines, either within or outside of particular discursive formations, and which they understand as needing

---

65. Franczak (2019, 251).

66. A discussion of this is in Chapter 2.

67. This discussion of boundary riders is adapted and developed from Demetrious (2013, 29–31).

68. The popular public relations conceptualization of practitioners as "boundary riders" describes their functioning at "the edge of the organization, serving as a liaison between the organization and the external groups and individuals" (Grunig and Hunt 1984, 9).

69. Foucault (1972, 131).

to be covered or opposed, respectively. One way in which practitioners might do this is to map out and promote the coherence of a given discursive formation:[70] a coherence that can be facilitated by its presentation in storied form. Alternatively, they might construct dichotomies in order to limit social or individual resistance to such formations, for example, through polarized constructions, such as a championed "silent majority" pitted against a stigmatized "vocal minority."[71] In addition, powerful PR entities might delimit public critique of corporate or political practices as obstructive, negative, or ill-informed, or nullify such critique through an array of techniques, including the vexatious disputing of opposing positions, or the active promotion of ignorance through the suppression or obfuscation of evidence.

The result of the construction of a dichotomy between the privileged, hegemonic position, and those that would oppose it, is to preclude the permeation of ideas and issues in all their complexity and contradiction into the realm of public debate.[72] The role of public relations boundary riders is thus to fortify and monitor the boundaries of privileged discourses on behalf of the client, both to maintain those discourses' seeming integrity and to keep out new statements that might open up a space for alternative views. This has troubling implications for the substance, mood, and imaginative scope of public language strategies and practices, and the potential for the meaningful public engagement in critical local and global issues they might stimulate.

---

70. For Foucault, thought is always constrained by the discursive boundaries enabling the formation of concepts (Foucault 1972, 59).

71. McKenna (2019).

72. However, activist opponents of hegemonic positions can also focus on social contradictions: the so-called breaks and tears that constitute apparently coherent discursive formations, and thereby seek to reconstruct those formations as legitimate objects for dispute or argument. This gives rise to practices like spying, infiltration of civil society groups, targeted intelligence gathering, and the use of "dirt files" that breach privacy, covert donations and inducements, in kind or in cash, that buy influence or expedite process, cover-ups, threats, and intimidation and vilification through extreme language and media framing. For example, see Demetrious (2013).

The culminating effects of the public relations industry in policing discursive boundaries is illustrated by events in the latter decades of the twentieth century, when despite its best efforts to avoid controversy, the traces of its handiwork became visible and were met with scathing social critique.[73] In the face of this increasing pervasiveness, informed individuals over the 1970s and 1980s set out to expose this activity for wider audiences, namely those outside exclusive business and political cultures, privy to its machinations. Civic and academic champions, often directly or indirectly affected by the events at hand, publicly "named and shamed" the public relations firms and practitioners involved in cover-ups, smear campaigns, and illegal activities, placing a spotlight on their interventions through critical publications. Perhaps unwittingly, universities were complicit in buttressing the public relations industry's grip on power. They rolled out franchise-style US public relations courses, which delivered a predigested curriculum that was linked to business expectation and self-interest. Overall, these studies valorized an uncritical approach to market expansion and the growth of personal wealth. Nonetheless, in the 1990s, a slight shift in disciplinary focus occurred within universities.[74] The rise of a critical stream of public relations research occurred as academics opened investigations into public relations' wider social and institutional impacts.[75]

73. Sixty years prior, public relations, as a business practice, was largely unchallenged by society. In this circumstance, the industry pursued an aggressive market-based agenda with a sense of righteous impunity and pilloried those who blocked or criticized. Examples are the public relations firms working for the tobacco industry that victimized individuals, some of society's most conscientious and contributing citizens, for speaking the truth about the harmful effects of tobacco. See Demetrious (2016a).

74. The confusing impacts of the legitimization of public relations within the academy led to a "project aimed to set in motion a movement to reform the field of public relations. The practice of public relations is increasingly recognised as central to political and public life and has a massive, sometimes co-ordinated, global impact. However, the discipline of public relations lacks intellectual credibility with other fields. While islands of research and theory exist, there is no formal linkage and no established network to drive radical reformatting, let alone institutionalise it in sustainable form" according to Jacquie L'Etang (2009, 15).

75. This has had the effect of expanding the remit of public relations research to include an investigation of its power relations, gendered practices, and relationship to race and privilege, as well as other less conventional agendas.

The untidy sprawl of ideas and awkward rationale of public relations serve to support multiple interpretations and may explain a general lack of interest in the area. This contributes to a situation in which complaints of public relations malpractice or misconduct receive little or no attention, let alone reprisal.[76] The optimistic assertions about the utopia to come may well be seductive or comforting, but in the meantime, the earth's temperature rises, millions of people around the world are displaced or held in detention as they seek refugee status, and the most vulnerable in society are further disenfranchised. Since its inception as an institutional practice in the early twentieth century, public relations has regularly weaponized words and communication to intervene and undermine civil society members and groups seeking to thwart the strategic agenda of big business. This is despite setting in motion and maintaining the avoidable health crisis caused by smoking, and the damaging of public discourse by circulating countless mistruths and deceptions. I thus conceive public relations in contemporary global culture both as an institutional site *and* as a normalized and normative mode of everyday practice: one that is not only the preserve of public relations organizations or professionals, but also a ubiquitous and habitual mode of communicative activity, that has been variously harnessed and refined in the service of neoliberal reason, and the language strategies and practices it informs. The next section explores the relations of power and institutional structures propping up these cultures.

---

76. Added to this, public relations firms are often highly resourced, meaning that they have vast amounts of money and power to spend on campaigns and strategies, which creates an advantage for business (see Demetrious 2013).

SPEAKING PRAGMATICALLY: QUESTIONS OF POWER AND LANGUAGE

Whether a politician jostling for popularity, or a pugnacious right-wing commentator, the current normative conditions in public debate tolerate a parade of demonstrably ill-informed speakers, who spread lies or conspiracy theories, and promote hateful or intolerant rhetoric. Indeed, the utterings of such loud and increasingly antagonistic "truth tellers" are widely carried and amplified in contemporary media cultures.[77] But an underlying reification unifies and legitimizes these speakers: they represent a form of truth, and are therefore rational.

The communicative conditions in which public relations language practices operate have worked to facilitate this self-contradictory phenomenon in knowledge formation. In this, the idea of rationality is central, both in terms of what it does, and what it appears to do. This is because communicative conditions imply a form of rationality, which promotes action. As oxymoronic as this may sound, rationality does not necessarily imply knowledge, because "knowledge" is deemed rational in relation to the norms and conditions of the time. Take for example, former US president Donald Trump's supporter base,[78] which holds to an "America first"[79] "truth." Such people may acquire knowledge formed through a

---

77. For Habermas (1984), the term "rationality" presupposes an association with knowledge. But herein lies a fine distinction: for Habermas rationality does not imply knowledge, but rather how the "speaking and acting subjects acquire and use knowledge" (1984, 8).

78. See Demetrious (2020). "Trump's base" refers to an unwavering loyalty by often male, older, white, married, less educated constituency, casualties of contemporary US society that were overlooked or disaffected with mainstream political approaches and opposed to "political correctness" or "PC" ideas and language. David N. Smith (2019, 212) argues that this voter group is characterized by "racial resentment, antifeminism, and hostility to immigrants—that have long been associated with authoritarianism.."

79. See Finley and Esposito (2019, 9) who write about the rhetorical appeal of Donald J. Trump's "America first" agenda, which used offensive and racially charged language to promote insular ideas about US protectionism: "Not surprisingly, millions of Americans have been receptive to this position. Indeed, Trump is celebrated by his base as a patriot who challenges a globalist (neoliberal) elite that threaten American sovereignty and the interest of the American people."

self-referencing prism of cultural fragmentation, characterized by biased political or partisan media sources, like *Fox News*,[80] in combination with other market-based promotional cultures. So pervasive are these, that they may produce the content on the screens they watch, or promote the voices that they hear, and this interpretation of truth is replicated and reinforced time and time again through friendship, consumer activity, entertainment, government, and other services they access, such as charities, and even in the protest modes they adopt.[81] Therefore, a multitude of media, increasingly available on digital devices, immerse us with words, images, and symbols, which give the appearance of communicative action in ways that discourage intersubjectivity. And what appears relatively normal and rational within this sphere is sensed as knowledge.

Central to these problems is the inability of people, who are subjected to cultures that support these market-based distortions, to separate this. In these conditions, politicians, media commentators, journalists, and experts may present overlapping associations between a "personal truth," in the guise of "common sense" to the public to shape beliefs of "knowledge." These conditions are primed to give rise to populist rhetoric that is accepted as "truth." Simultaneously, such impoverished repertoires may work to override the conditions that support "communicative action,"[82] such as coordinating to reach consensus or building mutual agreement through clear interactions and strong social relations conducted with a level of autonomy. Despite being developed in very different

---

80. Writing about the rise of Trump's candidacy in the 2016 US election and the role played by media conglomerates like *Fox News*, for Plitzko (2018, 2) "it had become an unpleasant fact and quite normal for the public that the media landscape produces newspapers and television channels with biased opinions and selective reporting over the last decades."

81. Plitzko (2018, 2) makes the further point: "The right-wing press continues to support his political behaviour, making *Fox News* and *Breitbart* potential industry role models for conservative ideas in other countries throughout the world."

82. Geoff Boucher (2011, 69), explains that communicative action is "the core" Habermasian idea of reification through colonization of the lifeworld by the system as "the problematic intrusion of the logic of the anonymous functional social systems of economy and administration, into social processes of renewing cultural knowledge, social norms and socialised personalities that can only be successfully performed through communicative interaction."

communicative conditions, the Habermasian idea of communicative action remains relevant and powerful today. For Byron Rienstra and Derek Hook, the central premise of the idea is based on an individual's lucid self-possession, which requires them "to have clear, unfettered access to their own reasoning, possessing clear preference rankings and defendable rationales for their goals and values."[83] Rienstra and Hook point out that "[w]ithout such understandings, agents would have no reasons to extend or defend their positions in a discursive interchange; no validity claims are redeemable between communicative participants if the agent cannot access, substantiate or understand their own rationality."[84]

The effects of this central assumption shape ideas of belonging in a deliberative democratic society in far-reaching ways, but can also be distorted. For example, when media commentators espousing conspiracy theories and hateful views claim "rationality" because they attract millions of views, shares, and followers who subscribe to their ideas, then they are undermining the precepts of cultural knowledge that are based on self-possession, open-mindedness, and mutual understanding.[85] But this nuance may be lost in the process, so in leveraging off the idea of authentic communicative action, these querulous individuals may gain a higher order of credibility for their views in society. Not surprisingly, they often cause offense in putting forward these distortions, and become the focus for blame. However, attracting controversy and attention may serve only to obscure structures, like media industries, that are working in tandem to strengthen and support them.[86] And when such language strategies and practices are

---

83. Rienstra and Hook (2006, 1).

84. Rienstra and Hook (2006, 1).

85. Christiano (1997).

86. Over many decades in the United States, the rise of right-leaning news media has worked, not just to hold these cultures in place, but to eclipse other examinations of power. For Bartlett (2015, 1), the launch of the twenty-four-hour *Fox News* in 1996 hit upon a winning formula to appeal to Republican voters, and as such, the term "*Fox News* effect" has been used to refer to the framing of voter division (Bartlett 2015, 8). The hugely powerful Koch network is central to right-wing media like *Fox* and conservative US politics, because it "coordinates big money funders, idea producers, issue advocates, and innovative constituency-building efforts"

informed by and joined to the discourses of neoliberalism, which has developed a stabilizing connectedness in society, they come to dominate.

Once in place, the public relations/neoliberal monoculture works to limit ideas and discourage discursive struggle, or even the questioning or interrogating of those speaking, not just because of the ferocious antagonism, but because of this semblance of a generally applicable truth. The instrumental rationality, once in the vernacular, gains legitimacy and acceptance. It comes as no surprise, then, that many of Uwe Poerksen's catalog of plastic words,[87] like "information," "management," "planning," "problem," "solution," "exchange," "future," "growth," "relationship," and "trend," appear regularly in public relations texts, such as planning and campaign strategies, media releases, and key messages.[88] Once circulating in these communicative conditions, these words "wander back, authorized and canonized, into the vernacular, where they become dominant myths and overshadow everyday life."[89] There they rest, seemingly benign and featureless, but actively reducing ideas and deadening language with a range of often expected, but sometimes unexpected, effects.

PR AND "COMMUNICATION" INDUSTRIES

One plastic word of singular interest is "communication." "Communication" works as both an emblematic plastic word in vernacular, and as a core

---

(Skocpol and Hertel-Fernandez 2016, 681–683). Mark Deuze (2009, 243) discusses media industries as structures that influence "the increasing rationalization and (thus) homogenization of all forms of public communication (including news and entertainment) in the hands of fewer and fewer multinational companies."

87. Poerksen (1995, 23). A plastic word has these attributes: it originates from or links to science; it is a "key for everything"; it is a reductive concept; it is ahistorical; it has strong connotations that promote function, and seamlessly and smoothly create a sense of uniformity; it has a dominating and deadening effect on speech (it replaces its synonyms); it is international in scope; and in its elevation as a speech act, it works to deny expression and gesture.

88. For Poerksen the "whole list comprises perhaps not more than thirty or forty words" (1995, 25).

89. Poerksen (1995, 4).

concept underpinning a whole industry, which in turn produces the plastic words that establish these reductive language conditions. This striking feature serves to both embed and structure rationality that promotes the role of markets and profit-making, while at the same time diminishing the oversight of regulators or non-market institutions in contemporary society.[90] Hence, "communication" has properties that unify thought and action toward market-based ideas in two quite different but dynamically intersecting ways, both as a product itself and as a market-based power structure. As a plastic word and concept, "communication" is all-encompassing. It speaks to the future, it covers nearly every aspect of human interaction, and it is propelled on an industrial scale though the occupations of advertising, digital marketing, journalism,[91] and of course public relations. These institutions forge the words to fortify the linguistic frameworks which shape humankind's reality and serve to reify, and to produce more of that reified meaning at the same time, which works to provide a web of reference points for knowledge formation.

Public relations, as the unseen champion of the neoliberal vision, has been central to this. Working both as discursive mode and institutional site, the public relations industry is a sentinel and highly specialized promoter of neoliberal discourse in texts, vocabularies, and concepts that in turn confer its increasing authority, status, and legitimacy. This constitutive cycle ensures that the ongoing production and legitimization of neoliberal vocabularies and concepts, which embed culture to economy,

---

90. As Wendy Brown (2019, 82) writes: "The neoliberal dream was a global order of freely flowing and accumulating capital, nations organized by traditional morality, and market, and states oriented almost exclusively to this project. Nailed to the requirements of markets that are neither self-stabilizing nor enduringly competitive, the neoliberal state, with its commitment to freedom and legislating only universal rules, would also protect the traditional moral order against incursion by rationalists, planners, redistributionists, and other egalitarians."

91. Though many would argue that journalism is the exact opposite of this, Habermas argues that the public sphere has degenerated in tandem to journalism's service of commercial networks of power. He argues (1995, 170–72) that, in the twentieth century, critical debate about such things as public affairs, social problems, health, and education has been exchanged for instant or sensational news, such as disasters, sport, social events, and human interest. He argues that individuals feel disempowered because they do not examine their own life experiences but defer to the mass media on personal needs and difficulties, as a higher authority.

continues uninterrupted. Propelled by the globalization of public relations and other communication industries, the spread of neoliberal visions and structures has been far-reaching and unrelenting. The globalized spread of neoliberal communication industries has been in motion since the 1980s, in tandem with the radical expansion of commercial industries such as telecommunications, audiovisual, television, and print.[92] Sue Curry Jansen argues that public relations' global expansion can be traced to two points: first, in the postwar period, and then from the 1970s onward, in the wake of the second neoliberal wave:[93]

> The rapid expansion of the public relations industry beyond corporate practices into almost every field of endeavor, including government, politics, education, religion, charities, health care, the arts, sports, food, fashion, finance, volunteer work, even criminal justice, raises fundamental questions about the privatization of the public sphere, the capitalization of public expression, inequalities in the distribution of communication resources, market censorship, and the future of democracy. The proclamation by PR enthusiasts that we are all in PR now, with the implicit assumption that this is somehow an equalizing force, which democratizes PR and washes away its history and efficacy as a tool of elite control, is not supported by the evidence.[94]

92. Dal Yong Jin (2008, 358) writes, "During the 1980s, the politics of neoliberal communications reform took hold in dozens of nations, following the US and UK. The initial marginal steps to liberalize markets began in 1984 in the telecommunications sector with the divestiture of AT&T in the US and subsequent privatization of British Telecom (BT) in the UK. Further, within the audiovisual sector, the transformation began in 1985 when the US television industry experienced several significant corporate takeovers on a scale not seen since the 1950s."

93. For Curry Jansen (2016, 9) this happened in stages: "America exported the corporate public relations industry to the rest of the world in two great waves. The first wave followed World War II and the reconstruction of Western Europe. The second, even more dramatic expansion, took place after the Cold War with the ascent of neoliberal globalization and the emergence of China as a major—by some measures even dominant—global economic power. The rise of the environmental movement in the 1970s and the corporate attempt to contain it also stimulated the international growth of PR, especially in Anglo-American spheres of influence."

94. Curry Jansen (2016, 158).

Rather, it has resulted in a default market-based orientation and, as Peter F. Drucker points out, "the new reality" has happened in seemingly unremarkable ways.[95] It has worked.

How do people make sense of this shimmering hall of mirrors, this strange, self-contradictory phenomenon, where a distortion of truth is reflected, back and forth, so many times that it appears to be something real—more real than the thing it distorts? Communication industries, like public relations, extract meaning from language in political and public life, so that it is weakened and does not work well to motivate or raise debate and circulate ideas to address the deep problems of society. But while a communicative void remains, it may be filled with competitive rancor and rage, longing, and fear for the future, serving to pit us against each other and harden stances. And the ongoing damage deepens these divides, for as Will Davis argues: "Viewed from within the neoliberal framework, those regions, cultures, individuals now routinely known as the 'left behind' are not simply unfortunate or inefficient: they are less morally worthy because they are less competitive."[96] This discursive insularity may discourage not only political struggle, but also empathy from seeing the world as relational and interdependent, and in doing so, builds tolerance for its dehumanizing effects.

The proliferation of plastic words in contemporary society dominates everyday vernacular and, in the process, strips language of nuance and variety in public debate. Individuals do not have the words to say what they need to say. In such cases, the Habermasian public sphere,[97] as an

---

95. Drucker (1989).

96. Davies (2017).

97. In this, Habermas's concept of the public sphere, as a center of self-interpretation that promotes the good of its members, brings into relief a gray, shifting, and indistinct area of commercial, state, and civic activity concerned with representation and authority, which is therefore relevant to this discussion of seemingly innocuous plastic words. He explains how the process of public debate and citizen discussion clarified issues of social importance. And yet, if rational agreement arising from exchanges of different opinion has disappeared from the public sphere because it is ousted by public relations, what is the social effect of this?

accessible jumping-off point in everyday life for people to critique and share ideas, becomes a desert that is devoid of diversity and originality, marked by a distinctive form of market-based rationality, that is not interested in real political struggle.[98] The scope of sites like the public sphere, not just for the celebration, exploration, and circulation of ideas, but as part of a politicizing process, is immense. However, instead it displays depoliticizing and anti-political characteristics.[99]

Plastic words like "strategy, "development," "growth," and "progress," propelled by the public relations industry, configure the arguments individuals express, the news stories they watch, the advertisements to which they yield, and perhaps even the graffiti they read. I argue that the tight embrace between public relations and neoliberalism, as a central site embedding this culture, is neither fanciful nor far-fetched. In discussing the impoverishment of public language, Poerksen identifies the "experts" who produce and transmit messages laden with plastic words as "functionaries,"[100] and argues that they do so by creating a sense of anticipation of expansion, both fear and excitement for space and the future. But for Poerksen, first and foremost this is because:

---

98. William Davies (2014) defines neoliberalism as "the *pursuit of the disenchantment of politics by economics*." Meanwhile, Wendy Brown (2019, 56) reminds us that the "political" is differentiated from "politics" as a "theatre of deliberations, powers, actions, and values where common existence is thought, shaped, and governed."

99. Rousiley C. M. Maia (2018, 150) argues that the nexus between depoliticization and anti-politics should receive more attention in deliberative democratic theory and writes, "Democracy is facing several challenges nowadays. These challenges stem from the large and widening gap between governors and the governed, the rise of anti-politics, and the nationalistic, discriminatory and explicitly anti-human rights agenda of several populist political representatives [...]. Thus, amongst the challenges for deliberative democrats is the need to understand interactions and tensions in public communication, across formal decision-making institutions and informal settings and wider publics."

100. Poerksen (1995, 87) profiles these experts as having, on the one hand, a sense of limited time but, on the other hand, as generating the anticipation (both fear and enthusiasm) for the future and its global expansion, the ability to divert the citizenry's gaze and abstract pain and suffering from their experience, by invoking the language of science, the economy, and administration, to smooth away the rough edges of realities that jar consumers' sensibilities or confront their ethical lives.

Our basic impulse is to be in motion; the experts contribute in various ways to a general mobilization. But in a world so thoroughly mobilized one also needs some people who provide security and perform exorcisms. The language of the experts imitates stability and secures the journey into the future.[101]

However, there is another reason. Typically the public relations industry is built on this type of expertise. Its practitioners excel in producing persuasive, future-oriented political texts that smooth away rough edges. In this, the rise of the public relations industry in the service of the neoliberal project is a critical but under-theorized motivating force, propelling these patterns of language in the vernacular and in the public sphere. A complex byproduct of advanced capitalism, these deadening public relations language practices have a significant effect on transforming political culture. Corroborating the critical role of public relations to the economic sphere, Sue Curry Jansen (2017), reports that Richard Edelman, CEO of one of the largest public relations corporations, said: "PR is 'the organizing principle' behind many business decisions [. . .] and functions as 'the cutting edge of corporate power.'"[102]

As I have argued, public relations is the most abstracted and elusive communication industry, and as the instrument of neoliberal free-market ideas, it has quietly co-opted the associations of communicative action. To understand the power and reach of public relations language practice, it must be understood as a self-referencing industry to produce and proliferate plastic words.

On the one hand, public relations language practices embed optimistic and bountiful visions of the future in a multitude of texts within society, government, and business. On the other hand, the gravitational pull of these meanings set the course for a market-based rationality, and the

---

101. Poerksen (1995, 88).

102. Curry Jansen amasses a rich trove of empirical work exploring the global growth of the public relations industry and its implications; see (2016, 18).

complex process avoids a wider representation of voices that constitute critical public opinion. In doing so, Sue Curry Jansen's work argues that public relations' objective is to mediate the media:

> It inserts itself between the event and the report of the event, compromising or displacing the roles of reporters and editors by controlling the flow of information through press releases, strategic uses of language, staging events, promotional campaigns, third party endorsements, and other techniques [. . .]. PR actively conceals its persuasive efforts from public view whenever possible. In doing so, it violates fundamental norms of democratic discourse: transparency and accountability.[103]

Mimicking the original intention of the public sphere, the political presence of public relations within public debates goes largely unnoticed.[104] However, this undermining and atrophying of real public debate is not the only effect. Big business and industry, through their prolific lobbying and publicity, have in effect sponsored the rise of the far right. Thus, for Wendy Brown, the neoliberal experiment, like Marxism, has failed, a victim of its own success:

> Democracy has been throttled and demeaned, yes. However, the effect has been the opposite of neoliberal aims. Instead of being insulated from and thus capable of steering the economy, the state is increasingly instrumentalized by big capital—all the big industries, from agriculture and oil to pharmaceuticals and finance, have their hands on the legislative wheels. Instead of being politically pacified, citizenries have become vulnerable to demagogic nationalistic mobilization decrying limited state sovereignty and supranational facilitation of global competition and capital accumulation. And instead of spontaneously ordering and disciplining populations, traditional morality has become a battle screech, often emptied of substance

---

103. Curry Jansen (2017, 10).

104. Habermas (1995, 194).

as it is instrumentalized for other ends. As antidemocratic political powers and energies in constitutional democracies have swollen in magnitude and intensity, they have yielded a monstrous form of political life—one yanked by powerful economic interests and popular zeal, one without democratic or even constitutional coordinates, spirit, or accountability, and hence, perversely, one without the limits or limitability sought by the neoliberals.[105]

To comprehend the forces that have impelled political life to became "monstrous"[106] and "antidemocratic," as Wendy Brown laments, the production and proliferation of public relations language practice, in its full discursive, sociopolitical, and cultural complexity, offers considerably more as a site for exploration and understanding.

COMMUNICATION IS NOT NECESSARILY COMMUNICATIVE

In contemporary society, "communication" is not action-oriented in ways that lead to mutual forms of consensus in a Habermasian sense. Rather, all-encompassing "communication" has insinuated into everyday vernacular to project an aura of future-oriented market-based authority to subsume nuanced meanings in public conversations. In doing so, "communication" as an industry and a word may be a powerful driver in styles of debate that produce "non-public opinion"[107] for self-serving political purposes. Within this logic, it is the colonization of communicative spaces, in particularized, professional, and policy settings, that is crucial.

---

105. Brown (2019, 42).

106. See Noam Chomsky in relation to the "monstrous" communication industries, particularly public relations: "We have huge industries, public relations industry, monstrous industry, advertising and so on, which are designed from infancy to mould people into this desired pattern." Noam Chomsky speaking in *The Corporation* (2003).

107. Habermas (1995, 244).

These may be found in public debates, in blogs, in the personal postings on social media sites, and in what we watch on screens, listen to, or turn from, and in the discussions that take place in classrooms, in cafes, and in neighborhoods. These settings are where vivid and pivotal power relations are at play, and where resistance and possibility may be activated or muted.[108]

The neoliberal diminishment of language in general through the practices of public relations to understand discursive struggle and hegemony may be well trodden in parts. But a focus on the taut relationship between public relations, secrecy, and publicity in capitalist society may yield interesting new territory. Anne Cronin (2020) reveals: "Secrecy and transparency are centrally important ideologies and practices in today's capitalist societies and are intimately linked to the work of various sectors of the PR industry. If practices of secrecy actively create and reshape social relations, then PR's implication in those practices requires depth analysis."[109] This compact of publicity and secrecy works, in tandem with intrinsic and extrinsic public relations practices, to contain discursive exit and entry points by maneuvering "publics" toward the warm glow of a market-based logic with consensual sounding plastic words. This works to obviate the need to engage with a critical interpretation of a message necessary for knowledge formation in the Habermasian sense. The authority of these words, messages, and narratives impels "publics" to ward off action that may lead to consensus and mutual agreement. Rather, what emerges is an essentialized instrumental approach to interpreting success or achievement in communication, evaluated on the level of circulation, "cut through," or exchange value. This chilling effect on media has been especially prevalent since September 11, 2001, and the terrorist attacks on American home soil. For Nancy Snow and Philip Taylor,[110] during "the so-called 'Global War on Terror,' authoritarian values of secrecy, information

---

108. Fairclough (1989, 43–76).

109. Cronin (2020, 232).

110. Snow and Taylor (2006, 390).

control and silencing dissent would appear to take precedence over democracy, the First Amendment and a free press." They argue that in this culture, openness and transparency override "the public's right to know."[111]

But some rethinking of assumptions in such open cutlures may be in order. In outlining her ideas of communicative capitalism, Jodi Dean suggests that, within contemporary settings, "communication" that leads to mutual forms of consensus in the Habermasian sense is a an naïve fallacy:

> Instead of engaged debates, instead of contestations employing common terms, points of reference, or demarcated frontiers, we confront a multiplication of resistances and assertions so extensive that it hinders the formation of strong counterhegemonies.[112]

Dean illustrates her point about the limitations of the Habermasian idea, with the example of the failure of deliberative politics and public debate around the US decision to invade Iraq in 2003.[113] This example suggests that no matter how much serious, well-grounded public debate there is, that is both civil and respectful, it is not enough to change politics today. Therefore, the idea of communicative action as a socially constitutive and relational activity that works for the common good may well be obsolete. While a level of pessimism in contemporary networked conditions may be warranted, the Habermasian idea of communicative action still offers a path, and an ideal to uphold as an alternative in how language practices may shape the various contexts of citizens' lives. It also helps

---

111. Snow and Taylor (2006, 390).

112. Dean (2008, 102).

113. Dean (2008, 101): "Even when the White House acknowledged the massive worldwide demonstrations of February 15, 2003, Bush simply reiterated the fact that a message was out there, circulating—the protestors had the right to express their opinions. He didn't actually respond to their message. He didn't treat the words and actions of the protestors as sending a message to him to which he was in some sense obligated to respond. Rather, he acknowledged that there existed views different from his own."

to understand the varied purposes of public language, their modalities and ethical effects. Recognizing how the global public relations industry produces and circulates meanings to construct Peter F. Drucker's "new realities" may go some way to understanding how this affects the acceptance of a market-based idea of democracy. It may also shed light on how the public relations industry acts as a fence to keep some ideas in and some ideas out, and as a corollary, how to upend its unconscious power.

The next chapter casts a light on the intricate weave of relationships between public relations professionals and advocates of the free market, including economists, wealthy elites, assorted media professionals, and publicists, during the early decades of the twentieth century in the United States. The aim is to highlight the ways in which a mode of "telling" the neoliberal story emerged in this setting that is now embedded in the vernacular of a globalized world; and to show how it had its prototypical origins in the combined efforts of an increasingly public relations–oriented machinery, working in tandem with key neoliberal figures to influence public opinion. Designed to bypass or override democratic processes in their exalting of the free-market society as the natural way of things, key organizations and individuals employed a range of quasi-propagandist modes of communicating to help lay the ground for deploying and echoing language strategies and practices, which have become so pervasive in the twenty-first century that they appear ordinary and unremarkable.

2

Communicating the "Practical Faith"

The Historical Neoliberal and Public Relations Nexus

The postwar period established public relations as a distinctive neoliberal communicative mode which championed the idea of "freedom" as a cause and served as a platform for a vehement opposition to the threat of "left" economic policies. Its tenor, approach, and features were intimately linked to the "volatile time of crisis, between World Wars and amidst the Great Depression"[1] which Rowe et al. describe as the first wave of neoliberalism. However, its emergence at this time was not an accidental occurrence whereby a handful of public relations counselors with conservative convictions, or close ties to prominent elites, made an impact. Rather, the relationship between big business, neoliberal ideology, and public industry over the postwar decades was conceived and worked purposefully as a tight-knit network to form an acute understanding of how language could be harnessed to achieve their aims. Such communicative alliances provided fertile ground for the successful nurturing of neoliberal ideas linked to action plans. As seen in the previous chapter, this mode has burgeoned and has characterized many social, cultural, and political arenas in contemporary settings, outside the institutions of public relations. Therefore,

---

1. Rowe et al. (2019, 153).

the durable language practices established in the cradle of the postwar period have ongoing implications, not just for resistance and possibility in communicative action, but for how "communication" is distributed and amplified, as well as understood and analyzed. The neoliberal voices active at this time, and the tension and struggle between them, may go some way to explain the failures of public debates today.

To explore these themes, this chapter will first map key economic and political events which gave impetus to the 1947 formation of the Mont Pèlerin Society (MPS). The eminent Austrian economist and intellectual Friedrich August von Hayek[2] planned and presided over the society,[3] and in time saw it become a powerful and permanent home for a transnational neoliberal network, seeking to undo progressive political agendas focused on collectivism. Closed and selective, MPS would unite isolated individuals to rejuvenate the unpopular and seemingly outdated ideas about business and growth to influence public opinion. As such, it worked over many decades not just to promulgate particularized ideas about "human freedom" and "free enterprise" in the liberal tradition, but to thwart others.[4] The MPS can be understood loosely as a club, dedicated to bringing like-minded, but isolated individuals together in a membership. Not only would MPS provide a forum to network and critique ideas about individual rights, society, and collectivism, but its followers, in their own often privileged and powerful capacities, would work to advance key ideas about free market economics, small government, and personal liberty. It is difficult to ascertain the MPS's intended and unintended influence in politics, the economy, and society, but its members were remarkably effective

---

2. Referred to hereafter as "Friedrich Hayek."

3. According to the Mont Pèlerin Society (2021, n.p.), "[a]fter World War II, in 1947, when many of the values of Western civilization were imperiled, 36 scholars, mostly economists, with some historians and philosophers, were invited by Professor Friedrich Hayek to meet at Mont Pelerin, near Montreux, Switzerland, to discuss the state and the possible fate of liberalism (in its classical sense) in thinking and practice."

4. Today, the Society's explicit aims are to keep watch for the dangers of "the expansion of government, not least in state welfare, in the power of trade unions and business monopoly, and in the continuing threat and reality of inflation" (Mont Pèlerin Society 2021, n.p.).

in using this platform to gather movement of these ideas. Thus, a core tenet of the MPS became the production of meaning, not just in talking among themselves, but in changing the opinions of the broader population by purposefully meddling with the public imagination.

To trace the mode of embedding this ideology in communication, I focus on three proselytizers of the free market in the United States during the 1930s, 1940s, and 1950s. First, I look to James P. Selvage, a New York–based public relations practitioner active from the 1930s, who enjoyed close relations with powerful corporate and Republican figures and who authored the booklet: "A Look Ahead at Public Relations." His pugnacious style, and his dexterity in working in radio, print, and film, made him an articulate spokesperson for free enterprise and a fierce opponent of the New Deal policies of President Franklin D. Roosevelt's administration. Next is a critical reading of Friedrich Hayek's 1949 essay, "The Intellectuals and Socialism," as a call for, and endorsement of the communicative purpose, approach, and tenor of the neoliberal project. Lastly, I explore the folksy parable "I, Pencil," by Leonard E. Read, a loyal champion of the ideal of a free-market economy and founder of the first conservative think tank in the United States, the Foundation for Economic Education (FEE). Drawing on samples of their respective texts, I trace the movement of the word "freedom" as it emerges as a distinctive neoliberal object, as it is reiterated, energized, and embedded in language practices, in ways that avoid the appearance of heavy-handed propaganda. Thus, the chapter demonstrates that the intimate interrelationships of public relations and neoliberal interests are not only long established, but also highly nuanced, sometimes at odds with each other, and that the struggles that played then, continue to play out now. Nonetheless, in the pre- to postwar decades of the twentieth century, an overarching belief in classical liberalism united the group, and a storied form of neoliberal reason emerged in nascent ways, with distinctive modes, discourses, and vocabulary. This neoliberal proto-narrative, which served to unite, integrate, and guide interpretation, was subsequently patterned, reproduced, and used in innumerable settings by the burgeoning, transnational communication industry.

THE DELIBERATELY OPAQUE RELATIONSHIP BETWEEN PUBLIC RELATIONS AND NEOLIBERALISM

The Great Crash brought the epoch of prosperity to a sudden and dramatic close, and the Depression discredited its primary symbols.[5]

In the wake of the stock-market collapse in 1929 and the onset of the Great Depression, a radical break in role of the US federal government manifested. In 1933, President Roosevelt developed a set of strong public spending policies to counter the crisis. The milestone idea of government directing capitalism signaled "an acceptance and regulation of the modern corporation."[6] Whether the reformist ideas of British economist John Maynard Keynes[7] directly influenced Roosevelt's social vision and policy reforms is moot.[8] But the New Deal's big spending government programs to counter the damaging effects of the Great Depression did break with economic orthodoxy.[9] This had a mixed response. On one hand, for some Americans, the "government-sponsored cultural projects" awakened a new consciousness and imaginative scope in arts like painting, music, literature, history, and newer forms of practice like photography, which "furthered an adventure in national rediscovery."[10]

---

5. Jones (1971, 714).

6. Cowie and Salvatore (2008, 8).

7. See Angus Burgin (2012, 3), who writes: "Keynes articulated an understanding of capitalism as a mode of social organization that demonstrated both irreplaceable merits and undeniable flaws [. . .]. He envisioned a public sector that would engage in limited but forceful interventions to ameliorate the problems that were engendered when individuals were left to act alone."

8. Price Fishback (2016, 390) argues that there is doubt in a direct association between the New Deal and Keysian economics, saying that "[a]lthough Keynes's ideas were in circulation by 1933, the lag between academic advances and their use in policy tends to take decades." Nicholas Crafts and Peter Fearon (2010, 298) state decisively that "[t]he New Deal was not Keynesian. Neither fiscal nor monetary policy was used as a tool for economic revival."

9. See Angus Burgin's (2012, 39) discussion of American economists who, at the time, believed that New Deal policies would lead to "authoritarian collectivism."

10. Jones (1971, 711).

For others, the New Deal policies were wild and dangerous, and would lead to "authoritarian collectivism."[11] Another defining characteristic of Roosevelt's interventionalist policies, salient to this project, was the highly resourced publicity operations and public communications used to support the popularization of the reform programs.[12] This potent combination of publicity and New Deal politics did not go unnoticed. Indeed, it served to fuel the business fraternity's growing alarm over the government's power to intervene in the market. John W. Hill, founder of the public relations firm Hill and Knowlton, said: "It is one thing for the public to have the power of evaluating dollars in terms of *products*, as it chooses this or that in a free market [...]. It is enormously different for Public Opinion, *via* government to emerge as the sole standard back of the dollar system by which corporate management computes the value of goals, measures the efficiency of work, and judges the worth of its enterprise."[13]

In this context, the National Association of Manufacturers (NAM) mobilized industry and business to launch extensive public relations campaigns in the 1930s, which aggressively opposed the popular Roosevelt New Deal, and instead promoted the profit imperative for business through small government and anti-regulation. The cost, volume, and scope of NAM's publicity operations to counter the New Deal were on an unprecedented scale and forged an ongoing and purposeful relationship between public relations and neoliberalism:

> The central theme of NAM public relations material was that industry's managers were the true leaders of the nation. The public interest, and

---

11. Burgin (2012, 39).

12. Moloney (2006, 43). He argues that, in 1936, the Roosevelt administration employed "146 full-time and 124 part-time public agents who issued 7 million copies of 48,000 press releases."

13. John W. Hill, cited in Karen Miller (1999, 12). Miller writes that "Hill & Knowlton" formed in 1933, and that their approach to public relations "was strongly influenced by the Depression and the New Deal, watershed events for the agency and its first clients" (1999, 9).

especially the workingman's interest, was safe in their hands. Business was on trial.[14]

The NAM backlash marks not only one of the biggest public relations offensives in history, but also Hill and Knowlton's rise to become a global behemoth.[15] As such, it is an example of the tight embrace between economic power, ideology, and public relations, as the conscious harnessing of discursive forces to propel meaning and disrupt knowledge formation.[16]

Setting the powerful nexus in motion was the Colloque Walter Lippmann, held in 1938. According to Francois Denord,[17] this was "an international congress held in Paris, consisting of twenty-six businessmen, top civil servants, and economists from several countries." Among these were members of "a rising new generation of liberal economists," including Friedrich Hayek and Ludwig von Mises.[18] The Colloque was significant because "[f]or the first time, neoliberalism was defined by a set of postulates that constituted an agenda."[19] Nearly a decade later, in 1947, Friedrich Hayek would establish the MPS's remodeled ideas about

---

14. Tedlow (1976, 34). Indeed, the sheer scale of NAM's public relations tactics marshaled in response to the New Deal is notable. In particular, the "the American Way Campaign" in 1936, designed "to challenge the fundamental social assumptions of the New Deal and to project a picture of American business as a system—through its normal routines—responds to and meets the concerns and aspiration of ordinary Americans. The key was to present a case for American business not from the customary vantage points of the stockholder, but from 'the mass man's point of view'" (Ewen 1996, 304).

15. The Depression decade decimated many businesses, but Karen Miller highlights that "public relations was one of the few growth industries of the era" (1999, 14).

16. This nexus is illustrated by the close associations that formed in this period. For example, NAM solicited John W. Hill's help to orchestrate a strike-breaking propaganda campaign: "In the Little Steel strikes, the unions faced what the committee terms 'a campaign of hostile propaganda'" (Cutlip 1994, 467). Stuart Ewen (1996, 358) corroborates Hill's influence in activating a deep divide in anti-union communication rhetoric and campaigning.

17. Denord, cited in Mirowski and Phewe (2009, 45).

18. Denord (2009, 48).

19. Dernod describes this agenda as "the use of the price mechanism as the best way to obtain the maximal satisfaction of human expectations; the responsibility of the state for instituting a juridical framework adjusted to the order defined by the market; the possibility for the state to

free-market capitalism, linked to this agenda.[20] However, the MPS membership at its first meeting differed considerably from that of the Colloque Walter Lippmann. While the Europeans remained central, "[a]lmost half of the participants in the MPS founding conference in 1947 came from the United States."[21] As a network, this group of intellectuals, businessmen, politicians, and academics were far from uniform in their views and approach. Yet despite their differences, within this forum a consensus of sorts was formed: one based on shared beliefs about "free markets, limited governments, and personal liberty under the rule of law."[22] Over the following decades, and while mostly unseen, the MPS and its members would continue to meet, plan, and flourish, promulgating a form of rationality. It was one based on future-oriented ideas of market-based prosperity and freedom, and small government, particularly in the United States,[23] and it led "to the creation of a comprehensive transnational discourse community."[24] In its own estimation, the MPS has played a decisive role in furthering classical liberal philosophy in the "battle of ideas" around history, society, and economy, but "has done more than just keep liberal ideas alive . . . [I]t has expanded and deepened liberal philosophy and spread liberal thought across the globe."[25]

The affairs of NAM and the MPS have been discussed both singularly and associatively, but in the main, they stop short of recasting "public relations" as both discursive practice and an institutional site, as central to neoliberal history or the furthering of the neoliberal agenda.[26] I argue,

---

follow goals other than short-term expedients and to further by levying taxes; the acceptance of state intervention if it does not favor any particular group and seeks to act upon the cause of the economic difficulties" (2009, 49).

20. Mirowski (2015, 429–430).

21. Plehwe (2009, 17).

22. Feulner cited in Plehwe (2009, 2).

23. See "Draft Statement of Aims" in Mirowski and Phewe (2009, 23).

24. Plehwe (2009, 5).

25. Eamonn Butler (n.d.).

26. Burgin (2012).

however, that public relations practices have been pivotal in providing the communicative mode for embedding the neoliberal reason in other domains, and that this aspect has been overlooked in its significance and is more generative and explanatory than previously understood. Neoliberalism, in the emergence of a key institution—the MPS—provides a cultural marker to understand and to trace the expansion of this discourse through public relations firms, think tanks, and other media organizations and their products. In undertaking this exploration and analysis, Kim Phillips-Fein's[27] excellent historical and sociological work illuminates the public relations industry's intimate intertwinement with the neoliberal project at this time: a relationship which mainstream public relations scholars largely ignore.

A small army of individuals in the 1940s and 1950s worked in various ways to shift the American people's political and economic views favorably toward a free-market perspective. Henry Hazlitt is one such figure. A business journalist, Hazlitt was not especially political, but the New Deal gave him the impetus to change, and in time, he developed strong ties to key business institutions and wealthy individuals in order to spread these ideas.[28] In 1947, Hazlitt would become a founding member of and then long-standing and active participant in the MPS and early think tanks.[29] His book, *Economics in One Lesson*, written in 1946, shows a sharp insight into the propagating impacts of public relations practices that he used to "peg" meaning that leads to knowledge formation. He writes that "special interests," such as businesses, use scientific language repeatedly and insistently to create a dense and impenetrable mindset, which, once in place, becomes unthinkable to oppose; this is utilized to wrap up and make more palatable a message that may seem "absurd."[30] However despite being

---

27. Phillips-Fein (2009).

28. Henry Hazlitt attacked the New Deal in the press with gusto, which may have had a politicization effect as his writings increasingly defended the free enterprise system (Tucker 2009).

29. Miller and Dinan (2008, 63–64). Hazlitt was involved with the FEE and the American Enterprise Institute (AEI). See Surma and Demetrious (2018).

30. Hazlitt (1978, 57).

extraordinarily effective in championing the neoliberal cause, public relations strategies such as Hazlitt's were not something openly lauded or even acknowledged in mainstream public relations texts. Miller and Dinan (2008) argue that this is no accident: "The efficacy of PR has, in fact, been largely suppressed from the historical record."[31] Like Phillips-Fein (2009), Miller and Dinan state that the MPS had not only a strong awareness of the power of publicity and public opinion, but also a desire *not to be seen as propagandists*.[32] This suggests that in public relations there was a distinct stratagem to submerge the association to neoliberal forces, such as the MPS.

This purposeful compact of publicity and obscurity is illustrated by the staging of the first American meeting of the MPS in 1958. Organized by the public relations firm Hill and Knowlton, the Princeton meeting was to be a grand affair with lofty speakers, such as Ludwig von Mises, and panels with papers by Milton Friedman. But offstage, the Princeton meeting hosted real tensions between the founding European intellectuals of the society and the conservative US donors, who had staged and paid for the meeting. The MPS, for the Europeans, had high theoretical ambitions, and its independence was integral. They did not want to relinquish its integrity only to see it become a joke, or a clumsy vehicle for propaganda; but at the same time, modifying the public "mind" required the support of the wealthy American businessmen. The reluctant partnership had the potential to upend. As it eventuated, this was not the case: "On the contrary, the connections between the business world and that of think tanks and intellectual organizations would only deepen over time."[33] The first American MPS meeting provides a site to trace the relationships between Friedrich Hayek and Ludwig von Mises, and key figures in the NAM and the FEE. Intentionally or unintentionally, keeping hidden the extent of public relations' involvement with conservative political movements, such as NAM

---

31. Miller and Dinan (2008, 1).

32. Scott M. Cutlip makes no reference to the Mont Pèlerin Society or Friedrich Hayek in his (1995) *Public Relations History: From the 17th to the 20th Century: The Antecedents.*

33. Phillips-Fein (2009, 296).

and the MPS, does make sense if understood in relation to the selective way in which neoliberals distilled their beliefs. Like Miller and Dinan, I argue that a symbiotic relationship between neoliberalism and public relations has been at work since the mid-twentieth century, which has been both directly and indirectly suppressed. The identification of this layer of activity in the postwar period makes a substantive difference to scholarly understanding of the scope and significance of public relations language repertoires in shaping the neoliberal project.

"Public relations counsel" James P. Selvage is another instructive figure in the postwar period, busily instilling free-market ideology in the American political imagination. Like Hazlitt, Selvage was widely respected by his peers and intimately connected with several institutional sites, including NAM, and other public relations business networks, such as the Wisemen association which was founded in 1938 by John W. Hill of Hill and Knowlton and "who met monthly in New York on an invitation-only basis."[34] Selvage was also notable for his embrace of a range of different creative mediums, including radio, film, and print, to bring home messages about the virtues of capitalism and free enterprise to everyday Americans, and even to schoolchildren.[35] In partnership with Morris M. Lee Jr., also previously at NAM, he produced the fifteen-minute radio program "The American Family Robinson," "which centered on the lives of the Robinsons of the manufacturing city of Centerville, caught up in the problems of the Depression. With businessmen portrayed as heroes and labor organizers as villains, the clear message was that the free enterprise system would set things right."[36] Other material he produced included a movie short called "America Marches On" and booklets for schoolchildren, such as "You and Industry."[37] Seemingly with no ethical compunctions, Selvage used these

---

34. Miller Russell (2014, 315), Opdycke Lamme (2014, 10), Surma and Demetrious (2018, 98).

35. Reference for Business (2021).

36. Selvage is quoted as saying that the purpose of the show "was to serve as industry's effective answer to the Utopian promises of theorists and demagogues at present reaching such vast audiences via the radio." Reference for Business (2021, n.p.).

37. The Museum of Public Relations (2021).

cultural products as vehicles to implant political mindsets in the public, and in doing so, showed a gleeful propensity to harness and exploit the power of language. The extent of his willingness to regard the "public" as a resource and extract value from it is evident in an address in New York, when Selvage advised his audience that doing just this would support American business entering a new phase of growth. In the following extract, note also the conversion of "the public" into "publics":

> I affirm with confidence that tomorrow belongs to the man who thinks in terms of the public—the public embracing his employees, his stockholders, his customers, his neighbors surrounding his factories, often the national body politic—and his government. These are the groups that are going to take a lot of pleasing in the years that are just around the corner. These are the publics about whose relations to industry modern business leadership is giving the most intense thought.[38]

In 1984 mainstream US public relations was defined as "the management of communication between an organisation and its publics."[39] However, this definition does not capture the ways that Henry Hazlitt and James P. Selvage either thought about or used communication practices through thick networks that were linked to political organizations like think tanks, or through film, radio, and other creative forms of communication. In the postwar decades, figures like Hazlitt and Selvage considered it essential to capture the public imagination in a political struggle which was increasingly framed as "do or die." Implicit in this was a powerful but incongruous underlying logic: the individual's right to pursue freedom as a cause to defend, and a utopian promise of a better and more prosperous

---

38. Wright and Christian (1949, v.) Referring to Selvage as a "widely respected" public relations counsel, this quote foregrounds the Preface of the 1949 book, *Public Relations in Management*, by J. Handly Wright (director of industrial and public relations at Monsanto Chemical Company) and Bryon H. Christian (professor of journalism at the University of Washington).

39. Grunig and Hunt (1984, 8).

future, while at the same time deferring to an elite to control thinking and action. The associative ethical reasoning endorsing this position was that "the market knows best," not deliberation or political struggle. Therefore, from the outset, the inconsistency of neoliberal reason active within democratic frameworks necessitated the vigilance of public relations practices, to monitor and manage public dissent, or interest in these frequent breaks in logic.[40] Elements of this neoliberal narrative, over the ensuing decades, and fashioned around the shifting idea of "freedom" linked to the economic sphere, would be augmented or fortified by distinctive plastic words, like "future," "growth," "development," and "resource."[41]Over time, this assemblage would work to dominate cultural imagination and create public predisposition and many *entrée* points for neoliberal political positions. Hence, a simple, all-encompassing, future-oriented proto-narrative emerged that could fit any purpose. It was the story of an individual's endeavor, faith, prosperity, and freedom, through the power of a market unfettered by government and regulation—a story that remains largely in place today.[42]

PROSELYTIZERS OF THE FREE MARKET: THE PROMISE OF FREEDOM

Peering into the abyss ahead, Hayek determined to form a society committed to persuading the intellectuals, and hence the masses and their political leaders, to change course. This society would bring

---

40. See Demetrious (2008) for a fuller discussion of two distinct ways in which public relations works to maintain a semblance of coherence in the public sphere to suppress the emergence of other coherences.

41. Poerksen (1995, 62).

42. Naomi Oreskes, Erik M. Conway, and Charlie Tyson (2020) discuss the rise of neoliberalism in the United States over the period 1935–1940 and how the metaphor "tripod of freedom" was used to underpin narratives. They say that this "was the claim that American democracy rested on three legs—representative government, civic and religious liberty, and free enterprise. Like a tripod, it would only stand if all three legs were intact and strong."

together for mutual enlightenment and encouragement the leading figures of classical liberalism.[43]

Neoliberalism influenced public relations, and public relations influenced neoliberalism. And this nexus produced a proto-neoliberal narrative that set the discursive groundwork for receptivity for many decades to come. To illustrate how the emergent proto-neoliberal narrative over this period was fortified, I trace the movement of "freedom" as an element of speech and a contextualizing idea in three respective publications: "A Look Ahead at Public Relations" (Selvage 1942); "The Intellectuals and Socialism" (Hayek 1949); and "I, Pencil" (Read 1958). These works use the word "freedom" to designate a political and ideological divide, which not only grows in prominence and connotative significance, replacing the more awkward terms "free market" and "free enterprise," but also becomes deeply embedded within a story of market-based salvation and bounty to elide its acute contradictions within this logic.

"A LOOK AHEAD AT PUBLIC RELATIONS"

James P. Selvage's treatise is not only a call to arms so that "America can fulfill its destiny as world leader" in promoting "the American Way of representative free government and honest free enterprise," but a call to champion the pivotal role that PR language practices would play in making this happen: "now and tomorrow." Originally delivered as an address to The Advertising Club of Worcester and then published as a booklet, Selvage promises, on the one hand, a prosperous and bright future, which has recaptured the spirit of enterprise; while on the other hand, cautioning about the battle against "opponents in economic philosophy" who are versed in the art of propaganda. His treatise barely uses the word "freedom"; rather, he makes references to "free enterprise" and "free market." This short extract gives a sense of its fervent flavor:

43. Higgs (1997).

> We are selling America itself to Americans who have forgotten what America has symbolized in the past as the envy of every other nation in the world—and what it must continue to symbolize—else freedom and its blood brother, free enterprise, will perish from the earth.[44]

Acutely aware of persuasive power, Selvage has no compunction about invoking racist and polarizing language to make his case. As the rhetoric swells, he refers at various times to "gospel," "sacred honor," "spirit," "preaching," and "belief," as he mounts calls to the defenders of the free market to be in readiness for the war within American borders, after the war outside. In this, he is referring to a war that is intrinsically bound up with public relations:

> If I am correct that public relations, including advertising, must win or lose the battle for free enterprise and representative government, then business and industry, in turn, have the right to ask of us "are you who labor in this field equal to the task?"[45]

As the excerpt below demonstrates, discursive defense, fortification, and attack via public relations are also bound up in Selvage's concept of "freedom," precisely because either someone, or something, is threatening to carry off this most prized political right:

> The people have got to hate those chains [. . .] we will demand the casting off of our shackles and return the American people to the American Way of representative free government and honest free enterprise. And that is the big job of public relations now and tomorrow.[46]

---

44. Selvage (1942, 3–13).
45. Selvage (1942, 9).
46. Selvage (1942, 13).

Selvage's essay is significant in building rationale and discursive bridges that straddle the contradictory ideas of economic subjugation to individual freedom: key elements that underpin the proto-neoliberal narrative.

"THE INTELLECTUALS AND SOCIALISM"

Several years later, in Hayek's essay, the terms "free market" and "free enterprise" are absent altogether, while "freedom" appears many times. Meanwhile, other references to "free society" suggest that Hayek is effectively expanding the remit of "freedom" to embrace both the narrow idea of the individual in pursuit of gratification, and wider idea of common human purpose. Thus connoted, "freedom" is used in a variety of ways in Hayek's essay, invoking the idea of trade, commerce, and bounty, but also as a higher ideal. In word and concept, "freedom" is elevated beyond the mundane to attain the status of something that is both taken for granted, or even squandered in the misguided allure of socialism, but immanent to the pure idea of human happiness:

> Does this mean that freedom is valued only when it is lost, that the world must everywhere go through a dark phase of socialist totalitarianism before the forces of freedom can gather strength anew? It may be so, but I hope it need not be. Yet, so long as the people who over longer periods determine public opinion continue to be attracted by the ideals of socialism, the trend will continue.[47]

In this essay Hayek argued that a layered and staged approach was required to popularize and spread ideas about individual choice and market freedom more broadly. To facilitate, this dissemination process would harness a group of elite scholars and experts, consisting of intellectuals

---

47. Hayek (1949, 382).

or "second hand dealers of ideas"[48] who would act as intermediaries and reinterpret and filter neoliberal ideas to the "masses" in the voice and style that made sense to them.[49] While not directly referring to public relations, Hayek made the point that in gaining public support, it was vital to avoid any suggestion of persuasion, lest it be construed as undemocratic.[50] In this approach, Hayek's MPS movement was "far less doctrinaire than the conventional narrative would suggest."[51]

As such, journalists, publicists, radio commentators, writers of fiction, cartoonists, and artists feature on Hayek's list as "carriers of new ideas outside their own fields."[52] Hayek postulated, "What qualifies him for his job is the wide range of subjects on which he can readily talk and write, and a position or habits through which he becomes acquainted with new ideas sooner than those to whom he addresses himself."[53] Moreover, it was imperative to be bold, optimistic, and motivating in order to challenge "the socialists," who for Hayek had the "courage to be Utopian."[54] To counter their appeal, therefore, Hayek declares: "we must be able to offer a new liberal program which appeals to the imagination. We must make the

---

48. Perhaps counterintuitively, by many standards, Hayek defines the term "intellectual" as not having any originality or high expertise. Rather, these second-hand dealers of ideas had to be quick and nimble thinkers as well as persuasive communicators well-versed in the latest trends, and moving confidently within a range of social, political and business networks and settings. (1949, 372).

49. Hayek writes: "These intellectuals are the organs which modern society has developed for spreading knowledge and ideas, and it is their convictions and opinions which operate as the sieve through which all new conceptions must pass before they can reach the masses" (1949, 347).

50. Ironically, Hayek believed that part of the problem for the conservative right was that it had engaged in good faith with the idea of democratic society, and that accounted for its lack of success. He writes: "the more conservative groups have acted, as regularly but unsuccessfully, on a more naive view of mass democracy and have usually vainly tried directly to reach and to persuade the individual voter" (1949, 372).

51. Burgin (2012, 9).

52. Hayek (1949, 372).

53. Hayek (1949, 418).

54. Hayek (1949, 432).

building of a free society once more an intellectual adventure, a deed of courage."[55]

Hayek's call to action carries several clues pointing to the deliberate agenda to enable the rise of neoliberalism. Imagination and "the courage to be Utopian"[56] to transform popular thinking is no overnight caper, but a long-term and patient endeavor in building support. To make this happen, academic weight was needed to carry Hayek's ideas into action.[57] Hence learned and erudite individuals were another band of crucial second-hand dealers in ideas, valued for their position of authority and access to elite enclaves: a potential which Hayek argued that so far only the left had laid effective claim to.[58]

FEE is the oldest free-market organization in the United States and was established in 1946 by Leonard E. Read, to study and advance the freedom "philosophy." Accordingly, with its persuasive free-enterprise agenda and extensive reach into networks both internationally and in the United States, the FEE was an ideal vehicle to transfer knowledge with authority that aligned with Hayek's views.[59] Setting these ideas in motion in 1949, Read released Ludwig von Mises's book, *Human Action*, through FEE.[60] While not itself of great note, this distribution of neoliberal ideas shows precisely the kind of back-handed approach Hayek recommended. Despite its length, the distribution of this work was well thought out and

---

55. Hayek (1949, 433).

56. Hayek (1949, 432).

57. It is not accidental, therefore, that over time Hayek should seek the help of a range of American business supporters like business journalist Henry Hazlitt and others such as John Davenport, a journalist, editor, author, and freelance writer, and Jasper Elliot Crane, "the MPS's most active business supporter in its early years" (Phillips-Fein 2009, 283).

58. Hayek's intense desire was to see organizations like FEE flourish and provide a model for other private organizations to replicate in spreading ideas about freedom and free markets. He wrote: "The number of such institutions which breed intellectuals and increase their number and powers grows every day" (Hayek 1949, 373).

59. Hayek (1949, 373).

60. Ludwig von Mises's *Human Action* was published in 1949.

extensive.[61] FEE purchased 1,140 copies of von Mises's book "in order to send a copy to each of the country's university and college libraries."[62] Such action would preserve von Mises's expertise as the original font of knowledge and provide for the propagation of ideas. As Hayek's (1949) paper demonstrates, and as Philip Mirowski points out, the conditions for neoliberalism's existence "*must be constructed* and will not come about naturally in the absence of concerted political effort and organization."[63]

"I, PENCIL"

The lesson I have to teach is this: *Leave all creative energies uninhibited*. Merely organize society to act in harmony with this lesson. Let society's legal apparatus remove all obstacles the best it can. Permit these creative know-hows freely to flow. Have faith that free men and women will respond to the Invisible Hand. This faith will be confirmed. I, Pencil, seemingly simple though I am, offer the miracles of my creation as testimony that this is a practical faith, as practical as the sun, the rain, a cedar tree, the good earth.[64]

First published in 1958, the parable-cum-essay, "I, Pencil," was written by Leonard E. Read, one of the "founding fathers of the Mont Pèlerin Society,"[65] and founding member of the think tank FEE.[66] Assuming the

---

61. In 1949, Jasper Crane wrote to Read, complaining that the book's "880 pages" made it daunting to tackle: "I suppose I ought to read it. But I cannot claim to be anywhere near the peak of the intellectual pyramid" (Crane 1950, 131).

62. Correspondence between Jasper Elliot Crane and Leonard E. Read (Crane 1950, 131).

63. Mirowski (2015, 234). Emphasis in original.

64. Read (1958, 11).

65. Liberaal Archief (2004, 16).

66. "The Foundation for Economic Education (FEE), is the oldest free-market organization in the United States, was established in 1946 by Leonard E. Read to study and advance the freedom philosophy. FEE's mission is to offer the most consistent case for the first principles of freedom: the sanctity of private property, individual liberty, the rule of law, the free market, and the moral superiority of individual choice and responsibility over coercion." Read (1958, 14).

voice of the humble pencil, Read relates the all-compassing story of a pencil as a "profound lesson" in logic for skeptics of the free-market society. Describing the harvesting of raw materials and the complex chain of globalized production processes required to make the pencil, the narrator declares that this gathering of forces to produce a lead pencil is a "miracle" of the invisible hand of capitalism. Written with a homespun inflection, and rich with religious metaphors, there is no doubt about the seriousness of Read's intentions in writing "I, Pencil." This seemingly simple tale makes a claim to veracity on a grand scale, and is designed to show the "moral superiority of individual choice over coercion" in encouraging the flourishing of a free market.[67] In this relatively obscure document, a particular kind of neoliberalism was emerging, a communicative strand that created powerful new social spaces and that, in following decades, would be buttressed by the suppressed forms of propaganda, such as public relations, in ways that had a profound and enduring impact.

Nonetheless, "I, Pencil" and publications like it, produced by FEE from its inception, were apparently designed to avoid any hint of the influence of public relations and propaganda. It contains no references to free market, free enterprise, or free society, but has four references to "freedom." While this frequency seems modest, the framing and underpinning weight ascribed to "freedom" is far from casual or incidental. At the outset of the homespun allegory, Read lays out the ideological and moral position in no uncertain terms for the reader: "If you can become aware of the miraculousness which I symbolize, you can help save the freedom mankind is so unhappily losing"; he follows with a galvanizing statement: "Freedom is impossible without this faith."[68] The political significance of Read's seemingly unsophisticated tale is underscored by Milton Friedman in an afterword, written in 1976, who remarked:

67. Read (1958, 14).
68. Read (1958, 9–10).

I know of no other piece of literature that so succinctly, persuasively, and effectively illustrates the meaning of both Adam Smith's invisible hand—the possibility of cooperation without coercion—and Friedrich Hayek's emphasis on the importance of dispersed knowledge and the role of the price system in communicating information that "will make the individuals do the desirable things without anyone having to tell them what to do."[69]

Read's parable is significant for its hegemonic potential, not just in the movement of meaning around the word "freedom," but in its choice of narrative features, intended to be absorbed into public language, to explain and spread "the basic idea that human freedom required private property, free competition, and severely limited government."[70]

FREEDOM, OBEDIENCE, AND THE HUMAN CAPITAL OF KNOWLEDGE PRODUCTION

Hegemony held the neoliberal project in place, and public relations held hegemony in place. The identification of conservative, like-minded "intellectuals" in Hayek's sense, who had expertise in their field and held sway of public opinion formation, became imperative to advance the neoliberal cause for the long term. With a focus on the power of public opinion,[71] and with the professional direction of A. D. Williams Jr., director

---

69. Friedman (1958, 12).

70. Friedman (1958, 13).

71. Lippmann ([1922] 1991, 29) writes: "Those features of the world outside which have to do with the behavior of other human beings, in so far as that behavior crosses ours, is dependent upon us, or is interesting to us, we call roughly public affairs. The pictures inside the head of these human beings, the pictures of themselves, of others, of their needs, purposes, and relationship, are their public opinions. Those pictures which are acted upon by groups of people, or by individuals acting in the name of groups, are Public Opinion with capital letters."

of public relations[72] for FEE, Vice President Henry Hazlitt remarked that within a short time of the think tank's establishment in 1946, "a stream of publications began to pour forth": "There were more than a hundred in the first few years. Some of these were one-page leaflets, some small folders, some moderate length pamphlets, and some were in effect short books."[73] In step with this mission, on forming FEE, Read had embarked on a prodigious publication campaign to raise economic or political issues in journals, pamphlets, books, and radio programs to "advisory and study groups in every state and in every community in America—*not* political action groups."[74]

Thus, in FEE, not only was there a strong emphasis on producing and implanting political meanings in the public imagination through publicity, but there was also a concerted effort to influence political decision-makers. In this work, FEE soon encountered the then-fledgling team at Hill and Knowlton, a public relations firm that would go on to become a key driver in the notorious tobacco industry campaigns in the 1950s.[75] Charles White, an officer of FEE and president of the Republic Steel Corporation,

---

72. According to Hazlitt (2006, 39), "FEE opened its doors on March 16, 1946. Most of the spring and summer was spent in the library, as renovation continued on the main building. The staff, as of September 1946, consisted of Leonard Read as President, Herbert Cornuelle as assistant to the President, W. M. Curtiss as Executive Secretary, Baldy Harper as Economist, Orval Watts as Editorial Director, and A. D. Williams Jr. as director of public rélations." These decisive and distinctive links between FEE and PR show that the organization was not only characterized by a neoliberal ethos, but also systematically focused on producing publicity to influence and shape public opinion to further these ideas as a core function. This activity is notable for the extent of its proliferation and its relatively early adoption. For Scott M Cutlip (1961, 368) the years 1945–1960 saw enormous growth in US public relations practice and education; a survey in 1956 by the Public Relations Society of America Education Committee found "that the number of colleges offering the subject had tripled in 10 years."

73. Hazlitt (2006).

74. Hazlitt (2006).

75. Hill and Knowlton was established in 1927 and continues to trade under that name as a worldwide public relations agency, following its acquisition in 1987 by global communications colossus WPP Group (Miller 1999, 177). In 1953 Hill and Knowlton consolidated its reputation as a clever, hawkish and dexterous PR firm when it aggressively confronted public concerns sparked by scientific evidence circulating in the mass media alerting people to the insidious and harmful effects of tobacco products. According to Allan Brandt, in strategizing its

had organized for Read to distribute FEE publicity relating to competitive enterprise via the firm.[76] FEE's early tendency to bypass conventional democratic channels and communicate ideas in hand with other corporate bodies, such as Hill and Knowlton, allowed it to operate outside the purview of traditional politics. This had the effect of constructing a new space that gave FEE entrée to domains at a safe distance, including politicians and educational institutions.[77]

Leonard E. Read was described as "handsome, strongly built, articulate, suave, well-groomed, energetic, and well-spoken."[78] FEE vice president Henry Hazlitt suggests that this charismatic quality inspired the respect of Hayek. Indeed, according to Hazlitt, it was Read's activities that set the MPS in motion.[79] Despite these inflated statements, it was the men who participated in the Lippmann seminar meeting of 1938 in Paris who would later form the core of the group that became the MPS, less than a decade later.[80] While Hazlitt believed that Hayek admired the Americans, such as Read, Hayek seems to have regarded entities such as FEE as having a somewhat dubious value in establishing the intellectual credentials of the

---

approach, the firm's president John W. Hill was sceptical about using advertising to influence public opinion, as it could be clearly seen as vested interest whereas: "the best public relations left no finger prints" (2012, 64). In challenging the veracity of the medical science that was causing alarm, Brand argues that Hill understood that it was critically important to "declare the positive value of scientific skeptisim of science itself" (2012, 64). Karen Miller (1999, 128) writes, "By 22 December, the agency had developed a PR program, and on 4 January, 1954, it announced the creation of the Tobacco Industry Research Committee through a newspaper advertisement headlined 'A Frank Statement to Cigarette Smokers' and signed by fifteen cigarette manufacturers, tobacco warehousers, and growers' groups."

76. Charles White refers to Leonard E. Read's business with Hill and Knowlton (1946, 67).

77. "This organization has been in operation for a little over four years, and prepares, publishes and distributes pamphlets and booklets presenting one side of issues having legislative significance. They are tax-exempt as an educational institution, and donations to them are deductible by the donor in determining his net income [. . .]. The Foundation for Economic Education has distributed close to 4,000,000 pamphlets and booklets in the last four years." House Select Committee on Lobbying Activities (July 18, 1950, 1).

78. Opitz (1998).

79. Haziltt (2006, https://fee.org/articles/the-early-history-of-fee/).

80. Jones (2017, 6); Plehwe (2009, 4).

MPS, owing to their tendency for simplistic proselytizing. According to Phillips-Fein:

> Although Read admired Hayek tremendously and adopted his vision wholeheartedly, Hayek and others in the MPS had long been wary about the FEE and about its strength in the American free-market intellectual scene, viewing the FEE as an overly strident, simplistic organisation that alienated as many people as it persuaded. Karl Brant for example, wrote that the FEE was "radical" and issued "cheap propaganda."[81]

Nonetheless, Read's prodigious publishing and networking activities in FEE must have shown that, with concerted effort, it was possible to launch a valuable counterpoint to the growing orthodoxy of John Maynard Keynes's economic theories and to collectivism.

That FEE placed a great deal of weight on the power and potential of communication to change mindsets is unmistakable, and points again to the submerged and divergent ways in which public relations was working at the time. To illustrate, in the FEE's early days, Read harnessed the professional relationship he had already forged with Ludwig von Mises to spread the word.[82] Read's invitation to von Mises to join the FEE was motivated both by their shared ideas about libertarianism and about the best approach to gaining broad social acceptance of those ideas through influencing public opinion. In 1943, von Mises and Read had corresponded and had discussed the place of publicity and persuasion in the battle for ideological supremacy between socialism and capitalism. They agreed this was tantamount and could be achieved by the appearance of a lofty appeal to a select group: the business elite and intelligentsia.

---

81. Mirowski and Plehew (2009, 293).

82. Margit von Mises, wife of "Lu" (Ludwig von Mises), wrote in her memoir: "It was a touch of genius combined with a shrewd sense of business that caused Leonard to associate Lu with FEE. It was the best idea he ever had, for he knew pretty well that if he could anchor the most eminent fighter for the free market to his foundation, not only the existence of the foundation was assured, but it would arouse the widest interest all over the country" (1976, 98).

> The masses, those millions of voters who are supreme in democracy, have to learn that they are deluded by spurious doctrines and that only market society and free enterprise can bring them what they want: prosperity. But in order to persuade the crowd, you have first to convince the elite, the intellectuals and the businessmen themselves.[83]

Clearly, words mattered. As such, FEE spent considerable thought, time, and money on the preparation of its communications. Read, for example, refers to the writing process as "in the mill," and that those draft publications were read "many times by me and other members of the staff."[84] But this communication activity must be understood in relation to the MPS's clear ambivalence about the value of a cheap propagandist approach in achieving a radical counterpoint to Keynesian economics. For Hayek, as for many of his colleagues in the postwar period, the wide-ranging appeal of what he calls "socialist" ideas in democratic countries poses an enormous threat and obstacle to the possibility of circulating, and attracting attention to, ideas about freedom and the free market among the mainstream population. To influence people on a large scale, Hayek recognizes that he and his fellow neoliberals must set in motion "a truly liberal radicalism."[85]

RAMIFYING WORDS: SIMPLICITY AND THE NUISANCE OF NUANCE

While a proto-neoliberal narrative emerged over this period with the simple goal of straddling several contradictory positions to ensure a sense of unity, it did not always succeed. Internal tensions within conservative

---

83. Margit von Mises (1976, 94).
84. Leonard E. Read to Mr. Charles M. White (October 7, 1946).
85. Hayek (1949, 432).

ranks over the use of clumsy propaganda, rather than subtler or more intellectual forms to shape opinion, were far from expunged, and as discussed, were particularly evident between the more extroverted US businessmen members of MPS and their more restrained European counterparts. On one hand, Hayek wanted to maintain an integrity of his economic theories and build authentic respect for their intellectual merit, but on the other hand, he was desperate to generate widespread public acceptance and uptake. Therefore, he advocated that the neoliberal language practices for knowledge formation should not tinker with socialist ideas at the edges, but wholly upend such discussions. The aim was to table an alternative utopian reality which was optimistic, seductive, and powerful in reorienting public opinion, to focus on creating desires for individual gratification over the collective good. However, Hayek's clash of ideas may have had a confusing effect for the ground troops.

Correspondence between Charles M. White, president of Republic Steel, and FEE's Leonard E. Read, in 1946, reveals internal tensions over *Roofs and Ceilings*, a "twenty-two-page treatise on the evils of rent control penned by Chicago School economists Milton Friedman and George Stigler in 1946."[86] In this terse exchange, White writes to Read that he was "terribly embarrassed several times about the reference in your *Roofs and Ceilings* pamphlet to the division of the wealth."[87] The irritation by White is very clear, as is his specific threat to abandon his association with FEE if his instructions to reduce the words and make the text more readable and engaging were not observed. After describing the pamphlet as "bull," White throws an ultimation: "If we can't boil this stuff down to short simple statements, I just can't be part of your show."[88] A part of Read's reply is instructive to understand these internal tensions in shaping the neoliberal narrative. He replies that *Roofs and Ceilings* was read many times, but "[o]versimplification of an idea is as dangerous as half-truths. Some

---

86. Boylan (2014, 4).
87. C. M. White (October 4, 1946).
88. C. M. White (October 4, 1946).

ideas are complex and ramified."[89] Read's response points to two preferred strategies to manage the reader's reception of the text: first, dissolving meaning with a light-touch approach that disguises a more radical intent, and second, "ramifying" or fortifying words to close off the many subterranean paths and branches that may be taken.

The wrestle between Charles White and Leonard Read over *Roofs and Ceilings* shows that, in practice, within the class identified as "second-hand dealers of ideas," there was pressure to flatten out meanings and nuance into bland simplifications. In addition, there was pressure to understand the "masses" as herds directed by a key group of experts, rather than as citizens who should be encouraged to think and form views by a dialectic process. Hayek's advocacy for a "utopian" narrative propelled the new ideology of individual choice and market-based freedom—which implies happiness—forcefully and successfully through these methods. Filtered through a hierarchical and phased communicative process, crude renderings of multifaceted ideas were applied to communications. In this, the hallmarks of public relations language strategies were established: a political mode predisposed to the compression of language, which connoted positive, futuristic terms that simplified complexity, in order to convert the public into "publics."

Leonard E. Read's profile as leader and key communicator in FEE and his role in MPS help to show the tension between his preference for detailed conceptual and explanatory material, and others' criticism of his work in matters of language and style for shaping "public opinion." At some point, Hayek must have reluctantly come to terms with the idea that manufactured forms of communication management, like public relations, were necessary to gain wider trust and belief in the mismatch of neoliberal reason in democratic society. In this, I have argued that there is an association between public relations practices and neoliberalism that is stronger and more complex than previously acknowledged. A distinctive neoliberal communicative mode emerged from this era, which has

---

89. Leonard E. Read (October 7, 1946).

unusual and largely unacknowledged design elements, but that has been propagated and active in hidden and subtle ways.

THE GREAT FORCES SHAPING OUR FUTURE

In the following decades, the global expansion of communication industries embedded neoliberal discourse beyond the United States.[90] In Australia, swallowed up by Hill and Knowlton in the late 1950s, was a locally grown and politically conservative public relations agency, Eric White and Associates.[91] Written by Thomas James Dwyer in 1961, this extract not only reveals the raft of powerful ways in which public relations was being enacted in transnational contexts, but also how local practitioners initially grappled to make sense of it:

> Like most new and unfamiliar tools PR was handled in the early years with a strange mixture of indecision, distrust and awe. The purpose and function of the tool were not always and everywhere understood. There were some managers who regarded PR as a type of jemmy to be used in prising open the doors to free advertising space. Others tried to wield it as a bludgeon to lay low opponents and critics. Others believed it to be a delicate surgical instrument designed for operating on the minds of people and condition them to new processes of thoughts. Others saw it either as an expensive time-consuming gadget or a diabolical monster from the improbable pages of a management science fiction novel, sent to bedevil honest

---

90. In 1958, a brochure was produced by the Public Relations Society of America, prophetically titled *The Great Forces Shaping Our Future*, to promote the National Public Relations Conference of November 5–7 of that year. Wisconsin Historical Society (2021).

91. Eric White and Associates was founded in 1947. According to Eric White's biography, together with his business partner Don Whitington in the 1950s, "EWA had an office in Melbourne, and took over the Australian operations of Hill & Knowlton Inc. and other American agencies. With different priorities, the pair went their separate ways in 1957." *Australian Dictionary of Biography* (2021). By 1971, Hill and Knowlton had fully acquired Eric White and Associates,

businessmen already plagued by regulations, labour shortages and financial stringencies.[92]

Dwyer's reflections on his early encounters with public relations language practices are highly instructive. That the "public relations" industry had arrived, with an all-encompassing, future-oriented aura of power, is unmistakable. That it used an odd mix of ideas that could mask brutality and that were highly strategized and opaque is also evident. That distinct public relations language practices, based on a spectrum of neoliberal voices— from Selvage, to Hayek, to Read—had been imported to Australia, and were set to work in submerged but potent ways, is undeniable.

Big business in postwar America encountered very different cultural and communicative conditions than in previous eras, such as in the "Gilded Age."[93] Nonetheless, the postwar period proved to be bountiful for public relations language practices to develop, especially in bedding down into the public imagination an overarching neoliberal protonarrative which used an interplay of history and fiction to straddle tricky contradictions. In this, both the word and the conceptual rendering of "freedom" has primacy for its discursive potency. Despite the social and economic conditions which favored the left and collectivism, public relations flourished in new modes and associations over this postwar period and disseminated the neoliberal narrative. It is hard to underestimate the impact that this relationship between big business, neoliberal ideology, and the public relations industry had on society. Together, a cartel-style partnership ensued, that was deliberately hidden and was designed to give

---

although it traded under the name "Eric White and Associates" but it continued to function under its original name until the mid-1980s." Ciarlante, cited in Crawley and Freeman (2012, 3).

92. Dwyer (1961, 7).

93. The "Gilded Age" refers to an era of industrial expansion in the United States, approximately 1870–1900, a moment in history when "golden opportunities" seemed in abundance. Andrew B. Arnold (2014, 1) writes: "This was an age, it seemed, in which the technological and financial limitations of the past were all falling away. Unimaginable riches and magical new technologies tantalized observers."

the free-market operators an advantage over public organizations and public services.

The field of public relations as a distinctive discursive mode is not a random development; its relationship and entanglement with neoliberalism are deep and historical. Some may argue that this is tangential; however, I argue that this entanglement was a purposeful strategy, and thus, I am seeking to re-evaluate the historical activity, drawing on literature and archival evidence to do two things: first, to acknowledge that this association existed; and second, to understand how it contributed to the formation of a distinctive communicative mode, which has endured and has characterized many social, cultural, and political arenas. The practices of public relations have long sought to control contradictions to maintain their harmonizing control over highly contested social and political issues. Unless scholars commit to the large task of exploring and critiquing the communicative dimensions of the neoliberal project, then we may fail to develop a more comprehensive, ethically oriented assessment of its discursive and rhetorical practices and effects, and, by extension, neglect the critical task of responding meaningfully to its ongoing impacts.

3

"We Need a New Narrative"

Neoliberalism and Public Relations Language Practice

In 1967, *The Society of the Spectacle* provoked a critical discussion of the deadening effects of mass communication, claiming that news, propaganda, advertising, and "the actual consumption of entertainment" had become a prevailing force in society, making, shaping, and distorting economic, social, and political realities.[1,2] In tabling this, author Guy Debord argued that capitalist power and cultural products had assumed a level of authority which in turn subdued critique and built political passivity, dynamically anchored to the imaginary through "the accumulation of spectacles."[3] This media spectacle is at once a by-product and intimately linked to the forces of capitalism. But it is the self-referential, reifying characteristics of this spectacle that produce shared meanings, which make it so remarkable, so durable. The spectacle appears as general truth and is packaged with a corporate

---

1. "We need a new narrative"; Bonchek (2016).

2. Debord offers a range of ways in which this illusionary spectacle manifests, but does not specifically mention the public relations industry (Debord and Nicholson-Smith 1994, 13).

3. For Debord, this passivity generated by spectacles is bound up by both the product and its purpose: "The spectacle manifests itself as an enormous positivity, out of reach and beyond dispute" (Debord 1994, 12–15).

"gloss"[4] of rationality. It acts as a hold to bring together disparate phenomena in an all-encompassing embrace, which is warm, glowing, and glorious. For Debord, this illusionary phenomenon is understood through a collection of its products, such as images, but also as "a social relationship between people that is mediated by images."[5] His lens opens a plausible analysis of the culturally hegemonic effects of capitalist society as seen through its byproduct, mass media. Written several decades after the postwar period, his work may serve also as a historical marker—a stake in the communicative ground—to illustrate some of the culminative effects of neoliberalism and public relations in producing the "mediated social relationship" of the "spectacle."[6]

The chapter explores the construction of meaning, interpretation, and action, through the lens of neoliberalism and its instrument: public relations. In doing so, it builds on the previous chapter, in which I argued that this relationship has endured, through a dominant storied mode of communication, based on a proto-narrative the emerged in the United States over the postwar period: the story of an individual's endeavor, faith, prosperity, and freedom, through the power of a market unfettered by government and regulation. This proto-narrative has worked to embed canonical market-based ideas on an immense scale, while at the same time, deterring or subduing cultures that support dialogue and debate. This chapter asks: How do public relations language practices become compelling in this world? And what makes these both predictable and acceptable today? And how do they work to create tolerance of ideas that run counter to humanism and science? In response, I draw on narrative theories[7] that cast light on the power and significance of plastic words[8] as units of meaning that are linked within language structures, to show

---

4. Debord (1994, 16).
5. Debord (1994, 12).
6. Debord trans. Donald Nicholson (1994, 12).
7. Bancroft (2018); Phelan (2014); Tamboukou (2013).
8. Poerksen (1995).

how public relations, as an instrument of neoliberalism, takes possession of and shapes meaning so comprehensively. It is the harnessing of this discursive power by public relations industries, through the modality of narrative, that opens understanding in this area. In attempting to open a specific and differentiated meaning, I refer to these malleable public relations language practices, which quietly intimate market-based logic in communicative realms, as "neonarratives."

Neonarratives cohering around the economic idea of "freedom" have insinuated their influence in all areas of life, and their hallmark vocabulary—plastic words, such as *development, competition, security,* and *prosperity*—consistently circulate to determine meaning in the decisions that society makes. In public, professional, and private domains, this vocabulary enjoys enormous currency. Such words, their meanings, and the intangible economic fears and desires that they unquestionably connote, function by promulgating and authorizing specific truths. It appears as the only way to think about things. Increasing its power and authority as common sense, such narratives open from countless sites to soak in and dissolve threats from other wayward ideas or concerns. Neonarratives are language structures that rely on a complex interplay of meaning, which refers to the real and imaginary, to tradition and history, in order to arouse action, and to gesture toward an interior "truth" contingent on the economic sphere. But they are not the only public relations practice of speaking and writing. Exposition, argument, and description are used in media releases, brochures, reports, proposals, campaigns, speeches, and research—but these are absorbed by, or fold into, a hybridized and controlling neonarrative structure.[9] Now deployed not only by those who directly support the neoliberal agenda, but also by those who would claim to resist it, neonarratives are put to work in ways that merit closer scrutiny[10].

---

9. Cleanth Brooks and Robert Penn Warren discuss the powerful properties of narration that can "absorb other modes" (1979, 190).

10. Public relations activities routinely deployed by industry practitioners, such as media campaigning, lobbying, or issue management, to control and shape the public's opinions and produce "knowledge," are intrinsically political, frequently manipulative, and should always be scrutinized for the risks they pose, and the harm they may cause, to individuals, groups and

Consequently, this chapter reflects on narrative and its function as a powerful and, arguably, too often reductive modality of meaning-making, with a range of ethical implications.

In this, I aim to show the ultimate purpose and the paradox of harnessing neonarratives: to close off possibility and the will for inclusive and communicative exchange and democratic public debate. Because to keep public opinion alive, in the Habermasian sense, is to argue *against* two apparently incontrovertible truths of neoliberal reason: first, that the market is all-knowing, indissoluble, and coherent; and second, given that the market knows best, that there is no place—and no point—in deliberative and engaged political struggle over what might improve life for the planet and for all. Thus, as the neoliberal project denies the inherently interdependent and social nature of human beings,[11] so does it deny the social nature of language, that is, to engage in inclusive forms of political struggle: to deliberate, argue, feel, understand, and reimagine the world. For Henry A. Giroux, "[t]his means rethinking the very meaning of the political so that it can provide a sense of direction but no longer be used to provide complete answers."[12]

In exploring these themes, I draw a line between these problems, and the public relations domain that carries implications and raises ethical questions that are central for practice. Public relations language practices work to generate acquiescence and political control within the many public conversations and debates, and in the contest of ideas. But how is this done so successfully, and in such a widespread way? Applying the idea of dialogue in Habermasian discourse, Fiona Robinson argues that

---

society. However, some public relations activities may tend toward a politically benign or adopt a more ethically enlightened approach, perhaps because they are mobilized around a socially unifying cause, such as community welfare, disaster relief, or charity work. Yet despite this, the mode of public relations that has prevailed over the twentieth century and into the twenty-first, which has progressively been harnessed by the neoliberal project, and which is now also firmly embedded in the vernacular of mainstream culture, is one that champions powerful financial and corporate interests, even as it may purport to be socially inclusive and ethically sensitive.

11. Mary V. Wrenn discusses that the denial of the "essential social nature" of human beings is at the core of the key enabling myths of neoliberalism (2016, 454).

12. Giroux (2004, 133).

the application of feminist ethics of care crucially repositions the idea of marginality, from the edges to the center. This implies an acceptance from the outset, that these unequal conditions are not an aberration of an ideal, but the normative reality. Therefore, these barriers are not there to be overcome; rather, dependence and vulnerability are to be understood as a regular—but not inevitable—part of human social life.[13] Therefore, it is the way in which those "publicly competing opinions"[14] in the Habermasian public sphere were already, and still are, always unequal which is such an important consideration. The interrelationships of this, understood through the responsibilities of care, must be acknowledged in understanding the ethical implications of neonarratives.

To tackle this, the chapter draws on a Foucauldian framework to develop an alternative, richer description, that shows the distinct ways in which forms of public relations work in the Habermasian public sphere, in the service of neoliberal agendas that promote simplistic, self-focused, and autonomous relationships to society.[15] Specifically, it looks at how this is done through language practices, to suppress the emergence of other coherences and discursive formations, particularly in relation to social change. The challenge is, therefore, to set in motion an alternative approach to communicating in the public domain: an approach that guides the critique and (re)ordering of discursive material, within the uncertain terrain of the twenty-first century. Identifying the critical dynamics of communicative practices may open new research trajectories, which may draw attention to, avoid, or preclude these unethical consequences. In turn, this may build other forms of rationality and knowledge.

Produced by the public relations industry, neonarratives as discursive constructs are linked to specific social and historical postwar contexts,

---

13. Robinson (2011, 847).

14. Habermas (1995, 195).

15. Mary V. Wrenn and William Waller discuss that "[n]eoliberalism postulates a specific vision of human nature. Individuals are self-interested and proceed in the service of this self interest in atomistic, individualistic terms. This conception is often assumed as self-evident truth and is a part of a simplistic argument in favor of autonomy" (2017, 1).

to which today's industry consultants and practitioners dynamically intersect with, and reflex toward. I argue that one such historically situated moment is within the crucible of the neoliberal thought collective, given impetus by the Mont Pèlerin Society (MPS).[16] It was also when the appearance of a distinctive, simple, all-encompassing, and future-oriented story manifested in the public sphere, saturated in neoliberal rationality. Taking root within the cultural and communicative conditions in the United States, this *story* was of an individual's endeavor and faith to achieve prosperity and freedom, through the power of a dominant, market-based society, assisted by government as administration. In communicating this storied sequence of ideas more broadly, the appearance of heavy-handed propaganda was to be avoided at all costs.[17] This ensured that a layer of communicative activity continued unabated, one which had strong hegemonic purpose, was partially submerged, and was not acknowledged either by industry, or the very forces it championed for its success. Hence, meanings were silently embedded by the neoliberal proto-narrative, in a range of popular genres, from political editorials in newspapers,

---

16. From the 1940s to the 1970s, an influential transatlantic network of "businessmen and fundraisers, journalists and politicians, policy experts and academics" worked to revive and popularize seemingly outdated ideas about free enterprise and small government, and at the same time, take aim at opposing left-leaning collectivist or socialist ideas (Steadman Jones 2012, 134). The diverse, and at times uneasy, alliances in this network led to the effective and global dissemination of neoliberal ideas to infiltrate policy settings through a range of communications, including think tanks. "But in the immediate postwar decades, neoliberal thought might have been confined to academic circles were it not for the growth of a network to spread its message of individual liberty, free, markets, low taxes, deregulation and limited government on both sides of the Atlantic" (Steadman Jones 2012, 134–135). Thus, the first meeting of the Mont Pèlerin Society in Switzerland in 1947, which "held this group together," is an important marker in spreading these ideas (Steadman Jones 2012, 135).

17. For Hayek, one of the principal challenges that he and his fellow neoliberals faced in the postwar period was influencing people on a mass scale. He was quite clear that he did not want transparent promotional tactics that people could see through. To address this, he identified the pivotal role of "intellectuals" who, in his view, wield power by "shaping opinion" over the long term, without the heavy-handed sense of propaganda (Hayek 1949, 317). It was therefore critical for conservatives to find respected individuals in society to influence the public. Hayek called these "second hand dealers in ideas," and included scientists and doctors, as well as a range of publicly focused professionals, such as "journalists, teachers, ministers, lecturers, publicists, radio commentators, writers of fiction, cartoonists, and artists" (Hayek 1949, 372).

to radio scripts, children's books, and family television. These language practices are centrally entwined with a specialized form of storytelling. Neonarratives are particularly powerful social constructions, because this modality as knowledge formation unlocks "the embrace, apparently so tight, of words and things, and the emergence of a group of rules proper to discursive practice."[18]

NEOLIBERALISM, PUBLIC RELATIONS PRACTICE, AND NEONARRATIVE

There is no story unless our attention is held in suspense by a thousand contingencies.[19]

To understand the power and reach of neonarratives in the public sphere, the delimitation of public imagination to the confines of market-driven culture, emanating from innumerable points in society, must also be understood. Hence for Maria Tamboukou[20] the study of language practices is not about a search to unlock the truth, or to bring to light hidden meaning. Rather, it is through an investigation of power and discourse, by "uncovering layers of distortions/constructions and is directed to the future rather than to the past."[21] In this, she asks the reader to consider the following: "How has our present been constituted in ways that seem natural and undisputable to us, but are only the effects of certain historical, social, cultural, political and economic configurations? By revealing this contingency, we become freer to imagine other ways of being."[22] Hence, the conceptualization of neoliberal language practices, as products of immense economic privilege and force in postwar US society, give way to

---

18. Foucault (1972, 49).
19. Ricoceur (2009, 277).
20. Tamboukou (2013).
21. Tamboukou (2013, 2).
22. Tamboukou (2013, 2).

an interpretation of power, in the Foucauldian sense of "producing truth, knowledge and ultimately the subject."[23]

From many viewpoints, the dynamics of storied language formations are rich sites for investigation. James Phelan shows how narrative's ahistorical ubiquity, as a form of temporal truth, not only opens its capacity as an object of inquiry with "finite means (setting, character, event, plot, and a wide array of techniques)";[24] it is also the process through which meaning, distortion, and construction are revealed:

> Narrative is not just an object to be interpreted and evaluated but also a way of interpreting and evaluating. To tell a story about an experience is to give that experience shape and meaning by setting it off from other experiences, placing it in the grooves of an intelligible plot, and judging its agents and events.[25]

Narrative formations are thriving and proliferating beyond the usual domains, such as fiction, or the lived experience. In public relations contexts, they are widespread as a means to push "publics" along a course toward a real and imaginary outcome.[26] This growth in narrative scripts in diverse settings is explained by Lindsay Holmgren, who argues that "a version of narrative" emerged in the economic sphere in the late 1980s, which placed events, "such as monetary shocks, within temporal frameworks that help to unveil particular, more or less fiscally liberal narratives, in part by aligning them with actual policy shifts."[27] While this conceptualization

---

23. Tamboukou (2013, 4).

24. Phelan (2008, 167).

25. Phelan (2008, 167).

26. For Paul Ricoeur, narratives generate episodic anticipation of events which impel us to attend: "To follow a story is to understand the successive actions, thoughts and feelings as displaying a particular directedness. By this I mean that we are pushed along by the development and that we respond to this thrust with expectations concerning the outcome and culmination of the process. In this sense, the 'conclusion' of the story is the pole of attraction of the whole process" (Ricoeur 2009, 277–278).

27. Holmgren (2021, 193).

of narrative in the economic sphere is criticized as an analytical tool for its subjectivity, Holmgren argues that "it is precisely the subjective human quality of a narrative approach that gives monetary theory—and ultimately policy—the depth and relevance it requires, emphasizing the urgency of understanding narrative reception by the flesh-and-blood audiences who are directly affected by policy changes."[28]

Aside from the application of narrative to a range of atypical settings like commerce, there has been an explosion of interest in this field, and a surge of narrative applied in various forms across government and civil society, and with individuals who have the digital tools to share meanings. Mäkelä et al. discuss that "[t]he current storytelling boom across various spheres of life encourages actors from individuals to businesses and institutions to instrumentalize stories of personal experience, but the search for a 'compelling story' is often blind to the possible downsides of experientially and emotionally engaging narratives."[29] In making sense of this booming storied language formation, Mäkelä et al. discuss that it attaches the narrative to new reality, while at the same time, it "blocks exchanges, and saturates symbolic space with its series and stories."[30] No longer primarily concerned with distribution of knowledge and past experience, it "shapes behaviors and channels flows of emotion," and establishes narrative systems where individuals both identify and conform to the rules established.[31] This disarticulation of narrative from the retelling of authentic past experience to purposeful market-based rationality distribution is significant. It points to movements in academic understanding of how the modality is being applied, and how it might be analyzed from different standpoints. Increasingly, activism, which for so long put up resistance to public relations language practices,

---

28. Holmgren (2021, 193).

29. Mäkelä et al. (2021, 139).

30. In this section, Mäkelä et al. cite the work of Amy Schuman (2021, 139).

31. Mäkelä et al. (2021, 141).

subscribes to "story-telling and social change,"[32] a mode heavily inflected by ideas of personal empowerment, where "you" can "change the world" and "move forward" with "compelling messages that connect with your target audience."[33]

Many well-meaning people, groups, and advocacy organizations are using public relations language and communication practices this way, but they are caught in a slipstream, and are compelled to draw on a narrow font of knowledge that potentially bounds action to a stripped-back set of market-based ideas. It follows that they are less likely to embed meaning from a wider repertoire of ideas. Once such a discursive monoculture is built, this cycle ensures that politics revolves around the same questions, and the same answers. While there are many variables that may influence the extent to which this situation prevails, it is fair to say that, increasingly, there is a receptiveness within activism to understand advocacy within the language and ideas of public relations. Reductively, totalizing knowledge within neoliberal rationality, the fragmentation is reinforced by information technologies like social media, which connect in the idea of the "personal" or "self"; this works to powerfully embed these values, and fracture shared understandings that had previously been united by memory and a vastly wider pool of ideas.[34]

32. *Storytelling and Social Change: A Strategy Guide* outlines the "sacred bundle" of stories: the "nature-of-our-challenge story," the "creation story," the "emblematic-success story," the "striving-to-improve story," and the "where-we-are-going story" (WorkingNarratives.Org Story-Guide 2021).

33. Fenton Communications (2009).

34. Jill Walker Rettberg (2014, 35) discusses the proliferating idea of the sharing/personal cultures in terms of selfies, blogs, and wearable devices: "Digital self-presentation and self-reflection is cumulative rather than presented as a definitive whole (J. W. Rettberg 2014, 5). A weblog or social media feed consists of a continuously expanded collection of posts, each of which may express a micro-narrative, a comment that expresses an aspect of the writer or an image showing a version of themselves."

"A STRATEGIC NARRATIVE IS A SPECIAL KIND OF STORY"

In contemporary business and organizational cultures, the idea of coupling the humanness in "telling a story," as a hegemonic business strategy for managing resistance and acceptance in commercial relationships, has taken root.[35] Referring to these as "strategic narratives," business consultant Mark Bonchek posits that:

> The cornerstone of a strategic narrative is a shared purpose. This shared purpose is the outcome that you and your customer are working toward together. It's more than a value proposition of what you deliver *to* them. Or a mission of what you do *for* the world. It's the journey that you are on *with* them. By having a shared purpose, the relationship shifts from consumer to co-creator.[36]

"Strategic narratives," such as Bonchek describes, may be used in business writing extensively, but they are fettered to "texts, such as arguments, committee reports, and descriptions, whose overall structures are governed by nonnarrative principles."[37] The upsurge of "non-narrative," stemming from neoliberal language practices within business settings and digital conditions that support the culture of self, must lead to a consideration of market power and resourcing, and how this, in turn, controls that power through this modality. This thickening entwinement between business and narrative is an important trajectory, and its analysis is assisted by Corinne Bancroft's conception of the braided narrative in fictional settings. She argues that "[a]s the term and image imply, braided narratives are comprised of multiple narratives that twine together to form a novel."[38]

---

35. "A strategic narrative is a special kind of story"; Bonchek (2016).

36. Bonchek (2016). Italics in original.

37. Phelan (2008, 168).

38. Bancroft (2018, 266).

As such, there are profound ethical considerations for those who create narratives, from their plots, and tensions that they smooth over or highlight, to (dis)continuities they create, and the relationship to the reader.[39]

And because these narratives are tangled up within many and various discourses and settings, they generate new and different effects. For Bancroft, this change profoundly complicates the ethical implications of such practices. She argues that in braided narratives the number of narrators multiply ethical positions "but also create a productive tension between situations and narrators."[40] In this way, for Bancroft, readers are "claimed by not one, but multiple narrators, resulting in a complicated layering of calls and questions that we must negotiate in order to even make sense of the novel."[41]

Braided neoliberal and public relations language practices are co-constructed by very powerful interlocutors, who have been harnessed to open vast political influence.[42] And this collaborative process is highly significant in understanding its potential for shaping anti-political representations. For Effron et al., "this is collaborative enterprise underpins the importance of narrative communication as a mediator of change."[43] Narrative more broadly not only scaffolds the imaginary or fictional to

---

39. In this, Bancroft discusses an ethical schema by James Phelan, consisting of four positions within story worlds on which to focus ethical questions: first, in relation to the characters; second, between the narrator and the audience; third, the implied author; and fourth, "that of the flesh-and-blood reader in relation to the set of values, beliefs, and locations operating in situations"; (Phelan, cited in Bancroft 2018, 272).

40. Bancroft (2018, 273).

41. Bancroft (2018, 272).

42. Barney Warf discusses the Trump administration and neoliberalism's failure to contain the coronavirus, and how *Fox News* presenter Sean Hannity joined with him to shield this incompetence to the public. He wrote: "The coronavirus has seeped into every crack and fault line in American society, exposing deep and long-standing class and racial inequalities. A country that should have been well prepared to combat the pandemic instead found itself hamstrung. Combined with a formidably ignorant public fed a daily diet of misinformation from conservative outlets such as *Fox News*, many people became impervious to scientific advice and opinion" (Warf 2021, 9).

43. Effron et al. (2019, 334).

the real but develops the conditions to politically intervene to disrupt the formation of meaning. But neonarrative formation does this by drawing the reader unwittingly into the economic realm of the public sphere, a social space already supporting unequal conditions. Hence there are two important ethical dynamics in the idea of co-construction: first, "author-audience interaction," and second, the "rhetorical nature of the narrative act" to mediate change and alter reality.[44]

So, while stories or narratives draw on something largely understood to be authentic, universal, and intergenerational, which gives them extraordinary power and momentum, this is not always the case. Rather, multiple forms of narrative can co-exist and understanding this helps to clarify context and power.[45] I apply this idea to public relations language practices and argue that, the simplified idea of narrative form is often invoked to sign post and plot neoliberal meaning in political media contexts. This subtle interplay between what narrative "should be" but 'isn't' in part, explains how the partnership between neoliberalism and public relations works side by side with authentic narrative to establish organizing frames to make sense of the world. Mäkelä et al. illustrate this in relation to the narratives crowdsourced through channels of social media. Politically motivated narratives can attract millions of views and shares. They argue that:

> The narrative phenomenon that we call the viral exemplum, which ought to be understood as a collision of forms rather than a form in itself, contributes to post-truthfulness in the contemporary public sphere as it shields itself from fact-checking and criticism on three levels—those of experientiality, representativeness, and normativity.[46]

---

44. Effron et al. (2019, 334).
45. Groves (2012, 39) refers to this as "multinarrativism."
46. Mäkelä et al. (2021, 155).

Public relations produces texts that regularly draw on narrative traditions, such as plans of action with situation analyses, target public profiles, key messages and talking points that are distributed in social media postings, briefings, campaigns, and lobbying. These narrative forms appear in undetectable and in more explicit ways to press the reader to act and think in market-based ways, that may have the effect of suppressing critical thinking.[47]

THE PUBLIC RELATIONS REPERTOIRE OF PLASTIC WORDS

I argue that one way in which public relations and neoliberalism work together is by establishing a repertoire of coherent textual forms, that work within different contexts. These textual forms sit under an overarching neonarrative which interweaves discourses—of the economy, wealth, freedom, individualism, and security, for example—and which are "glued" together by what may be identified as keywords, but what Uwe Poerksen prefers to call "plastic words."[48] The power of plastic words is chiefly accrued from their being abstract, ahistorical, context-independent, ambiguous, apparently universal, and adaptable, across a range of discursive domains. In harnessing the notion of plastic words, both as key terms and as a means of camouflaging the flawed coherence of neonarratives, I aim to show how a relatively circumscribed vocabulary, assembled in storied form, has become integral to the neoliberal project. It has done this by signaling neoliberalism's central precepts and by weaving them into narratives as shorthand, as markers of authority and control.[49] Such words have become so ordinary that they often fail to provoke reflection

---

47. Phelan (2008).

48. Poerksen (1995, 6–7).

49. Indeed, Hayek himself noted the influence exerted by what he called "catchwords": terms that capture unspecific, or imprecise, or less understood ideas (1949, 424). For a development of this discussion, see Chapter 2.

or critical scrutiny, given their ubiquitous, everyday usage. Plastic words serve to reorder a unique kind of dispossessed and autonomous language practice, that resists being attached to a time or place, or embodied in life. I argue that the unreflective use of plastic words contributes to the depoliticizing effects of neonarratives more generally.

FREEDOM

"Freedom" excites an individual's imagination to see their different selves, bigger, bolder, more purposeful, and successful. It becomes a critically important key word in the neoliberal narrative, to deliver market-based logic in palatable, problem-free form, and that promises bounty and/or reward. In this abstracted and ahistorical position within the vernacular, the word "freedom" disguises or makes invisible its politically connotative implications, and yet they are still there. As such, it is critical to note the bridge between the terms "free market," "free enterprise," and "freedom."[50] The idea of "free market," in particular, has established economic academic traditions that invoke positivist[51] scientific method to investigate and explain the social world. In this sense, "freedom," as a conduit to the notion of "free market," represents "a mingling of spheres" which promotes the "mathematization" or the intensifying datafication of everyday language.[52] Thus, "freedom," as economics in the neoliberal sense, is absorbed into

---

50. Chapter 2 traces the movement of meaning in three texts, situated in the postwar period.

51. Positivism is a paradigm that upholds the idea that a testable hypothesis will produce a social fact and truth. However, Foucault (1972, 202) argued that naïve, restrictive, and hidden ideologies underlie positivist thought. Positivism is associated with a view that "the structure and functioning of society could be mapped to a biological model" (Harper 2011, 3). If all parts perform their separate functions and work together, it will survive as a "healthy" or "well" society. Structural functionalism and positivism were highly influential in early communication research and institutional practices, which sought to explain behavior and to provide the means for its predication and control, for example, media-effects research. However, by the second half of the twentieth century, critiques of positivism challenged its "core premises and practices," and as a result, communication researchers looked for other methods (Lindlof and Taylor 2002, 9).

52. Poerksen (1995, xvii).

the everyday, and positions the subject in relation to these unrevealed connections.[53]

The word "freedom" does not appear in Poerksen's catalog of plastic words. But with its established links to the functionalist economic sphere, weight, and authority, reductive but elastic usage, positive resonance, and "ahistorical naturalness,"[54] arguably, it is normatively working this way, and as such, a potent and unique variant. With its provenance in philosophical and sociopolitical spheres,[55] the term "freedom," since the postwar period, has been used for example to describe consumer goods, cultural products like songs, books, and movies, and various political and religious organizations. As such, it is a universal sign, alive and glowing, while at the same time, unremarkable. For Poerksen, in reducing and flattening out diversity of meaning, plastic words become "the master key to the everyday [. . .] and they open doors to enormous rooms. They infiltrate entire fields of reality, and they reorder that reality in their own image."[56] Thus, plastic words encompass generality: and "freedom" does just this. It makes other words, like "duty," or the shouldering of the "burden of responsibility," sound slow and cumbersome, dated and obsolete. Notions of dependability, or reliability, which are implicit in any society that can offer freedom for individuals, seem like dead weights,

---

53. In a celebratory edition of "The Freeman" (1981), George Koether, a public relations practitioner, journalist, speech writer, and a former student of Austrian School economist, Ludwig von Mises, selected and arranged excepts from his landmark book, *Human Action* (1949). In this special edition, Koether distills von Mises's ideas into an alphabetical list of fifty-nine subjects, from "Accounting and Advertising" to "Wages and War." He writes: "In these extracts I have sought to capture the essence of his thought on a number of topics, but for purposes of brevity and ease of comprehension sentences have been shortened and juxtaposed, words eliminated, paragraphing changed and punctuation sometimes altered. Yet, with the exception of a very few words in brackets, every word in these extracts is pure Mises, every word is taken from *Human Action*" (Koether 1981, 517). This compression of von Mises's sprawling thesis into a number of subject headings is noteworthy not just for the signification of key ideas that had endured over that thirty-year period, but to show, in a Poerksenian sense, how the road to "canonization" was trodden.

54. Poerksen (1995, 25).

55. Eagleton-Pierce (2016).

56. Poerksen (1995, 4).

holding the individual back from reaching their potential. "Freedom" is future-oriented, and promises an unshackling from dull obligation; in that sense, it is youthful and always emergent. Thus, the all-embracing idea of "human freedom"[57] is tied to the notion of entrepreneurship, selfishness, and competition in a market economy, and can be understood to be at the center of neonarrative practices. Adopting the notion in this sense might set in train a belief that if "freedom" is politically available, it provides everyone with the same opportunity, the same resources, and the same benefits. Therefore, conditions such as exclusion, threat, inequity, or disadvantage become far less problematic.[58] Indeed, unease around these matters might be alleviated or removed entirely. And disparaging or challenging the interpretation of these ideas can be brushed away, or crushed, as either propaganda, insanity, delusion, or oppression. Thus, the brutalizing and imaginary properties of this word are simultaneously implanted in discourse. As with other plastic words, there is a quiet aura of anticipation around "freedom." In that sense, the word can be analyzed as always arousing appetites and wants, and that enterprise and commerce can always satisfy that need or desire.[59] Words like "freedom" work, because they diminish complication and co-construct passivity and acceptance.[60] "Freedom" does not just make life simple, smooth away problems, and tantalize with a glimpse of what might be for good or ill; it becomes a living thing, as if propelled by the very laws of nature. Importantly, it

---

57. Offering a critical assessment, Jodi Dean (2008, 48) says that "[r]edefining social and ethical life in accordance with economic criteria and expectations, neoliberalism holds that human freedom is best achieved through the operation of markets."

58. In examining the provenance of the word "freedom," Eagleton-Pierce (2016, 83) argues that "[a]lthough this term is found in the eighteenth century, it only grew in popularity from the 1930s, with a notable conceptual take-off from the late 1970s." For Leary (2018, 96–97) "free market" emerged as a substitute term for capitalism, which had developed negative connotations as a socialist criticism. Significantly, the term "free market" gestures to an ideal: "a condition and an expression of inalienable political rights, of freedom in the political and even existential sense: 'The freer the market, the freer every man's choice as to what he will work at as well as what he will buy.'"

59. Poerksen (1995, 16).

60. Poerksen (1995, 102).

pulls people toward individual action, but not toward collective thinking. "Freedom" is a word that is both favored and harnessed by public relations, acting as an intermediary by intervening in the deliberation process, to control public opinion and manage both intrinsic and extrinsic contradictions. Within the closed frame of a market-based society, "freedom" is a singularly powerful idea, elaborated in a myriad of ways as neonarrative.

Other plastic words—such as communication, information, security, growth, competition, prosperity, future, development, innovation, resource, solution, market, flexibility, choice, and participation—are now so everyday as to sound politically neutral or nondescript. Produced for, and found in, news bulletins, speeches, reports, business emails, tweets, company website copy, briefing notes, government policies, funding applications, curriculum vitae, self-help manuals, and professional training modules, for example, the presence of such words in texts goes largely unnoticed. But something seems out of place if they are *not* present. Plastic words, in their now unobtrusive, commonplace—if not compulsory—entanglement in everyday language, and as shown below, in plastic neonarratives, typically signal currency and vigor. An emotionally ambivalent tension that exists within a response to these words, and their conceptual and semantic qualities, is that they may suggest something important, and yet can mean nothing in particular; they are of the moment, and yet necessarily ahistorical; they can present as incontestably coherent and sensible, though their integrity melts under scrutiny. Because terms such as "freedom" and "choice," for example, are able to fold in and smooth over—or smother—the jarring contradictions of neoliberal reason, they become powerful resources in the neoliberal lexical catalog. Indeed, plastic words, as Poerksen points out, "sound friendly, smooth, positive, and consensual, but, while not in themselves evil, they mask brutality. With a word such as 'development,' one can ruin an entire region."[61] The ethical implications, attendant on even the most apparently innocuous use of plastic words, are notable. Within a spectrum of

---

61. Poerksen (1995, 6–7).

neoliberal rationality, differentiation gives way to a conformity of ideas in opinion and imagination, in ways that lead to a particular and reductive and prescribed worldview.

A significant appeal of plastic words, not only to proponents of the free market, but to anyone seeking or asserting an authoritative voice in contemporary neoliberal culture, is their modular character[62] and their "semantic pliancy."[63] These words are adaptable to the discursive contexts into which they may be inserted. In their portability, such words become "historically disembedded"[64] and lose the meanings accorded by spatial and cultural context; they are thus transformed into "nature."[65] By extension, their abstraction enables mobility and modularity, and affords them the capacity to be connected with similar words, and thereby to form "verbal nets."[66] Crucially, such words are typically proffered as value-free.[67] They are general, connotative, positive terms; "they reduce all domains to a common denominator and sound an imperative and futuristic note."[68] Hollowed out and reduced to information bytes through their incorporation into discursive forms across institutional and public spaces, their generality may nonetheless induce passivity, or "consensus."[69]

Importantly, Poerksen notes that plastic words produce their effects both as semantic units and as concepts: "a way of imagining."[70] Indeed, he explains that plastic words are first and foremost concepts, and that these inform or anchor such vocabulary, or semantic units.[71] In order to

---

62. Poerksen (1995, 95). Poerksen likens such words to Lego blocks.

63. Poerksen (1995, 9).

64. Poerksen (1995, 22).

65. Poerksen (1995, 23).

66. Poerksen (1995, 59).

67. Poerksen (1995, 87).

68. Poerksen (1995, 102).

69. Poerksen (1995, 102).

70. Poerksen (1995, 28).

71. Poerksen (1995, 28).

clarify this distinction, consider the word "sustainability," which, while not appearing in Poerksen's list of plastic words, potentially qualifies as emerging, and one which may be regularly harnessed by the contemporary neoliberal vernacular. With its provenance in the social movements of the 1970s, "sustainability" has, in some contexts and uses, helped provide a resistant, discursive counterpoint to business-as-usual capitalism, and has carried some weight in policy debates about how to tackle social and environmental problems.[72] However, the affirmative semantic aura of this now prevalent term, and its associated forms ("sustainable," "sustainably"), means that in contemporary settings, it is regularly invoked for generalized purposes. On the one hand, the Australian Greens, for example, may refer to the development of renewable energy sources as sustainable (as compared with the continued mining of fossil fuels);[73] or, on the other hand, the Minerals Council of Australia may defend the mining of fossil fuels as enabling sustainable economic growth.[74] Moreover, "sustainability" is also anchored conceptually—though not necessarily historically, geographically, or culturally—in relation to a host of other terms in everyday language, such as "green," "organic," "environment," "economy," "growth," and "development." These terms both call up, and are often used to support, ideas that signal sustainability; at the same time, they maintain sufficient vagueness or ambiguity to forestall inquiry about, for example, how exactly the growth of the economy is related to on-the-ground practices that might ensure the survival of the planet.[75]

72. Andrew Basiago explores the significance of the term "sustainability" emerging in the early 1970s, and he reflects on its use as a methodological approach to processes of development by biologists, economists, and sociologists, among others. He expresses optimism about the social and environmental benefits of "sustainability analysis" as "a new decisional paradigm" (Basiago 1995, 119).

73. Australian Greens (2020).

74. Minerals Council of Australia (2020).

75. Andrew Nikiforuk (2019) critiques sustainability for its vagueness and vacuity, and its co-opting for "greenwashing" purposes. Nikiforuk draws on Poerksen's text to support his critique of language that obfuscates, and he is blunt in his condemnation of the use of language to camouflage market-driven objectives: "What sustainable meant in 1987 and means now is unlimited

In this way, then, plastic words serve to quieten or preempt a potential interlocutor's response, not because of what they mean, in situated contexts, but because of how their very ambiguity functions to make hazy the meanings and effects of the neoliberal-oriented discourses in which they are incorporated. As Poerksen puts it, "[i]n their usage the *function* of the discourse dominates, not its *content*. These words are more like an instrument of subjugation than like a tool of freedom."[76] Another way of putting this is to say that neonarratives are studded with plastic words that become a world, at once enthralling and bypassing the lived and imagined experiences of situated subjects, and the historical contexts they inhabit.

This cluster effect develops concepts that are highly resilient. Plastic words from one narrative context, which resonate with and correspond to the plastic words embedded in other narratives, have a colonizing effect. They produce the marketization of the imaginary. They thus seem to have taken on a life of their own in reaffirming, across diverse and sometimes disparate realms—such as health, education, finance, or welfare—a unifying mantra to instill the sense that there is no alternative to this way of neoliberal understanding, and that this is indeed the only natural and legitimate way of the world.

Although familiarity with and facility in using plastic words will often allow entrée or acceptance into powerful social, professional, and political groups,[77] plastic words also serve to deny language its purpose as historical or social practice, where this is understood as a space for debate, deliberation, dissent, contestation, or questioning. Thus, even when individuals would object to or challenge a particular plastic narrative or the discourses that inform it, their recognition of plastic words that have currency may well keep them at least passive, or acquiescent, or simply quiet. In this way, plastic words create a climate of consent, so that it becomes increasingly

---

industrial and technological growth, or more of the same old bullshit because 'the economy and the environment must go hand in hand, sustainably.'"

76. Poerksen (1995, 101). Italics in original.

77. Eagleton-Pierce mentions that neoliberal keywords, which he treats as plastic words, constitute "a kind of 'social glue'" (2016, xviii).

difficult to clear the clutter of words that often mask a dearth of meaningful practice.

In summary, then, this interspersion of plastic words across all manner of, often apparently unrelated, narrative contexts supports the work of not simply abbreviating, but also reducing language to data. It helps to make words and language matter primarily, and sometimes exclusively, in instrumental rather than processual, dialogic, or relational terms. Most importantly, the plastic words and concepts harnessed for neonarratives frequently cover over, or distract from, a focus on the intrinsic and extrinsic social and political contradictions, which might make such narratives interpretable in all their complexity and inconsistency, as well as make salient their ethical and social import.

"WE (DON'T) AGREE": FREEDOM, OBEDIENCE, AND THE PLASTICIZED NEONARRATIVE

In today's democracies, the plasticized neonarratives that seek to endorse, promote, and protect the dominant neoliberal system, and its raison d'être, undergo significant strain as vital, contextualized narratives. Their overriding focus is to extol the virtues of the market and to narrate the aspirational, competitive, and acquisitive trajectories, and happy consequences, of living according to its logic. Their distinctive lexicon of neoliberal-inspired plastic words is so adaptable that they are found not only in marketing and promotional texts, but also in texts pervading all aspects of human and social lives. From this standpoint, the opportunities for political, discursive struggle, for questioning, or interrogating the stories they tell, are drastically reduced, and these dominant stories maintain their stranglehold.

Constructed through discourse, power, and history, these now familiar plastic neonarratives do not emerge in a vacuum.[78] Accordingly, the idea of the "braided narrative,"[79] as one which expands the formal structure

---

78. Tamboukou (2013).

79. Bancroft (2018).

of narrative situations, is considered with James Phelan's[80] discussion of "non-narrative" formations informing the specific lived contexts in which they are today produced and circulated. As discussed in Chapter 1, such narratives are not interpretable or meaningful without support from government, private industry, public institutions, technologies, and media platforms,[81] which are already primed for and receptive to their discourses and their tenor. Thus, contemporary cultural spaces, both public and private, accommodate these narratives. Indeed, there is a "storytelling boom"[82] because people have themselves become attuned to the precepts and practices of neoliberal reasoning: whether in the imperative to evaluate the relationship between the planet, human, and nonhuman beings, in economic and ahistorical terms; to apply market-based calculations of value to all spheres of life; to extol the apparently inherent merits of competition, innovation, and private enterprise; or to affirm the primacy of the atomized, self-responsible individual.[83] Moreover, such narratives reciprocally reaffirm the market-based logic of those cultural spaces' own well-established means of self-legitimization.

So, what form do plastic neonarratives take? As with other dominant forms of cultural narrative, they do not appear once, in one place, at one time, and thereby make their mark. In fact, they tend not to exist in any single or unified form; nor may they even be immediately recognizable as belonging to the narrative mode. Barbara Herrnstein Smith makes a point about interwoven nature of narrative, which she describes as a discourse:

---

80. James Phelan (2008).

81. From another vantage point, Sean Phelan draws our attention to how, in contemporary settings, neoliberal discourses dependent "on media logic and processes" are working in the public sphere to reshape the very concept of "media," which for many people, is more central than ever in bringing political abstractions like "economy," "polity," and "society" to life. He argues that the anti-political characteristics of mediated neoliberalism work to cultivate hegemony within media contexts by drawing on "public relations source material," but that this is well beyond "a 'rhetorical' phenomenon" and requires more focus from scholars of media and communication to understand its sometimes baffling cultural and social effects (Phelan 2018, 542–548).

82. Mäkelä et al. (2021).

83. Holmgren (2021).

narrative discourse is not necessarily—or even usually—marked off or segregated from other discourse. Almost any verbal utterance will be laced with more or less minimal narratives, ranging from fragmentary reports and abortive anecdotes to those more distinctly framed and conventionally marked tellings that we are inclined to call "tales" or "stories." Indeed, narrative discourse is, at one extreme, hardly distinguishable from description or simply assertion.[84]

Submerged neonarratives may go largely unnoticed, but they are carefully shaped, disseminated, and modified to work across different temporal and social situations as stories, events, experiences, thoughts, ideas, beliefs, attitudes, and so on. What grants neoliberal-inspired narratives prominence and persistence is the appeal, power, reach, and resonance of the sticky-threaded webs or networks,[85] which support, (re)circulate, or extend them. But what also allows these "braided"[86] neonarratives to hold sway is the difficulty of dislodging them.[87]

IDENTIFYING AND ANALYZING NEONARRATIVES

In this section I discuss the notion that unfettered plastic neonarratives are now ubiquitously absorbed into communication cultures and are working seamlessly in counterintuitive ways that further the aims of neoliberal knowledge formation. From this submerged position, and founded to a core purpose of political intervention, they work to tether participants in public debates to a narrow set of cultural dispositions, vocabularies, and

---

84. Herrnstein Smith (1980, 232).

85. The notion of the network has also come to have strong associations with those involved in resistance or activist politics. This underscores the idea that the network is not the exclusive province of the powerful. However, see Jodi Dean's critique of the network, conceived as inherently "horizontal, cooperative and autonomous forms" (2019, 180).

86. Bancroft (2018).

87. Franczak (2019).

styles within market-based interpretations of the world, that not only fail to make progress but also lead to a circular path of ideas. Therefore, it is critical to reflect on what they consist of, how they garner hegemonic control, and how that control may be called into question, in order to uncover the implications for public debate and society.

While this may be the case, it would be a mistake to extol the idea of a portable template for neonarratives. Each of its market-based individual constitutive texts are authored, circulated, and modified, in particular cultural moments, and for the purpose of addressing particular audiences and interests. Nonetheless, and drawing on the work of Poerksen (1995), there are several recurrent and salient features of contemporary plastic neonarratives: a distinctive utopian tenor and an associated sense of atemporality; discursive coherence and an elision of the ethical; and technocratic framing. As noted, while industry, government, and activists may mobilize these narrative features in many different contexts and relations between civil, state, and market powers, they are anchored to a central purpose: as a public relations strategy to evade intrinsic/extrinsic contradictions that present as obstacles in public debate (Demetrious 2008, 2013). The neonarrative's characteristics are set out below.

UTOPIAN TENOR AND LIVING IN THE MOMENT

Neonarratives motion toward the moment and narrow the ways it can be thought about to influence what action is taken within a limited set of choices.[88] "Temporality" in this sense is what makes a story possible; neoliberal-inspired narratives regularly flatten out notions of time, through which history is muted, so that the worlds these narratives depict offer glimpses of a utopian future[89]—or the cautioning threat of

---

88. Luis Araujo and Geoff Easton (2012, 317) offer a detailed comparison of the various ways business narratives construct concepts of time, and this intersects with individual actors to "bring about their own versions of the future."

89. Rather than as a utopian project, Harvey sees neoliberalism "as a political project to reestablish the conditions for capital accumulation and to restore the power of economic elites"

a dystopian one—or are suspended in time, almost literally "in limbo," gesturing toward, as Peck and Theodore suggest, an "empty future."[90] It is these qualities that give neonarratives their sense of the (im)possible-real, the seamless, and the resolute. It is these qualities, too, that accord these narratives their dispossessed, ahistorical, and decontextualized sense of the unreal.

DISCURSIVE COHERENCE AND THE ELISION OF THE ETHICAL

The superficial coherence of plastic neonarratives typically results from elision of their internal contradictions, by either eliminating or co-opting (and making compatible) discourses that would otherwise trouble or disrupt the market-based treatment of and solutions to everything. In other words, they cover the "hole inside."[91] This is an example of how intrinsic public relations practices are applied to smooth over ruptures. Such promotional cultures supporting this practice have become generally accepted, as the incursion by market-based discourses makes alternative ways of thinking and reasoning increasingly difficult, and sometimes impossible.[92] However, plastic neonarratives do not abandon a commitment to

---

(2005, 19). Nonetheless, he also acknowledges ways in which the rhetoric of neoliberalism covers over this objective. See Chapter 2 for a discussion of Hayek's call, in 1949, to develop a utopian vision for the neoliberal project.

90. Peck and Theodore (2019, 263).

91. In stark contrast to the neoliberal nonnarrative, Maria Tumarkin (2018, 117) writes about authentic forms of narrative when "[y]ou must speak because the act of speaking, the narrative you make and remake with each telling, is what will keep you alive, what you'll hang on to, because this narrative covers, incompletely, too bad, the hole inside you. You must speak because if you don't, they win. If you don't, you have stopped fighting, given up."

92. Davies makes the point: "A recurring motif of neoliberal political critique is to extend metaphors, norms and measures from the economic realm of markets and business to the political realm of government. For example, the discourse of 'national competitiveness' borrows the language and methodologies of business strategy, and applies them to questions of national executive decision-making, representing political leaders as national CEOs" (2018, 274).

ethics.[93] Indeed, one of the reasons for neoliberalism's enduring strengths may well be its capacity to instrumentalize ethics, to fold the ethical into its discursive orbit, in order to, paradoxically, deflect or dilute ethical concerns and questions that would push beyond economized boundaries.[94]

TECHNOCRATIC FRAMING

Neonarratives appear to carry the weight of truth in framing interpretations of reality because they are an assemblage of plastic words interdiscursively woven with the language of science, standardization, and managerialism. Such technocratic styled discourse has singular characteristics: it "consciously presents itself as "above the fray," as a supplier of "facts," neutral and objective, free of all interests and values except truth, and it represents "its epistemic claims—often tacit—as objective knowledge."[95] The scientistic voice generated by this "closed discourse"[96] is impersonal, unambiguous, and sometimes dehumanized. In questioning such a neonarrative, it should be asked in a Foucauldian[97] sense: who speaks, who is sanctioned

---

93. Peter Bloom (2017, 3) puts forward a compelling case for the neoliberalization of ethics and the ways it has transformed ethical subjectivity so that citizens become "ethical capitalists."

94. For example, as a plastic word in the neoliberal lexicon, "responsibility," as a semantic term and as a concept, has come to be conceived in specifically individualized and managerialist ways, while its generalized associations with legal and juridical, as well as social and ethical, obligations remain relevant (Eagleton-Pierce 2016, 156–160).

95. As defined by Bernard J. McKenna and Philip Graham (2000, 235).

96. McKenna and Graham (2000, 226).

97. Foucault (1972, 50–55) outlines three stages in understanding enunciative modalities. First, ask why some statements are used together and not others: "Who is speaking? [. . .] Who is accorded the right to use this sort of language (*langage*)? Who is qualified to do so? Who derives from it his own special quality, his prestige, and from whom, in return, does he receive if not the assurance, at least the presumption that what he says is true?" (Foucault 1972, 50). Second, ask how the discourse gains its legitimacy, and to what institutional sites it is related. Third, ask what position the subject occupies in relation to other groups of objects. This suggests that investigators can identify what creates modes and links statements together, by looking at how the subject is positioned in society in relation to the statement and objects, what limits their dispersal, and how this is related to institutional sites.

to speak, who is being addressed, and whose interests are at stake in the speaking? These aspects are often not made readily amenable for consideration in such a narrative, since its statements are frequently declarative: assertions about the world *as it is* dominate, with apparently no need to situate explanations or defense of why or how they are so.[98] In technocratically oriented texts, frequent use of such preordained styles of abstractions can give rise to circular or self-referential commentary that gives rise to hegemony. These closed technocratic neonarratives succeed by curbing an individual's need to actively engage with the complexity, interpretability, and meaningfulness of the story at a visceral level. In this sense, neonarratives may unrecognizably, but irreducibly contribute to essentializing language in framing processes that "render events or occurrences meaningful and function to organize experience and guide action."[99] This is particularly relevant to collective action frames in social movements that engage with active and processual meaning-making to disrupt neoliberal ideas. If the activist group's discursive processes are taking place in a context that is saturated with neoliberal rationality, then the frame-alignment processes[100] are stymied in a cul de sac of ideas which have gained cultural resonance through "narrative fidelity," making the prospect of transformative social change ever more remote.[101] This may have the intended effect of moving individual subjects into a less politically assertive space by making it difficult for them to exercise their civic capacities, a strategy which works to minimize the production of politically empowering statements and promote a passive form of citizenship, that in turn will work to counter the social interconnectedness supported by social movements.

98. McKenna and Graham (2000, 236–237).

99. Benford and Snow (2000).

100. According to Benford and Snow (2000, 624), social movements deploy strategic efforts in framing that are "deliberative, utilitarian, and goal directed" and take place through four alignment processes: "frame bridging, frame amplification, frame extension, and frame transformation."

101. Benford and Snow (2000, 622).

NEONARRATIVES: PLIANT, HIGH-STRENGTH, RESISTANT

As discussed, before everything, the idea of neonarratives is developed from, and depends on, the foundations of intrinsic and extrinsic public relations contradictions: the specific language practices harnessed by the public relations industry, in its attempts to secure discursive coherence for its communicative practices, and in fending off alternative or oppositional voices and coalitions that seek to deflect or rebuff its political interventions. The processes and practices in deploying intrinsic and extrinsic public relations work relentlessly to propel language and ideas into the public sphere, and to structure interpretations through stories by linking to the distinct discourse of neoliberalism. This formation anchors specifically to plastic words to create a more complex narrative structure, which straddles and/or compresses a range of contradictory positions, and simplifies these into relatively dichotomous positions.

Goal-oriented neonarratives, where many single public relations texts converge to become one unifying text, are studded with plastic words that both position the subject and frame an economic interpretation of the world. They are the means to build consistent agreement through public opinion that gestures toward an enticing "new reality," one in which business, free from the constraints and interference of government, can expand and thrive, with benefits for all. Essentialist neonarratives are the bridges or connectors that assemble and make sense of, empty plastic words, such as *communication*, *information*, and *development*. However, without attaching to public relations' meaning-making processes that design interventions for knowledge formation (campaigns, plans, objectives), and to their textual products (social media posts, media releases, speeches, blogs, press conferences, etc.) that are distributed and then shared, neonarratives and the plastic words they carry may not work, or have any significant impact at all. In other words, they are entirely dependent on the driving neoliberal logic, political purpose, and meaning-making processes of public relations.

Public relations has been used by commercial organizations, over many decades, to confront social contradictions that threaten their interests.

These contradictions are often tabled by activists with opposing agendas. Positioned thus, public relations attempts, through neonarrative, to lead the subject—which could be an individual, but, more likely, "publics" targeted for social control—into a coherence that supports and naturalizes the logic of simple market-based society, built on wealth accumulation and small government. Given this, a further line of argument might be that the greater the number of breaks in logic that neoliberalists are confronted with in complex public debates, the simpler and seemingly more effective the neonarrative becomes, e.g., "climate change is a hoax,"[102] or a three-word slogan used to frame refugee debates, like "stop the boats."[103] Thus, in a "pincer move," intrinsic and extrinsic public relations practices are deployed as neonarratives to privilege specific discourses, and ascribe coherence to the practices, ideas, and attitudes they signal.[104] In this way,

---

102. Indeed, the anti-science argument of "climate denial" contains so many logical contradictions that this should have rendered this stance ridiculous and thus impotent. Take, for example, a Reuters "fact check" on February 19, 2021, which refuted: "A post has been circulating on social media saying NASA admitted that man-made climate change is a hoax as the sun is responsible for global warming, not humans. This claim is false: the NASA website has many pages explaining that human activities are contributing to climate change."

103. The Refugee Council of Australia (2021) discusses how, in Australia, this slogan was used to "demonise people seeking asylum, fleeing war and persecution; condemning them to indefinite offshore detention and torture in prison camps on Manus Island and Nauru."

104. Intrinsic public relations practices are those that seem to work within the rules, such as legal frameworks, regulatory codes, and normative social expectations. Such positioning often sidesteps nuanced ethical tensions that may arise, but because no rules are broken, or there is no rule, they achieve this neutralizing effect somewhat unobtrusively, without breaking bones, and in ways intended to not "in any way affecting the body of enunciative rules that makes them possible" (Foucault 1972, 153). More generally, intrinsic public relations practices are understood as political intervention in the public sphere, by carefully twisting the fine threads of truth to position meaning within fixed boundaries of neoliberal thought. These circulating practices, for want of a better word, are sometimes referred to as "spin" and "fluff." On the other hand, business and other organizations use public relations language practices differently, if they believe that statements issued by counter sources, or those who challenge them, will lead interested individuals or groups inside or outside the boundaries of the discursive formation. In the case of the latter, the organization acts aggressively to suppress or discredit the source, so that the source's statements are not distributed. I broadly categorized this as extrinsic public relations. An example is the public relations strategy deployed by the fossil fuel lobby, attacking a climate action group, for instance, by describing them as "extreme" or "unhinged," or by infiltrating the group to spy on their activities, thus breaking both the law and normative

public relations language practice may brush and burnish the idea of neoliberal rationality, simultaneously from different standpoints.

Two key areas are drawn out in summary of this discussion:

1) Public relations industries use narrative styles to manage intrinsic/extrinsic contradictions, and in so doing distort, and co-construct a "non-narrative" formation.[105] As a mediator of political change, these neonarratives are delivered through multiple narrators, and entwined in a complex "braided" structure, to map the boundaries of discourse that enable the policing of contradictions from numerous standpoints. This will vary according to where the individual contradictions lead or are located.

2) Intrinsic public relations practice can work on single issues, or as I have argued, in concert with extrinsic public relations practices, as neonarrative.[106] Embedding a convergent neonarrative within public debates sets up discursive walls in language and the imaginary. This leads to an understanding of public relations as a ubiquitous communicative mode, in the service of the neoliberal project, which is not restricted to the institutional site, but as a normalized and even normative mode of "everyday" communicating.

---

expectations of business, and its relationship to society. Extrinsic public relations may be used by organizations to choke high-threat challenges, set in motion by activists or others, in order to maintain the dominant discourse and "restore to it its hidden unity" (Foucault, 1972, 149).

105. James Phelan (2008, 168).

106. This refers to public relations' practice of "harmonizing intrinsic contradictions" within a single discourse, and by naturalizing and creating a sense of that discourse's coherence and integrity, as opposed to public relations' practice of "managing extrinsic contradictions" or oppositions, posed by alternative discourses to the one(s) it is privileging by asphyxiating, suppressing, or discrediting (as oppositional, negative, or false) those alternative discourses (Demetrious 2013).

The scope and reach of public relations language practice in furthering neoliberal rationality cannot be underestimated. As Wendy Brown says, neoliberalism is "undoing the basic elements of democracy," which include "vocabularies, principles of justice, habits of citizenship, practices of rule, and above all democratic imaginaries."[107] The neonarrative, both producing and sustained by these conditions, affects contemporary public discourse, policy decision-making, culture, and society, with a market-based rationality.[108] The creation of object by public relations industries in service of neoliberal logic, and the embedding of the statements that support the object via plastic words, and the dispersal of statements through a neo-nonnarrative, could work as a meta-theory, rather than apply to just one social phenomenon. This lens may bring in new ideas and complexity, and a more thoughtful analysis of how communicative interventions take place and succeed.

Today's communicative conditions tolerate and/or promote a predisposition in the subject, toward plastic words and neonarratives. The left and the right of politics use similar phrases, so everything is reduced to the same pattern of ideas, with a homogenizing effect. Plastic words hollow the meaning out, evacuate it from the text, assisted by the skilled interlocutor, be they a media commentator, think-tank spokesperson, or politician who follows the neonarrative script. Moreover, plastic words and neonarratives are not static, or frozen in time. They are subject to a range of cultural dynamics, as seen in Chapter 1, and particularly through the franchised communication industries that have spread across the globe. Thus, there are degrees of plastic words and neonarratives: emerging, established, and disestablished. Always in motion, they appear empty, but they are not; they appear flexible, but they are not. With little resistance, they promote a vision of the fulfilled individual through self-interest, a

---

107. Brown (2015, 17).

108. Jodi Dean (2008, 103) points out that "[w]hat enhances democracy in one context becomes a new form of hegemony in another. Differently put, the intense circulation of content in communicative capitalism forecloses the antagonism necessary for politics. In relatively closed societies, that antagonism is not only already there but also apparent at and as the very frontier between open and closed."

state that diminishes a view of wider social responsibilities. The corollary is to elide ethical complexity, to silence.[109] Vernacular language has been transformed, and narrative as public relations language strategy has been central, but public relations has also lost control of this process. The enveloping discourse produced by intrinsic or extrinsic public relations practices in concert, through the modality of neonarrative, sets in motion the cultural expectations of the subject to ensure they are malleable. If plastic words lay down the tracks, then neonarratives are the trains which transport the subject, via emotion, to the destination. In this work, they are indispensable. But within the public sphere, neonarratives develop energy, dynamism, and reach quite apart from their original purpose and producers' intent.

This chapter has not discussed lobbyists, think tanks, peak bodies, political interest, or front groups. Nor does it examine politicians, plutocrats, activists, journalists, media personalities, nongovernmental organizations (NGOs), corporations, or other social actors or sites. Neither does it discuss the weaknesses and failures of public debate in relation to groups and individuals using digital media, and the associated trolls, bots, algorithms, or other media platforms. Yet, it goes to the heart of the dynamics shaping the failures of the public sphere, in ways not usually discussed. Politically potent public relations language practice and knowledge formation is little understood. But deconstructing the implicit neoliberalism in public relations research and practice, and understanding its spread, is urgent to comprehend the multiple ways its complex relationships are working to shape the reception, interpretation, and action on critical social issues.

The next two chapters take up the ways in which this phenomenon has found its way into communicative practice at government, institutional, public, and private levels, and has transformed public debates. I focus on the ways in which, whether self-consciously or not, all individuals harness

---

109. For Wrenn and Waller (2017, 1), "[t]hat individuals exhibit either selfish or other-regarding behavior, speaks to the surrounding institutional configuration. Capitalism is justified by the insistence on autonomy as the natural state of humans."

narrative, discourse, and plastic words, to depoliticize the very discussions which should be political, and that should engage the polity in a rich and productive debate. I will show how neonarratives embed public discussion about climate change, and the state of people occupying borderlands, and the discourses that structure them to do their work in these domains.

4
Happiness, Plastic Truth, and the Story of Climate

This chapter focuses on how the plasticized neonarrative of climate change denial,[1] has underpinned one of the most brutal and anti-human communication campaigns in history. It explores how PR language practices working on behalf of powerful market actors have used 'denialism', directly and indirectly, over many decades, to structure neoliberal rationality, narrow cultural sensitivities and deepen political divides. The effect of this has been to delimit the imaginary and shut down a richer more nuanced public debate about energy which in turn as contributed to inertia and policy stagnation . It shows that, together, public relations and neoliberal forces—particularly as represented by radical think tanks and secondhand dealers in ideas active in the run-up to the 1970s and 1980s, or the second wave of neoliberalism[2]—have shaped a story denying climate change. In this, plastic words such as "information" and "environment"

---

1. Núria Almiron (2019, 9) defines climate change denial as "the stance that advocates against the evidence posited for human-induced global warming." On the other hand, climate research advocates are accused of "alarmism," which is a disingenuous manufactured position and/or a false prophet of a new religion. See Joffe (2019), who states that Greta Thunberg has "a flawless public relations machine running in the background at all times."

2. This second wave of neoliberalism is an "era [that] has been associated so fundamentally and certainly with neoliberalism, when arguably this era indicates certain articulations and radical mutations of neoliberalism as contingent upon the political, social and economic context" (Rowe et al. 2019, 154).

become terms with ambiguous meanings, which are rendered apparently innocuous, and even benign or positive to undermine and discredit evidence-based climate science. To enclose discursive spaces, the chapter argues that this neonarrative lays claim to a "new reality" and works prodigiously to suspend climate action and to "transform history."[3]

The public spectacle of public relations industry responses[4]—seemingly sporadic, isolated, or incoherent—masks the presence and artifice of a neonarrative, which, in short, goes something like this: "Humankind" and "nature" occupy the same planet, but in separate and independent realms. Nature is plentiful, rich with "resources," and provides an abundance of wealth for the benefit and progress of humankind. However, climate change advocates—such as activists, scientists, politicians, and social critics—claim this utilization brings harm in the form of increased carbon dioxide emissions, and they are working to deprive humankind of the right to material happiness. In this, they are wrong. The market—free and limitless—provides *more and better* opportunities to compete for, extract from, and consume nature's bounties, and their promise of an innovative and prosperous future.[5]

This neonarrative of climate change denial has radically flattened out nuance and in this has created the *semblance* of discursive coherence,

---

3. Paul Ricouer (2009, 291) discusses fictional narrative as intrinsically circular as it is linked to history, both informing and shaping events that in turn become history.

4. Evidence continues to come to light of the coalition between neoliberal and public relations forces over the postwar period. Benjamin Franta (2018) writes that "[i]n the 1980s, big oil companies carried out internal assessments of how their products' emissions might affect the planet. Despite findings linking fossil fuels to ecological damage and global warming, the industry kept their data secret, and then lied about it, potentially dooming the rest of us as a result."

5. Free market advocate Vijay Jayaraj (2016) has produced an exemplary version of this narrative: "Those vilifying CO_2 as the main reason for a dangerous increase in global average temperature [. . .] are misled by faulty computer climate models that overestimate its warming effect. Sad to say, they are now misleading the public and policymakers. While doing so, they have also buried the undeniable benefits of CO_2. The benefits for world agriculture from increased CO_2 are estimated to be about $140 billion a year. This benefit is projected to increase in [the] next three decades. Radical environmentalists have misled people about the green greenhouse gas, carbon dioxide. The indoctrination of school curricula, the ignorance of the public, and the well-crafted lies of the radical environmentalists have wrongly demonized CO_2."

which encourages an optimistic understanding of a world with a changing climate, which is presented as no cause for alarm. Hence privatizing and profiting from the commercial exploitation of "the environment" is not such a bad thing, nor of much importance.[6] The chapter shows, in some detail, how the interpretive process leading to this point intersects with the seductive power of plastic words, which pose as "friendly, smooth, positive, and consensual," but which mask violence and serve to nullify dissent.[7] In doing so, it seeks to provide an alternative way to understand, in concept, what is giving energy to the seepage of neoliberal ideas into everyday language and into public debates—such as the impacts of rising carbon dioxide emissions—in ways that serve to disrupt and polarize the support required for the formation of meaningful policy directions.

Today, the climate situation is worse than ever. The Intergovernmental Panel on Climate Change (IPCC) is a body of the United Nations, and its assessment of anthropocentric climate change shows a significant escalation in the global warming levels since the agrarian societies before the industrial revolution. Its 2021 summary report details:

> Global surface temperature has increased faster since 1970 than in any other 50-year period over at least the last 2000 years (high confidence). Temperatures during the most recent decade (2011–2020) exceed those of the most recent multi-century warm period, around 6500 years ago[13] [0.2°C to 1°C relative to 1850–1900] (medium confidence). Prior to that, the next most recent warm period was about 125,000 years ago when the multi-century temperature [0.5°C to

---

6. Rachel Carson prophetically discussed a form of denialism in 1962, writing that "[t]he citizen who wishes to make a fair judgment of the question of wildlife loss is today confronted with a dilemma. On the one hand conservationists and many wildlife biologists assert that the losses have been severe and in some cases even catastrophic. On the other hand the control agencies tend to deny flatly and categorically that such losses have occurred, or that they are of any importance if they have. Which view are we to accept?" (Carson 1971, 87).

7. Poerksen (1995, 6–7).

1.5°C relative to 1850–1900] overlaps the observations of the most recent decade (medium confidence).[8]

Scientific consensus on climate research agrees that climate change is anthropogenic, and that mitigation and adaptation are urgent. However, despite the accumulating evidence taking this position over many decades, the public deliberation leading to policy consensus on the issue has foundered badly in the twenty-first century. The deeply ruptured positions on climate change have manifested in an often rancorous, unrepresentative, and paralyzing public debate, and can be traced to neoliberalism and public relations industry legacies. As a result, the position of climate change denial has worked to impede meaningful action, and characterizes contemporary public debate. Within the ranks of its powerful lobbyists, the climate change denial argument rests on a purported belief in the wisdom of the market, active antiscience, and an entitlement to sway public opinion by any "means" to achieve the "ends." Climate change denial works in public discussions by consuming energy and time in participants, be they scientists, activists, or economists, refuting misinformation and defending climate research or mitigation policies, such as a carbon pricing mechanism. This is precisely the point. It works. An example of denialism's political impact is in Australia, where, according to Marc Hudson, the country "once enjoyed a reputation as an exceptionally stable democracy: in the 32 years between December 1975 and November 2007, it had only four prime ministers; between June 2010 and August 2018, it had six. In most of those changes, climate policy has played a part."[9] Like the United States, the political significance of climate change denial in Australia can be understood in relation to the fact that it is a significant producer, and exporter, of fossil fuels, such as

---

8. IPCC (2021, 8). "Disclaimer: The Summary for Policymakers (SPM) is the approved version from the 14th session of Working Group I and 54th Session of the Intergovernmental Panel on Climate Change and remains subject to final copy-editing and layout."

9. Hudson (2019, 543).

black coal and brown coal.[10] Although fossil fuel industries are highly profitable,[11] they are the main contributors to increasing concentrations of greenhouse gases, leading to catastrophic climate change.[12]

Climate research shows that many human activities, which have become fundamental to the dominant economic and social organization of modern life, add to growing carbon dioxide concentrations and other greenhouse gases.[13] These activities include, but are not limited to, the burning of fossil fuels (e.g., to produce electricity, heat buildings, move cars, and produce goods), land clearing for agriculture and mining, the farming of livestock, and the application of fertilizer. Rising carbon dioxide emissions threaten the planet with catastrophic ecological and human problems. These include rising sea levels, more extreme weather, and changes to land stability and rainfall patterns, which will affect agriculture and food supply, habitability, and biodiversity, in ways likely to lead to future dispossession, inequity, global poverty, and conflict. This research emanates from society's most trusted institutions, such as the IPCC, Australia's national science agency the Commonwealth Scientific and Industrial Research

---

10. See Australian Government (2021c): "Australia has 6 per cent of the world's black coal EDR and ranks sixth behind USA (31 per cent), Russia (21 per cent), China (13 per cent), India (8 per cent) and South Africa (7 per cent). Australia has about 25 per cent of world recoverable brown coal EDR and is ranked first."

11. Coal is one of Australia's most important and profitable exports. According to a Reserve Bank of Australia's report, "[c]oal is one of Australia's largest exports, and has accounted for around one-quarter of Australia's resource exports by value over the past decade" (Cunningham, Van Uffelen, and Chambers 2019, n.p.).

12. In Australia, fossil fuels drive the rising CO_2 emissions. See CSIRO and Bureau of Meteorology (2020): "Despite a decline in global fossil fuel emissions of CO_2 in 2020 associated with the COVID-19 pandemic, this will have negligible impact in terms of climate change. Atmospheric CO_2 continues to rise, and fossil fuel emissions will remain the principal driver of this growth."

13. IPCC (2021, 4) states that "[o]bserved increases in well-mixed greenhouse gas (GHG) concentrations since around 1750 are unequivocally caused by human activities. Since 2011 (measurements reported in AR5), concentrations have continued to increase in the atmosphere, reaching annual averages of 410 ppm for carbon dioxide (CO_2), 1866 ppb for methane (CH_4), and 332 ppb for nitrous oxide (N_2O) in 20196. Land and ocean have taken up a near-constant proportion (globally about 56% per year) of CO_2 emissions from human activities over the past six decades, with regional differences (high confidence)."

Organisation (CSIRO), and the United States Global Research Program (USGRP). These institutions also agree that humanity has limited time frames to take mitigating action. Serious matters that concern the human and planetary survival abound in the twenty-first century, and yet, the neonarrative of climate change denialism glosses over these worries and leads the subject back to a calm and problem-free existence. So, what exactly is the plasticized neonarrative of climate change denial?

The climate change denial story, promoted by public relations and neoliberal forces, rests on the powerful idea that the realms of "the human" and "nature" are essentially separable from one another, and that plants, animals, minerals, and other earthly matter are sources of wealth. Therefore, nature's primary purpose is as a resource for exploitation, in order to achieve progress, which benefits humankind. However, bringing risk, uncertainty, and tension to this set of arrangements are "warmist" scientists, and their biased research in the escalation of greenhouse gas emissions, and/or the unbalanced "alarmists," advocating for mitigating climate action. They are the producers and communicators of faux science and biased information on the effects of increased concentrations of carbon dioxide, which is designed to undermine commerce and industry, and the vast systems that enable it, and in turn, threaten humankind's entitlement to nature's bounty. To defend this position are the neoliberal champions of freedom. They will rally to publicly expose faux science and pillory those individuals or organizations involved in its manufacture. In this story, the media—sometimes good, sometimes bad—is a constant source of suspense, curiosity, and expectation. Entwined, these storylines aim to persuade the subject to place trust in the champions of freedom and in the wisdom of the market, in order to ensure ongoing human wealth, happiness, and optimism.

The success of this neonarrative has ensured that translating climate research into new and related policy settings, to reduce greenhouse gas emissions through public debate, is slow, unsteady, and frustrating. It has been deployed by conservative forces, on an industrial scale, to impede policy work in the public interest. Thus, neoliberalism and its instrument, public relations, are identified as a pernicious and dangerous dynamic in this deliberation, in ways that represent more than a polarization or diversity of views. Indeed, its purpose undermines and threatens action and adaptation to confront the changing climatic conditions and its widespread effects.

To prise open new ground, this chapter explores how neoliberal ideas and language, which manifested within twentieth-century public relations industry processes and logic, have become naturalized in contemporary public debate, as the preferred strategizing and performative mode of communication. Deployed within a complex web of intrinsic and extrinsic public relations communicative practices,[14] the climate change denial story as a neonarrative is built on a series of decontextualized words, such as "freedom," "information," and "the environment," to achieve numbing effects. Voices of those who are intimately entwined with industry and commerce, such as media commentators, talk-back presenters, journalists, television hosts, authors, and opinion writers, engage in the ambiguous "game of telling."[15] In this, they propel an interplay of meanings fused with historical facts, critical oversimplifications, and inaccurate interpretations of climate science that maintain, fortify, and co-create the neonarrative of denialism. In doing so, they fend off threats from climate research findings and create a product which serves to mask the widening fissures in their own reality.

In engaging with this analysis, the chapter focuses on key historical moments in the latter decades of the twentieth century, when social contractions that threatened industry began to emerge. It identifies the emergence of the word "pollution" as an instructive starting point to trace this movement of meaning within these social contradictions. A later section of the chapter will focus on neoliberal media voices harnessed to

---

14. Distilled from research of activist practices, a non-market-based approach to this is described as "public communication." This style is political, but is open to, and permeated by, ideas that reveal the possibility of an alternative way of thinking about the world. Evidence of this permeation of ideas is the definition of new objects and the opening up of subject positions in ways that bring diverse groups of people together. For a full discussion, see Demetrious (2013).

15. For Paul Ricoeur (2009, 294) "the game of telling" is an "ambiguity of designating both the course of recounted events and the narrative we construct. For they belong together."

popularize these ideas, in ways that lead the public toward a mood of inertia and the stagnation of social change, in a powerful real-life example. Known as "Climategate," the 2009 case involves the public denunciation of scientists working in climate research at the University of East Anglia, and the delegitimization of their work. The chapter then examines this event in relation to plastic words, and how the term "environment" has become decontextualized and is working in contemporary vernacular to buttress climate change denial.

AWAKENING DISINTEREST: THE "GAME OF TELLING"

The climate research policy debate covers vast social, cultural, and historical terrain, and it is not possible to cover all the work that has been done in this area.[16] However, a critical point in understanding the foundering of public debate about climate, and how this interrelates with neoliberalism and PR practices, can be traced to the later part of the twentieth century, in the emerging public debates about the relationship between the human and the planet in late modernity. Interior meaning of the neonarrative can be unlocked by tracing the movement of the term "pollution," which has worked to give impetus to denialism.

In play since the 1950s, "pollution" was popularized by the US media as a politicized scientific and social concept, which then became absorbed in vernacular. For Michael A. Champ, it "became another 'dinner table' or 'news media' term that was relative to the social and political values of the day."[17] Hence, while "pollution" could by strict scientific definition be applied to *natural* events, such as volcanic activity, overall it denoted the harmful effects of *human* activity and industrial-production processes, such as air pollution, water pollution, and noise pollution. As a corollary, "pollution" connoted an ethical relationship to nature, and the potential

---

16. "[T]he game of telling"; Ricoeur (2009, 294).

17. Champ (2011, 7).

for corrective or remedial action to production processes to mitigate the local and global impacts.[18] The term "pollution," and its cultural and discursive field, continued to grow in the popular imagination in the later decades of the twentieth century, but for industry and business, so too did a growing unease about the reach and implications of these ideas.

Thus, in the later decades of the twentieth century, planetary degradation from human intervention precipitated public anxiety that a dystopian future might not be far away. The basis for such fear was propelled by powerful texts, such as Rachel Carson's (1962) *Silent Spring*, which broke new ground as a compelling and accessible scientific exposé of the chemical industry products like dichlorodiphenyltrichloroethane (commonly known as DDT).[19] Much has been written about Carson, her book, and the attacks on both; however, there is an illustrative twist within this discursive moment, which points to the early assembling of climate change denial to form a plasticized neonarrative.

To quell the politicizing effect of Carson's ideas, which represented a break in the prevailing neoliberal rationality, the Chemical Manufacturers Association deployed expensive public relations tactical responses. Mark Hamilton Lytle argues that this industry conglomerate "had at their disposal vast public relations and advertising resources and spent millions extolling the virtues of pesticides without ever acknowledging their toxicity."[20] Unsurprisingly, after Carson's book was published, detractors accused her of selective truth, misinformation, and distortion of fact, and of prosecuting a moral agenda divorced from science, which was antiprogress based on bias and zealotry.[21]

---

18. Champ (2011, 5).

19. Aronczyk (2018); Hass and Kleine (2003); Lytle (2017).

20. Lytle (2017, 57).

21. David K. Hecht (2012, 149) writes that "Carson's book attracted swift and vociferous denunciation from scientists connected with or sympathetic to the pesticide industry; much of it was both alarmist and *ad hominem*."

One of Carson's prominent critics, political scientist Charles T. Rubin, went slightly further. Deeply suspicious of Carson's "clarion call and dark warnings" as an "environmental popularizer,"[22] he wrote that even those who praised *Silent Spring* overlooked any deficiencies in the scientific argument, because they, first, sympathized with Carson's crusade, and second, put forward a rationale that "one piece of misinformation had to be fought with more misinformation." Therefore, Rubin believed that Carson's supporters intentionally protected her from any valid criticism of her research findings or thesis, by deploying their own, calculated "ecological PR" response.

> This tactic is apparently justified, to his mind, by the fact that "the extreme opposite has been impressed on the public by skilled professional moulders of public opinion." Such hostility to the existing business, industry and governmental establishments, which is only now showing signs of abating among some environmentalists, created a sense that ecological PR needs to fight business PR.[23]

Rubin's reasoning, which led him to coin the term "ecological PR," is significant for understanding how hardened cavalier attitudes toward industry critics may have influenced the self-protective tenor of denialism. Teasing out this point, Rubin believed that activists or critics intentionally adopted oppositional tactics, drawing on extant public relations logic and practices. However, there is no evidence available to suggest that activists, at this time, were using "public relations" in any equivalent or systematized way to industry. On the other hand, there is evidence, such as Rubin and Sachs's research, which showed that "mass media," such as newspapers, magazines, and wire services, were increasingly covering the

---

22. See Rubin (1994, 18). His intense scrutiny of "environmental popularizers" and their discursive power resonates with Hayek's notion of secondhand dealers in neoliberal ideas, as a critical nexus to build public support; however, in Rubin's case, the focus is on controlling/managing those popularizers who pose a threat to the neoliberal reason.

23. Rubin (1994, 36).

topic of environment, and concluded that industry must respond carefully to such criticism.[24] Therefore, despite Charles T. Rubin's baseless assertion, James E. Grunig, who at the time was both an influential and well-connected US academic, specializing in public relations at the University of Maryland, shared the view that activist organizations were a powerful counterpoint to industry.

> Public relations practitioners may be found working on both sides of environmental issues. Some may be in positions defending industry accused of polluting air and water or of wasting energy and valuable natural resources. Other practitioners, however, may represent activist organizations or governmental agencies which seek support for preservation of the environment. Often the second set of practitioners may communicate the accusations which create an environmental public relations problem for the first group of practitioners.[25]

Rubin's (1994) and Grunig's (1977) views provide insight into the origins of the hostile relationship between activists and public relations practitioners, which emerged in the later stages of the twentieth century. Today, this trenchant polarization is evident in relations between climate change denialists and climate change activists. But importantly, Rubin's and Grunig's views show that industry and public relations had, in a measured and strategic way, laid the groundwork for long-term confrontation and opposition, based on the view that it was fighting "fire with fire" via "ecological PR" with "industry public relations." Indeed, such emphasis suggests that in the ongoing work of public relations practice, the maintenance and deployment of neonarratives, like climate change denial, became central.[26]

24. Rubin and Sachs (1973).

25. Grunig (1977, 36).

26. To quell the politicizing effect of *Silent Spring*, which represented a break in the prevailing neoliberal logic, the chemical industry launched an aggressive extrinsic public relations campaign to discredit Rachel Carson's reputation and work.

In the 1960s and up to the 1970s, diversification of thought, and social change through collective action, presented as unifying, strong, and far-reaching.[27] This was so much so, that neoliberal defenders pushing an anti-environmentalist message did not manage to disproportionately influence public debate with disinformation, as has been the case since the beginning of the twenty-first century, when new media afforded a multitude of ways that denialism could gain social traction with the public.[28] In the late twentieth century, relatively open deliberations ruptured some assumptions about the rights of industry to pursue profit over people, and to chip away at the hegemonic truth upholding simple invocations of "progress." The ventilation of ideas supporting contrasting concepts of living were evident in public debate at this time. As such, an alternative stance on climate-related issues, such as air and water pollution, emerged from the growing green awareness movements, and made an impact on popular public opinion. Such environmental agendas for change were particularly visible in the early 1970s,[29] with influential publications such as *Limits to Growth* (1972) containing dire warnings about the threat of overpopulation and the depletion of resources, and which in turn inspired other books, such as *A Blueprint for Survival* (1972).[30] It was also evident

---

27. Tarrow (1988); Eley (1990); Herring (2001).

28. See Lockwood (2008).

29. Hays (1981).

30. *A Blueprint for Survival* was originally a 1972 edition of the print magazine *The Ecologist*, which had formed two years earlier and which had wide-ranging effects in spearheading the countercultural political movements. Bethany Hubbard (2012) writes: "A radical and influential issue, it was both a catalyst for political change and an eerily accurate outline of global issues we still face today. Published prior to the 1972 UN Conference on the Human Environment, in Stockholm, the "Blueprint" issue was so popular it reportedly sold about 500,000 copies, and was later published in book format. "Radical change is both necessary and inevitable because the present increases in human numbers and per capita consumption, by disrupting ecosystems and depleting resources, are undermining the very foundations of survival," wrote *Ecologist* founder Edward Goldsmith, Robert Allen, and a team of colleagues, who named self-sufficient smaller communities, like those of native societies, as a model for sustainable living. As part of a strategy for the future, this forward-thinking team outlined "The Movement for Survival," which would be spearheaded by "a coalition of organisations concerned with environmental issues." This movement would eventually lead to the formation of the Green Party.

in fiction. *The Monkey Wrench Gang* (1975) is a novel which blurred the idea of civil disobedience with industrial sabotage to counter the environmental crisis and inspired real-life protest movements.[31] Arguably, these discursive flows raised notions of the human and planetary interdependence and stimulated the public imagination. Moreover, the discursive undercurrents included public anxiety, anger, and a pressing need to understand why and how the state and industry had failed in their duty to protect this sacred alliance between nature and humans. Within these social and cultural conditions, the term "pollution" flourished and propelled a more nuanced view about the merits, risks, and ethics associated with industrial growth and human activity.[32]

At this time, two simultaneous, but oppositional themes collided: freedom and obedience. Second-wave neoliberalism was utterly "contingent upon the political, social and economic context," and in this sense the new and powerful voices speaking up to challenge industry seemed to be gaining the upper hand.[33] From the 1980s onward, the sociological themes to which "pollution" gave rise generated a widespread belief that humankind had to radically rethink the relationship with nature—urgently.[34] For example, Allan Bell argues that "[t]he greenhouse effect and ozone depletion were beginning to appear on public agendas from 1987."[35] In tandem with this, the idea of disruption to and interference in the "balance of life,"

---

31. To illustrate this cultural momentum, Robert Macfarlane (2009,. n.p.) states that "Earth First! was openly inspired by Edward Abbey's novel. Dave Foreman, one of the four founders, published a now-notorious manual for direct action entitled (1985) *Ecodefense: A Field Guide to Monkeywrenching*."

32. Champ (2011).

33. Rowe et al. (2019, 154).

34. E. Bruce Harrison (1992, 51) states: "Environmental issues remained fairly consistently a high priority for the national news media throughout the 1980s. Thus far in the 1990s, environmental awareness and news coverage have escalated sharply." Note that this second edition built "on the insight gained from the changes in environmental issues and attitudes since the publication of the first edition in 1988" (Harrison 1992, vii).

35. Bell (1994, 34).

"mother nature," and its consequences for "mankind" became embedded in the public imagination and public opinion.[36] The gathering momentum of "pollution" as a field, which was increasingly accessible on many societal levels, posed an unprecedented threat for the established trade and industry economic orders, as individuals and institutions moved. Behind these social flows, a crisis of faith was taking place in public relations. Ethical management theorist R. Edward Freeman's empirical research, published in the early to mid-1980s, is valuable for revealing that, at the time, public relations practitioners were not only using ineffective tools with "publics," but were not being taken seriously by the press, and were even regarded by their own as irrelevant and ineffective.[37] Arguably, these contingent conditions gave rise to mutations in public relations as it was deployed to arrest the slide, and to combat the idea of "ecological PR."[38] The public relations industry's articulation of the neonarrative of climate change denialism, in multiple sites, worked in tandem with this weaponized mode to stymie the orderly social transformation of society, to achieve lower greenhouse gas emissions, and to find alternative ways to coexist with the planet than might otherwise have taken place.

Certainly, the coagulating idea of climate change denial can be traced to 1988, when a testimony to the US Senate discussed the relationship of human activity to global warming. At the time, Philip Shabecoff reported that "Dr. James E. Hansen of the National Aeronautics and Space Administration told a Congressional committee that it was 99 percent certain that the warming trend was not a natural variation but was caused by

---

36. Beck's (1992) thesis of risk society and reflexive modernization discussed the momentum of ideas in relation to excessive industrial activity and overproduction, which lead to consequences such as pollution, acid rain, and radioactivity, and undermine capitalism's claim to progress in society. In these conditions, Beck predicts a massive public critique will take place and prompt a rethinking of the means, goals, and objectives of the scientific and techno-economic production process that led to the problems (Beck et al. 2000, 5–6).

37. R. Edward Freeman (1984, 219) reported that public relations practitioners said, "[t]he press is impossible; what we have been doing for the past 20 years, and doing well, just isn't enough these days."

38. Rubin (1994, 36).

a buildup of carbon dioxide and other artificial gases in the atmosphere."[39] Accordingly, "[s]hortly after James Hansen's June 1988 Senate testimony placed anthropogenic global warming on the public agenda in the United States, organized efforts to deny the reality and significance of the phenomenon began, reflected by formation the following year of the Global Climate Coalition (an industry-led front group formed to call global warming into question)."[40] By the 1990s, it was evident that neoliberalism-inflected industry and politics displayed a more aggressive and hostile form of anti-environmentalism, with no room for nuance and negotiation. The flattening out of meaning to bland simplifications in regard to planetary matters was assisted by the drawing of political demarcations, such as when, "[i]n 1994, a growing group of Republican senators were elected with links to the anti-environmental movement who explicitly declared their aim to be to undermine much of the environmental legislation passed in the 1970s such as the Clean Air and Clean Water Acts, and the Endangered Species Act."[41]

Despite interventions to stymie legislation that addressed the effects of pollution, nature and planetary themes were elaborated and popularized in many different spheres of society. Some examples include: civil society and protest activity, the legislature, the judicial system, arts and culture, and public debate. These fora provided platforms to compete with any emerging denialism agenda and tabled the need for urgent environmental action and mitigation strategies, such as the limitation of economic production, exploring renewable energy options, and aiming for supportable population growth. But equally, the embedding of this agenda strengthened and aligned the relationship between neoliberal actors and public relations. Public relations institutions and practitioners wielding hidden influence and power within media hierarchies, networks, and systems, and with privileged access to public platforms and "mass" audiences,

---

39. Shabecoff (1988).
40. Dunlap and McCright (2015, 300).
41. White et al. (2006).

were both willing and motivated to reinforce neoliberal stories and interpretive positions through a multitude of textual material. Public relations deployed many intrinsic and extrinsic tactical responses over coming years, from media releases, to "op-ed" pieces, to policy statements, public commentary, to monitoring and spying on "enemies" that may be working against the neoliberal narrative.[42]

The last three decades of the twentieth century saw an intensification of the animosity between the public relations industry and civil society, one channeled in more inventive and concealed ways. Again, there is much written about this,[43] so a few instructional examples are used to illustrate. Bearing in mind the view that "ecological PR" loomed as a threat to neoliberalism, in the 1970s, E. Bruce Harrison devised the idea of "greenwashing," to undermine the new environmental collaborations that were quickly taking root in better educated and socially aware Western societies.[44] "Greenwashing" was conceptualized as a corporate plan to "subdue" environmental NGOs and nonprofits that were partnering with business, regarding the funding advantages this arrangement brought;[45] "[t]he overall result was a series of deals that helped corporations deploy their power to subvert the environmental movement."[46] In the 1980s, the coal industry took similar remedial public relations action to change public opinion and to co-opt the mood for ethical environmental awareness. In doing so, they regularly deployed the trope, "clean coal," in a succession of public relations campaigns.[47] The idea behind "clean coal" was to counter the stigmatization of dirty coal for energy production and to

---

42. Beder (2006); Demetrious (2013).

43. Hager and Burton (1999); Shevory (2007); Peacock (2012); Demetrious (2013).

44. Rubin (1994, 36).

45. Today "greenwashing" is generally understood simply as dirty corporations deflecting media and community scrutiny by "masking their harmful actions against the environment with propaganda-driven rhetoric" (Donahue 2004, 19).

46. Hass and Kleine (2003, 273).

47. Hudson and Wright (2015); Demetrious (2017, 2019, 2019a).

introduce another socially palatable reality for "publics" concerned about escalating carbon dioxide emissions.[48]

By the 1990s, niche specializations in and around the fields of "environmental affairs," "environmental communication," and "environmental public relations management,"[49] set in motion by the implications of "pollution," had emerged fully. Together, these new public relations modes worked with "issue management" and were deployed to quell the regular and vocal public fallout associated with the operations of risk-producing industries, such as the chemical, mineral, and energy sectors.[50] Like the neonarrative of climate change denial, these strategic management functions smooth over problems to suppress open critique, in a changing world where favorable public opinion is central to business and organizational success. To illustrate, Peter M. Sandman's notion of "risk communication" was developed as a trouble-shooting counter-tactic to organized public outrage. Sandman argues "[. . .] many in industry and government have learned the hard way, ignoring or misleading the public is a losing strategy. The traditional attitude of experts toward the public in risk controversies is beginning to change because it has stopped working."[51] What is clear is that, at this time, CEOs and mangers in American corporations had a view that public relations activity, used in specialist ways, could perhaps turn things around for industry, or at least delay the policy shifts that sought to rein in their activity. This investment and belief in public relations as a viable solution to corporation's problems with

---

48. "The use of coal is the single largest barrier to limiting global temperature increase to no more than 1.5°C and is a central issue to the necessary decarbonization of economies and ensuring peoples' health" (United Nations 2019). Thus, coal industry public relations impacts on the reduction of greenhouse gas emissions.

49. Grunig (1977).

50. Peter M. Sandman developed the field of "risk communication" to manage or reassure what he argued was emotional alarm, evident in public opposition to a range of industrial activity, by using a formula: "Risk = Hazard + Outrage" (Sandman 1993, 1). First published by the American Industrial Hygiene Association, Sandman had been developing these ideas since the early 1980s.

51. Sandman (1993, 4).

the public are a notable shift from the rather tepid regard in which public relations was held in 1980s.[52] It shows that more, not less, investment in controlling how the public thought and reacted was required from corporations seeking to shield themselves from the mounting public scrutiny and resulting controversies that would affect their bottom lines. This was a pivotal moment in the cohering of public relations and neoliberal forces around a simplistic and implacable anti-science, anti-human communicative position.

The neonarrative of climate change denial asserts that the "human" and "nature" are wholly separate spheres as an organizing idea. To peddle this so that it loses its "paradoxical appearance,"[53] a neoliberal thought collective of powerful media networks,[54] with access to large public platforms and vast audiences and financed by many established and vested industry and business groups, launched into the vernacular the practice of denying anthropogenic-induced climate change. It is suggested that the main aim was not only to debunk the arguments about the environmental crisis and to reinstate the view that nature is primarily a resource for domination and exploitation, but also to promote a call for a utopian vision, promising a future regulated only by the free market, and emancipating the private individual from the burdens and constraints of red tape, and the interventions of government. The like-minded views and shared values of public relations practitioners and neoliberal forces were mobilized in opposition to the social flows that galvanized around the term "pollution," which was critical in laying the groundwork for neonarratives like climate change denial. Over time, this concerted attack had the effect of derailing

---

52. Freeman (1984).

53. Ricoeur (2009, 293).

54. In 2016 global coal producer Peabody Energy filed for US bankruptcy protection. Court documents in the legal process revealed how its public relations campaign to keep fossil fuels viable by promoting climate denial drew on a thick and submerged network of financial relations. Matt Kasper (2016, n.p.) reported that "the breadth of the groups with financial ties to Peabody is extraordinary. Think tanks, litigation groups, climate scientists, political organizations, dozens of organizations blocking action on climate all receiving funding from the coal industry."

rational public debate, which was necessary to find consensus on mitigation and adaptation policies to deal with growing anthropogenic carbon dioxide emissions and the changing climate.

The soothing effects of the neonarrative of climate change denialism are strengthened when the unfolding climate research is framed and represented as depressing and disempowering, which produces the inverse effect in the public of holding action at bay. Paul Ricoeur discusses this narrative feature as a *"split or cleft reference"* and "a way of relating to things which envelops, as a negative condition, the suspension of the referential claim of ordinary language."[55] Hence distressing headlines in daily media, designed to bring home the consequences of climate inaction, are common enough. Some examples of this are: "Climate change is worsening extreme weather events"; "Climate change is threatening our most treasured natural icons"; "Climate change isn't an intangible future risk. It's here now, and it's killing us";[56] "Climate crisis is greatest ever threat to human rights, UN warns."[57] But messages such as these play into denialism, as they are the antithesis to ideas of "freedom" and the individual's right to nature's bounty. As such, these climate realities actively repel interest. In this way, the "split" neonarrative of climate change denial referentially enlists, or at least invites, support from a gullible, disengaged, weary, or vulnerable public. It does this by gesturing toward a simple and reassuring story. Some of the media messages used to promote denial refrains include comments such as "the Earth's climate has changed before, but this is not due to 'man'"; "the science is not settled"; "the science is chaotic and unreliable"; "the opposite may be true, the world is cooling." Climate change denialists have also suggested that warmer temperatures may be good for the planet; that sunspots/galactic cosmic rays are the cause of some changes; and because "CO_2 is a small part of the atmosphere

---

55. Ricoeur (2009, 293).

56. Epstein (2019).

57. Agence France-Presse in Geneva (2019).

it can't have a large heating affect."[58] Such claims serve to promote a negative condition and suspend action by casting doubt on the authority of climate scientists' findings. And moreover, they buttress this negativity by insinuating that it is the scientists who have been manipulating the data, and that they are participating in a conspiracy to cover over the facts, for self-gain.

These confused conditions in public debate are ideal for public relations language practices and, in particular, neoliberal narratives to work. Moreover, neonarratives gain potency when they are linked to nostalgia and yearning.[59] The sticky braided threads, which combine to form climate change denial, gesture to yesterday's trouble-free world, as well as work to produce a powerful and tactical communicative response to destabilize this momentum around changing human and planetary relations. Dogmatic anti-science climate change denial voices offer the conviction which buttresses the neonarrative, reassures and makes life beautiful again, and subdues the voices of "environmental popularizers," whose words and warnings may be slowly resonating.[60] The sprawling neonarrative of climate change denial smooths over the rough and uncomfortable climate realities, to keep their "publics" safe and privileged. The next section focuses on the well-connected intermediaries that believe in a free society, and who are determined to influence the public, namely Hayek's (1949) secondhand dealers in neoliberal ideas.

---

58. Maslin (2019).

59. Writing about "otherness and difference," African American cultural theorist bell hooks (2006) discusses essentialism as a belief held by the individual that there are constitutive traits which determine how people speak, act, dress, and behave. In practice, hooks says that this is achieved by elevating and privileging a dominant narrative or history that invokes collective memory or "yearning," both in institutional and cultural contexts.

60. Rubin (1994, 18).

THINKING TANKED: WEAVING IN THE NEOLIBERAL SOUNDS

The climate change denial argument works to suspend meaningful action and policy development in response to climate research, and it has been remarkably successful. Indeed, according to Philip Mirowski et al.,[61] it has triumphed over its opponents on the left by confounding, exhausting, and paralyzing, leaving even the most ardent environmentalist to consider the role of geoengineering technologies, to adapt to climate change by artificial means, rather than by acting now to reduce greenhouse gas emissions. They argue that the denialists deploy multiple methods to prosecute their argument, and that they play the long game, buying time for the market to produce knowledge: "At each step along the way, the neoliberals guarantee their core tenet remains in force: the market will arbitrate responses to the biosphere degradation because it knows more than any of us about nature and society."[62]

Conservative think tanks are central to climate change denial's success because they have worked in tandem with the neoliberal project as intellectuals, in Hayek's sense, to supply something that resembles research[63] to public-facing secondhand dealers in ideas. Thus, denialism scripts are pre-packaged, ready, and available to media commentators, who can speak with a level of conviction on climate change denial in public debate by using public relations prompts, such as "talking points" or "key messages," while simultaneously rejecting elitist notions relating to the scientific research of bona fide experts. In this context, conservative private research organizations[64] comprise a "coherent political movement

---

61. Mirowski et al. (2013).

62. Mirowski et al. (2013).

63. According to Jordan Soukias Tchilingirian (2018, 163), "the think-tank intellectual thus becomes a handmaiden for elite interests, lacking in cognitive autonomy and scholarly rigour. As such think-tanks lack real credibility, and their knowledge is illegitimate."

64. For John M. Holcomb (2005, 553–554), since the mid-1970s, private research institutions have offered a greater diversity of political positions, but some of the most established and

embodied in the institutional history of the global network of think thanks: the American Enterprise Institute, the Cato Institute, the Institute of Economic Affairs, the Institute of Public Affairs, (the key Australian node of the network) and their dedicated spin-off counter science think tanks."[65] Riley E. Dunlap and Peter J. Jacques reviewed the links between conservative think tanks, such as the Competitive Enterprises Institute (CEI), the Heartland Institute, the CATO Institute, and the Marshall Institute, and the production of climate change denial literature; they found that the literature was mainly written by "a small number of contrarian scientists, primarily located in the United States, (who) played a critical role in planting and legitimating climate change denial within conservative circles."[66] Sitting at a distance from crass public relations, think tanks produce institutional rationality for knowledge formation based in the economic sphere, and are invested with weight and gravitas to counter climate research and the development of alternative policy settings. As such, they have played a key role in the neonarrative brushing and burnishing. Large and small free-market and socially conservative think tanks, and their network of political parties and groups, legislative lobbyists and influential individuals, powerful media, and business and industry players—the neoliberal thought collective—have provided, and continue to provide, financial and network support[67] in order for the dogmatic term "climate change denial" to be spoken with authority and momentum. By producing the plausible scripts for their secondhand dealers in ideas, neoliberal think tanks are thus intimately entwined with public relations and neonarrative.

Interlocutors like media commentators, talk-back radio hosts, journalists, and politicians work in many ways to broadcast the neonarrative of climate change denial. As discussed, to gain a level of intellectual substance, these

---

powerfully networked are conservative, supported by industrial interests, and fiercely pitted against any climate mitigation policies.

65. Mirowski et al. (2013).

66. Dunlap and Jacques (2013, 711).

67. White, Rudy, and Wilbert (2007, 125); Skocpol and Hertel-Fernandes (2016).

public disputes or denunciations may draw on the socially conservative private research produced by think tanks.[68] Hence, as the product of neoliberalism and public relations, the neonarrative of climate change denial is effectively propelled by conservative voices and their networks to stymie public debate and policy development. At the urging of the "champions of freedom," the contributions of interjectors—members of the public—who might wish to modify, ask questions about, challenge, or otherwise participate in the reshaping or reimagining of extant stories/narratives, are discouraged and/or rejected.

To pause on this point, it is not unwarranted to question just how this sort of obstruction of deliberation occurs in supposedly enlightened or at least functioning democratic societies. With this in mind, Chris Peters provides an insightful investigation of the rise of Bill O'Reilly, the influential US conservative commentator and vehement climate denier, who has appeared on *Fox News* for many years.[69] While he examines how O'Reilly gained sway with his audience, Peters's work shows how neoliberal voices that seek to enter and dominate the public sphere more generally can be interpreted more widely. In this project, he identifies some of the performative traits as: acting out their conviction within a construct of "the appearance of Enlightenment perceptions surrounding the proper exercise of reason and emotion";[70] purporting to be fair and balanced—journalistic ideals—while also redefining news with combative free speech or "exaggerated vitriol";[71] the predigestion of facts, rather than

---

68. The US-based Climate Investigations Center (CIC) provides case studies of scientifically biased individuals involved in public commentary on climate change denial. An example is Patrick Michael, former director of the Center for the Study of Science at the free-market fossil-fuel-funded Cato Institute. CIC (2020) writes: "Patrick Michaels, currently the Director of the Center for the Study of Science at the Koch-founded and funded Cato Institute, has built a career curating doubt about climate change science and its impact on our environment. His contributions as an 'expert' to the multi-pronged strategy to stall action on climate change have been subsidized for decades by the industries that have the most to lose from any such action."

69. Peters (2010).

70. Peters (2010, 840).

71. Peters (2010, 833).

presentation;[72] engaging in long-standing feuds, or "constant recurring themes";[73] presenting as the tribune of the people, by standing up for common sense and the little guy;[74] not actually presenting the news, but "determining what the viewer needs to factor in";[75] and acting as a conduit of facts, while performing a sense of "reality, factuality and fairness."[76] This and other research suggests that climate change deniers commonly embody remarkably similar character traits and discursive strategies.[77]

James Delingpole is a free-market media commentator, a neoliberal interlocutor, and a one-time online columnist for *The Telegraph* with no scientific expertise or formal qualifications. According to Phelan, "Delingpole sees the entire green movement, including the case for anthropogenic climate change, as simply a front for a socialist attack against the capitalist system."[78] His media performances, like that of other neoliberal interlocutors, often invoke the precept of speaking up for "the people" against a threat, using "free speech" to speak directly to those who have the "right to know." Hence, Delingpole can be understood, not as an individual, but as an instrument for producing neoliberal sounds that have been harnessed to politically intervene in public debate, in order to destabilize the momentum for climate action. In describing Climategate as a potent performative example of the neonarrative of climate change denial, and in showing how Delingpole propelled it into the public sphere, the analysis will focus on the discursive dynamics that converged in this debate in the hope of finding a way through this sociopolitical and cultural impasse.

---

72. Peters (2010, 834).

73. Peters (2010, 840).

74. Peters (2010, 841).

75. Peters (2010, 840).

76. Peters (2010, 839).

77. D'Cruz and Weerakkody (2015).

78. Phelan (2014, 124).

A BEAUTIFUL CURVE: THE REACH OF NEOLIBERALISM IN SHAPING PUBLIC OPINION

> At the beginning I called "Climategate" the biggest scientific scandal in the history of the world. And so it is, not so much because of what went on at the Climatic Research Unit at the University of East Anglia, but because the repercussions are so huge. Until "Climategate," our political masters were happy to present us, in the name of combating "climate change," with a bill so enormous—45 trillion—it threatens to wipe out the entire global economy. If "Climategate" succeeds in stopping this then it will no longer be a scandal. It will be a total bloody miracle.[79]

In November 2009, the media reported that over 1,000 emails belonging to the Climate Research Unit (CRU) at the University of East Anglia were stolen and made publicly available.[80] Climate change denialists claimed that the illegally accessed emails proved that there was an active conspiracy by scientists to falsify data pertaining to anthropogenic climate change.[81] In turn, the CRU email hackers were suspected of deliberately attempting to discredit the integrity of that university's climate research and the IPCC—a body established to provide expert scientific advice to government and others, about the natural and social impacts of the changing climate—and jeopardizing its funding.[82] Giving weight to this, the CRU email hack, with its high media prominence, was leaked to the

---

79. Delingpole (2009).

80. Bricker (2013, 218).

81. Booker (2009).

82. Carbon Brief (2011). There were other concerted attempts to discredit the IPCC. See, for example, Plehwe's (2019) illuminating discussion of a report published in 2013 and authored by the so-called Nongovernmental International Panel on Climate Change (NIPCC). Plehwe explains that this report, most of whose authors lack academic credentials in meteorology or climate-related fields, was designed both to mimic and to counter the IPCC's own report. Indeed, the NIPCC report "claims to present scientific results that contradict much if not all of the findings of the IPCC. What is more, the report argues that IPCC research works on the wrong premise

web just prior to the December 2009 United Nations Climate Change Conference in Copenhagen. This strategic timing was seen as an attempt to "undermine" the global call to action and the summit's credibility.[83] While the long-term impact of these events is hard to judge, at the time, an explosion in non-expert media commentary helped to reshape and construct a distrustful relationship between the public and the idea of bona fide climate science. Distrust was particularly seeded in the veracity of the data being used to inform the IPCC and Copenhagen summit's global position on climate policy. This CRU conspiracy narrative became a sweeping denunciation of all climate research, and a warning to the faithful that even the IPCC and the UN were in on the climate hoax.[84] The discursive momentum generated by this news was pushed along by neoliberal interlocutors like Delingpole, who took the opportunity to highlight the far-reaching financial ramifications of Climategate in ways that necessitated a direct appeal to the reader. Specifically, "[i]f you own any shares in alternative energy companies I should start dumping them NOW."[85] He claimed the candid email discussion proved that "warmist scientists may variously have manipulated or suppressed evidence in order to support their cause." Denialists thus professed such ideas *without*

(man-made climate change), ignoring the alternative hypothesis of natural climate change, which is held to be much more consistently backed by available data" (2019, 141–142).

83. Fred Pearce (2010, n.p.) reported that "Kevin Trenberth at the National Centre for Atmospheric Research in Boulder, Colorado, and IPCC chairman Rajendra Pachauri both said they saw it as an attempt to undermine the Copenhagen climate conference, that was due to take place two weeks later."

84. An economist and author of *Freedomnomics*, John R. Lott Jr. (2009) writes that "science depends on good quality of data. It also relies on replication and sharing data. But the last couple of days have uncovered some shocking revelations. Computer hackers have obtained 160 megabytes of e-mails from the Climate Research Unit at the University of East Anglia in England. These e-mails, which have now been confirmed as real, involved many researchers across the globe with ideologically similar advocates around the world. They were brazenly discussing the destruction and hiding of data that did not support global warming claims. The academics here also worked closely with the U.N.'s Intergovernmental Panel on Climate Change."

85. Delingpole (2009). Capitalization in original.

doubt and purported to reveal the real *truth* of the matter. As a corollary, Climategate came to connote the idea that individuals who value "freedom" should put their trust in the market, more so than any other form of social action to preserve these conditions. In doing so, the subject of their communication was being positioned to understand, not just that the climate scientists are conspirators of bogus research, but conspirators working to *deny* people's freedom in relation to the proto-plastic narrative established in the postwar period: the individual's right to pursue a utopian promise of a better and more economically prosperous future. Hence, neoliberal ideas, relating to individual freedom and a market-based society free from government coercion, were embedded and circulated within diverse discourses. The climate change denialists' attacks on the CRU scientists, and their climate research, cast a long shadow, and tarnished many other credible research institutions and policy processes, as these claims were repeated relentlessly in the media, time and time again.[86]

Catchphrases like "Climategate" draw individuals toward a vortex of sensations, emotions, ideas, words, and objects that construct the neonarrative of climate change denial. In that sense, neonarratives draw on something largely understood to be universal and intergenerational, which, as Tumarkin points out, gives them extraordinary locking power and momentum. Brett Jacob Bricker argues that "Climategate" fulfilled all these criteria.

> "Climategate" had all of the formal characteristics defining conspiracy but also the situational characteristics that completed the constellation. In particular, it concerned an alleged truth hidden by elites, presented a narrative of an investigative reporter being punished by elites and suggested that any normal person with enough fortitude could uncover and interpret the evidence (Fenster, 1999: 9). However, unique interaction of anti-elitism, existing ideology, a well-crafted charge, and a poor rhetorical response by those

86. Mangan (2019).

accused gave the charge of conspiracy in the case of "Climategate" particular resonance.[87]

The term "Climategate," and its connotations of conspiracy, meld with plastic words like "information" to build an aura and burnish the neoliberal neonarrative that is "consistent with the trend of skepticism of Anthropogenic Climate Change (ACC) theories in popular consciousness."[88] The sprawling term "Climategate" built on the now established genre chain, which began with the Watergate scandal,[89] with its associations of wrongdoing at the highest level. Despite the wild historical inaccuracy in comparing these events to Watergate, the catchphrase "Climategate" was loaded and weaponized, because it aligned with the neonarrative elements' foundational dynamics of the unfolding story, of an alleged diabolic deception on a global scale. This suggested an ideologically driven plot to overthrow capitalism, by environmentalists and climate change sympathizers. In shaping reality, Delingpole was represented in his media comments as the "champion of freedom," the "truth teller," and the "whistle blower," who was willing to reveal a political cover-up and expose an ill-defined link to an underground source, and the eventual downfall of the highest, untouchable authority. Phelan argues that Delingpole "stages a journalistic identification with the logics of accountability, transparency and information (the same holy trinity built into the governmentality of audit regimes)."[90] In tandem with this approach, the

---

87. Bricker (2013, 224).

88. Bricker (2013, 232).

89. The key dynamics of the "Watergate" scandal are explained by Donald A. Ritchie (1998, 50): "On 17 June 1972, police arrested five men who had broken into the Democratic National Committee headquarters at the Watergate office building in Washington, D.C. carrying wiretapping equipment [. . .]. *Washington Post* reporters Bob Woodward and Carl Bernstein published numerous articles that tied the burglars closely with the president's top staff. Other newspaper and television reporting indicated that the White House had paid 'hush money' to keep the burglars from talking and that Nixon's administration had engaged in a cover-up of its illegal activities."

90. Phelan (2014, 129).

idea of a momentous event is also present in Delingpole's performances. "Climategate" in this moment draws on orders of discourse that imply the shattering of illusions, the weakening of a fortress of power, and a step along the road to rebuilding the future in ways that are better, stronger, and real.

Delingpole—righteous upholder of the truth—appears to have been unconcerned about the criminal activity at the core of this matter. Indeed, he helped to fan the firestorm this story eventually became in the long-standing feud with climate scientists.[91] Again, his corruption of journalistic values moves from a presentation of actual facts to "determining what the viewer needs to factor in."[92] And it is Delingpole's own analysis which provides insight into how discursive practices contributed to the momentum of this issue to discredit scientists and climate research, at the same time as upholding a form of rationality, in order to raise the strength and stakes of the neoliberal cause. In the piece below, neoliberal Delingpole appears to relish the media frenzy and morphing of public debate into a media circus.

> It has been a weird, weird thing having a ringside seat at the messy unravelling of the greatest scientific scandal in the history of the world [. . .]. From a tiny germ of a story on a few specialist blogs, "Climategate" has gone uber-viral in a way few of us sceptics could ever have dared hope. As I write, the name has clocked well over 30 million Google hits, which for me has been a bit like being a proud parent watching his singing, dancing little girl suddenly grow up to become Madonna—for "Climategate" was sorta, kinda, partly my baby.[93]

---

91. Peters (2010, 840).
92. Peters (2010, 840).
93. Delingpole (2009).

In describing the success of his role in elevating this media interpretation, Delingpole's use of superlatives and sensation is untempered. Combined with the neonarrative, this contributes to the compression of meaning relating to social risk and technological impacts of climate change, thereby diminishing its complexity, and co-constructing passivity and acceptance with public relations "publics."[94] And through this process it becomes a disassociated "truth." For, as Ricoeur says, "[t]he historical event, thus torn form its initial setting, has lost its specificity in order to conform with a general concept of event, itself deprived of any particular relation to the act of narrating."[95]

In time, the CRU scientists were exonerated by a series of investigations.[96] Nonetheless, Climategate gained enough social traction to propel widespread reductive understandings that worked against legitimate climate research in society's interest. This example demonstrates how non-expert authority has been used effectively to create a cultural identifier, resembling an exposé of global proportions, rather than the hacked and stolen emails of East Anglia University CRU. Once channeled, Climategate was digitally dispersed to influence those members of society who were hesitant, undecided, or of two minds on climate matters, in ways that are designed to affect their political understandings. As such, the wild opinions of interlocutors, like online journalist Delingpole, were credited as an authority to speak on climate research over the institutions and individuals which society has conferred with the legitimacy to do so. Therefore, a non-expert interlocutor with an anti-science agenda gained credibility with the public, within a construct of "the appearance of Enlightenment perceptions surrounding the proper exercise of reason and emotion."[97] The Climategate example demonstrates an interpretive catchphrase that gained widespread media attention and take-up by those purporting to be standing up for common

---

94. Poerksen (1995, 102).

95. Ricoeur (2009, 276).

96. Union of Concerned Scientists (2009).

97. Peters (2010, 840).

sense.[98] However, this was not accidental and did not rely on the talents or otherwise of non-experts, like Delingpole. As I will aim to show, it relied on the embedded foundations of public relations language to develop its discursive momentum and power. The next section examines the plastic words and interlocutors that enabled Climategate to gain mobility within the public sphere.

"HOW CAN ENVIRONMENTAL COMMUNICATORS IN INDUSTRY OVERCOME DISADVANTAGES?"

Neoliberal interlocutor James Delingpole purports to be a champion for the individual's right to pursue freedom and to counter any threat or denial of this by government.[99] This appeal is augmented by selecting genre styles that support a mood of urgency and peril. Neoliberal interlocutors also rely on storied logic that entails a warm relationship of trust, between the "publics" as underdogs, and the interlocutor as their protector. In media delivery, stagey dramatic pauses and speaking directly to the camera/audience are used to underpin emphasis and build momentum. This is the "narrative of speech" that works hand in hand with "a narrative of action" to compound the signification process.[100] So too is making a show of rejecting "spin" and claiming the semblance of authenticity and truth as a "narrative crossing" to the "redescription of our historical condition."[101] These are complex dynamics, which are designed to resemble democratic ideals. As Peters points out, it is about the appearance of upholding journalistic ideals, such as balance and fairness, while at the same time redefining news with combative free speech or "exaggerated

---

98. Peters (2010, 841).

99. Section title quoted from Harrison (1992, 11).

100. Ricoeur (2009, 162).

101. Ricoeur (2009, 274–275).

vitriol."[102] Vast audiences, accessible via social media and legacy media, are both subject and susceptible to these discursive cues, which are designed to obfuscate truth and to stifle originality and future imaginings. This stagnation stops the public discussion from prising open new understandings of the world and keeps the neonarrative intact and safe.

Plastic words are pliant, portable, and commodified units of meaning used in public relations language practices, and assist secondhand dealers in ideas, like Delingpole, to do their work. Poerksen suggests that it is the slip-sliding imprecision of blank plastic words which makes them impenetrable. However, they are not benign or purposeless. Hence, while vernacular words like "freedom" and "information" have fields of associations and ideas, it is the reverberations between the specific plastic words with the subject that are the focus for analysis here. Climategate anchored to the neonarrative of climate change denial, in turn constructed an expectation of how the public should think and feel politically about climate research. For Poerksen, "information" is a significant word that exerts "a mesmerizing effect"; at the same time, it can offer the "impression of emptiness."[103] Hence, the fusion of this seemingly amorphous, malleable, but powerful word leads the subject toward a sense of inevitability, and acceptance of a neoliberal reality.[104] Illustrating this point is that the news reports of the University of East Anglia's Climate Research Unit's stolen emails framed it as "climate audit,"[105] over the criminal act that led to the disclosure.[106] Thus, the holy immanence of "information" as "a manifold reality"[107] is apparent in Anthony Watts's numeric description

---

102. Peters (2010, 833).

103. Poerksen (1995, 41–44).

104. Poerksen (1995, 5).

105. The stolen emails were referred to as "climate audit" when Anthony Watts released the story on November 19, 2009.

106. Poerksen (1995, 42) argues that "information" brings very particularly qualities to the vernacular. It "becomes superior to mere opinion, or only intuitively grounded suspicion, or even feeling. It is fortified with data. It can be checked. As a datum, it is the essence of the thing."

107. Poerksen (1995, 47).

of the "shocking" cache in this text selection: "The file was large, about 61 megabytes, containing hundreds of files. It contained data, code, and emails from Phil Jones at CRU to and from many people."[108]

This emphasis on "information" (bytes), with its specific associations with science and data, served to embolden the general hoo-ha of the climate change denialists. As Dana Nuccitelli wrote:

> After 1,000 of climate scientists' private emails were stolen and published online, snippets of text were taken out of context and misrepresented to falsely accuse the scientists of scandal, conspiracy, collusion, falsification, and illegal activities. Climate deniers and biased media outlets whipped up such froth over these misrepresentations that various organizations launched nine separate investigations to identify any possible scientific wrongdoing uncovered by the emails. They found none.[109]

Climategate grew rapidly in digital media contexts and created division and confusion in ways that undermine the very concept of rational and evidence-based public debate. The decontextualization of the emails made them free floating and open to (nefarious) interpretation. Hence, interlocutors like Delingpole could remove them without serious challenge from the historical moment where they meant something in relation to something else. This unmooring served to contribute to the manufacturing of ambiguous information, which could be used to buttress climate change denial.

Perhaps counterintuitively, it is proposed that the concept captured by the term "environment" underpins the catchphrase "Climategate." Used in a plurality of contexts, overwhelmingly, the "environment" has come to stand for something other than the human. With its provenance in science, it is this very lack of precision which makes "environment" a likely plastic word. On their own, words may be harmless, but when

---

108. Watts (2009).

109. Nuccitelli (2016).

they resonate across different discourses, such as neoliberalism, they incrementally or dynamically develop a logic and coherence in the form of the neonarrative, which leads to an ideologically invested destination that absolves human activity from any consequences of harm to the planet. According to Eagleton-Pierce, "[t]he rise of the environment as a central socio-political problem has coincided with the mainstreaming of ideas and practices associated with neoliberalism. With the planet facing multiple ecological stresses from rising animal extinction rates to global climate change, debate on the relationship between humans and natural surroundings has become increasingly animated and contested assuming an apocalyptic tone."[110] This is accompanied by a slight semantic shift in the twentieth century, when the world "environment" becomes "the environment," embracing a far wider context than simply organisms and natural world; it now denotes this in relation to harmful human activity.[111] This has resonances with Ulrich Beck's work that suggests that if the sociological is not included in the analysis of climate, then it is of very little value.

> The discourse on climate politics so far is an expert and elitist discourse in which peoples, societies, citizens, workers, voters and their interests, views and voices are very much neglected. So, in order to turn climate change politics from its head onto its feet you have to take sociology into account. There is an important background assumption which shares in the general ignorance concerning environmental issues and, paradoxically, this is incorporated in the specialism of environmental sociology itself—this is the category of "the environment." If "the environment" only includes everything which is not human, not social, then the concept is sociologically empty. If the concept includes human action and society, then it is scientifically mistaken and politically suicidal.[112]

---

110. Eagleton-Pierce (2016, 61).
111. University of Pittsburgh (2016).
112. Beck (2010, 254).

The term "climate change" is potent. It is destabilizing. It has a radicalizing effect on the society because it presupposes an economic redistribution of sorts, with winners and losers, and a challenge to market-based rationality. With the ominous prospect of this disruption, Beck's work suggests that connecting "climate change" with the word "environment" presents almost a no-win situation in public debate. Referring to the natural non-human world, "the environment" serves to further entrench demarcations and the battlelines where humans are pitted against nature. Thus unwittingly, the speaking subject, be they a politician, climate scientist, or activist group advocating for greater understanding of climate risk and its implications for the human world, may create a more fractured and distant relationship with the public. This is because implicit in their words are social hierarchy and division between advocates of this unseen enemy: nature. The potency of these addresses in public debate are critically important because it is the struggle over the definition of climate risk that is a precursor to a form of settled "knowledge." For Beck, "if this is the core understanding of risk, then this means that we must attach major significance to the media staging and acknowledge the potential explosiveness of the media."[113] Perhaps then, there is no more significant failure in public debate to address.

Plastic words are "a way of imagining" that is strangely reassuring, but can mask the violence occurring to humans and nature.[114] Neonarratives are scaffolded by plastic words, such as "freedom," "information," and "environment," which are implicitly linked to contradictions within neoliberalism, that can be traced to the word "pollution" and the notion of "ecological PR."[115] How then can everyday people, from the many different parts of society, contribute to tackling the problems identified through an invigorated political process?[116]

---

113. Beck (2010, 261).

114. Poerksen (1995, 28).

115. Rubin (1994); Grunig (1977).

116. Beck (2010, 255).

CLIMATE CHANGE DENIAL: DISRUPTING THE DISRUPTER

Public relations, in acting for special interests like industry or politics, produces climate change denial as an explanation and deploys this in neonarrative to work in many counterintuitive and subterranean ways. Climate action has been delayed, and these forces have set history on a particular course. Within their own criteria, they have been successful in fortifying a neoliberal interpretation position in the public imagination. The multiple acts of "telling" the neonarrative lay down stabilizing cross-references like sedimentary layers. Yearning also plays a significant dynamic in the appeal of climate change denial stories promulgated by interlocutors like Delingpole. Public relations plays a part in this; by enclosing differentiated individuals into "publics," it consigns them to a self-referencing type with a "family resemblance" that can be predicted and controlled.[117] It also helps interlocutors like James Delingpole that the mood and topic of climate change are largely framed as depressing and disempowering by "environmental popularizers."[118] The more the problem of climate change is discussed, the more dire and helpless the individual becomes, and hence the cause to take action becomes "politically suicidal."[119] Thus the "split" neonarrative that contests and trivializes climate problems becomes ever more alluring, comforting, and restorative.[120]

Implicit in calls to act on climate is that society has encouraged wasteful, consumption-driven lifestyles that have led to these problems. For some, this is a pejorative that has complex effects, as it implies that climate change advocates judge "us" as guilty: bad people who are selfish, greedy, or stupid. Denialists, like O'Reilly and Delingpole, harness this pessimism and use it in language games to conjure up nostalgia for a time

---

117. Ricoeur (2009, 288); Hughes and Demetrious (2006, 99).

118. Rubin (1994, 18).

119. Beck (2010, 254).

120. Ricoeur (2009, 293).

when these problems simply did not exist, thus deepening the cultural divide which appeals to a "particular form of alt-right politics in the United States, Australia, parts of Europe and Britain."[121]

There is simply no merit in the climate change denial argument. Its deep social and scientific contradictions mean that its call for inaction is not only absurdly illogical, but anti-human. This incongruity should have rendered the anti-science argument impotent, but it has not.[122] In finding a way through this, I argue that the public relations industry which supports denialism, and deploys interventions in public debates such as neonarratives, is not tangential. Rather, these discursive strategies centrally explain how climate inaction, emanating from many sites and voices, including scientists and those not directly associated with public relations, has been propelled on a visceral and imaginary social level. But arguments such as these, which are interpretive and critical, seem to fall away like leaves. The failure to claim this "truth" means, not only do these distortions and falsifications remain in place, but there is never a firm starting point for reform in this area.[123] Nonetheless, the growing significance of public relations and its discursive strategies as an explanatory theory for climate

---

121. Rowe et al. (2019, 155).

122. In 1989, the UK's conservative Prime Minister, Margaret Thatcher, promoted climate action to the international community at a UN General Assembly: "It is mankind and his activities that are changing the environment of our planet in damaging and dangerous ways. The result is that change in future is likely to be more fundamental and more widespread than anything we have known hitherto. Change to the sea around us, change to the atmosphere above, leading in turn to change in the world's climate, which could alter the way we live in the most fundamental way of all" (Vidal 2013, n.p.).

123. The contest for truth and verification in the climate change debate has provided a critical foothold for the discursive strategies of public relations to work. In their influential book *Merchants of Doubt: How a Handful of Scientists Obscured the Truth on Issues from Tobacco Smoke to Global Warming*, Naomi Oreskes and Erik Conway (2012, 206) discuss the couterintuitive dynamic affecting public opinion in which it becomes a powerful vehicle for misinformation rather than critical discussion and debate. This happens when a form of "truth that relies only on something that looks or feels like "proof", gathers momentum to erase rationality: "We think that science provides certainty, so if we lack certainty, we think the science must be faulty or incomplete. . . . History shows us clearly that science does not provide certainty. It does not provide proof. It only provides the consensus of experts, based on the organized accumulation and scrutiny of evidence."

inaction is emerging. For example, Robert Brulle and Carter Werthman's 2021 survey of US public relations firms in climate change policy debates, like Edelman, Glover Park, Cerrell, and Ogilvy, shows that there is pending litigation focusing on the promulgation of misinformation, and that the mood to make public relations more accountable for obstructing climate action is growing.[124] A new coherence, a new relationship of intelligibility along these lines, may eventually emerge in this space. However, the likelihood of any reformist movement needs to be considered in relation to the "trillions of dollars the fossil fuel industries and other vested interest reaped by slowing down meaningful change on the global warming issue."[125] Added to this, the vast profits gained from delaying action on climate, within a market-based logic, in turn support the legitimization of further misinformation campaigns by a "large number of organizations, including conservative think tanks, advocacy groups, trade associations and conservative foundations, with strong links to sympathetic media outlets and conservative politicians."[126] At best, reform may rather be a matter of de-privileging public relations and its many interacting texts, in the hope that this may help dissolve the constructed reality of climate change denial.

Neoliberal and public relations forces combine to bypass deliberation, and bypass authentic political struggle. Misinformation, division, procrastination, disengagement—an entwined, uncertain mass of interpretations, judgments, and statements—steer debate and decision-making toward a set of narrow choices. But explaining this as "spin" is not only limited, but may reproduce the very cultural pillars that support it. In responding to the impact of climate change, new ways of living, thinking, and communicating, which are more considerate of human actions, must be embedded. Collectively, these inroads could, in time, lead to substantive change. But while there is some cause for such hope (rather than optimism), global risks like climate change are frightening and transformative.

124. Brulle and Werthman (2021, 19).

125. Fessmann (2019).

126. Brulle (2014).

The global risks posed by climate change point not only to economic disruption, but to other consequences, such as statelessness and refugees as millions are exiled from their homes due to the crisis. In this reality, people are "confronted with the global other. They tear down national borders and mix the local with the foreign."[127] In the next chapter I explore the public debates surrounding people who occupy the borderlands.

---

127. Beck (2010, 259).

5

"Borderlands"

Public Relations and the Broken Moorings of Language

This chapter discusses how public relations language creates "new realities" in response to people crossing borders and moving in and between nation-states. The plight of displaced people, those who are stateless, seeking refuge, or who wish to become a member of another nation-state, is a defining public debate of this century[1]—a political shard which can be sharply at odds with national identities. Yet unlike "climate change denial," there is no single catchphrase that these social contradictions neatly cohere around. The dominant characteristic of this political debate is its unmooring, its long fingers and partial submergence. In this debate, it is this very disunity of public dispositions and viewpoints that defines it and leads to a narrowing path of cultural sensitivities. In framing this chapter, I draw on Gloria Anzaldúa's *Borderlands*[2] to explore how language,

---

1. Climate refugees will be the world's poorest and most vulnerable people. Droughts, fires, storms, and floods will affect food supply, leading to conflict and forcing millions from their homes and "[t]he insecurity created is the defining threat to global human rights in the 21st century" (Environmental Justice Foundation 2017, 40). These conditions will get worse. Alexander Betts says, "the pandemic has heightened the already difficult situation of forcibly displaced people around the world, whose number has been rising over the past decade, and is currently estimated to stand at 80 million (of whom 26 million are refugees)" (Skrdlik and Beney 2021).

2. Anzaldúa (in Cantú, Hurtado, and Anzaldúa 2012).

culture, and power are working to shape conceptions of social realities. Speaking powerfully from her lived experience of exclusion and liminality between the US–Mexican border,[3] Anzaldúa shows how this hybridized seam, this dislocated and yet connected space, can be used to unsee/see, and to build new understandings of, social realities in speaking up in defiance of hegemony.[4] As part of her larger argument, Anzaldúa stresses the arbitrary nature of oppressive social categories: "Borders are set up to define the places that are safe and unsafe, to distinguish us from them."[5] It is within this third space as an "outsider within,"[6] that I argue public relations practices work to narrow voter dispositions in ways that passively tolerate or accept exclusionist neoliberalist policy settings. In mapping this line, this chapter will examine the historical and geopolitical locus within which neoliberalism is situated, and the discursive relations that arise. In doing so, it will probe the spaces where public relations, detached from institutional sites, is working more broadly as concepts in thinking and social practice. It will show that neoliberal logic is driving meaning-making in metastatic ways, which affect the cultural flows in human rights and social justice matters. In summary, the chapter argues that while there

3. Anzaldúa writes that she was raised *"en el Valle De Rio Grande* in South Texas—that triangular piece of land wedged between the river *y el golfo* which serves as the Texas-U.S./Mexican border [. . .]" (in Cantú, Hurtado, and Anzaldúa 2012, 57, italics in original).

4. In their "Introduction to the Fourth Edition," Norma Elia Canu and Aida Hurtado (in Cantú, Hurtado, and Anzaldúa 2012, 7) explain that although Anzaldúa's ideas were situated in her own lived experience in South Texas, "her theory also applies to any kind of social, economic, sexual, and political dislocation. Her insights help us to understand the experiences of individuals who are exposed to contradictory social systems and develop [. . .] the agility to navigate and challenge monocultural and monolingual conceptions of social reality."

5. Anzaldúa (in Cantú, Hurtado, and Anzaldúa 2012, 25).

6. In the "Introduction," Norma Elia Cantú and Aida Hurtado (in Cantú, Hurtado, and Anzaldúa 2012, 7) discuss the layered construction of knowledge as an "outsider within," flowing from life in and between borders. Cantú and Hurtado write: "For Anzaldúa, the borderlands are important not only for the hybridity that occurs there, but also for the perspective they afford to their inhabitants. Living between two countries, two social systems, two languages, two cultures, results in understandings experientially the contingent nature of social arrangements. Thus, Anzaldúa asserts, living in the borderlands produces knowledge by being within a system while also retaining the knowledge of an outsider who comes from outside the system" (in Cantú, Hurtado, and Anzaldúa 2012, 7).

is a raft of seemingly unrelated phenomena in this debate, two threads connect them: public relations language practices and neoliberalism. The task is to identify ways public debate may be shaped and opened, for more human-centred, grounded, and empathetic understandings to emerge. As such, my focus is on the marginalized and social groups with diverse cultural positions, and their challenges within these conditions to disrupt the hegemony spawning from the circulating neoliberal language practices. To understand the configuration of the borderland field of ideas—namely, immigration, refugees, and statelessness—I apply a Foucauldian[7] analysis. Specifically, I consider how public relations language practices combine to represent them as "categories," to anchor widespread neoliberal dispositions and orientations and at the same time promote a particular relationship between culture and politics. I ask how this may diminish the public's expectations in human rights matters, harden stances, and build consent.

NEOLIBERALIZING EMPATHY

> The U.S-Mexican border *es una herida abierta* [is an open wound] where the Third World grates against the first and bleeds. And before a scab forms it haemorrhages again, the lifeblood of two worlds margining to form a third country—a border culture.[8]

Anzaldúa's metaphor of a wound, weeping and sore, to illustrate the indeterminant spaces wedged between the haves and the have-nots on the US–Mexican border, is an evocative one. It challenges the reader to understand more deeply, not just the jarring humanitarian matters affecting refugees, immigrants, and stateless people, but what this space is, and how the communicative realm is working to control and shape interpretive positions in these realities. So, what are the neoliberalizing dynamics in public relations language practices that are shaping the border cultures,

---

7. Foucault (1972, 56–63).

8. Anzaldúa (in Cantú, Hurtado, and Anzaldúa 2012, 25).

within which ideas about membership of the nation-state and inclusion play out? Time and time again, the populist political language represents the borders of nation-states as simplified binaries: haves/have-nots, in/out, safe/unsafe, legal/illegal, deserving/undeserving, and winners/losers.[9] Propelled and enforced by public relations, these rhetorical divisions are at the heart of a powerful neonarrative that embeds institutional and cultural sites alike.

The large neonarrative is a story of a nation-state (for example, Australia or the United States), and its economic development success (as opposed to failure) to establish progress that leads to the prosperity of its members. The beneficiaries of this "development" (hard work) will reap the bounty, but nonetheless, if the market forces were left free, opportunity and advantage would be available for other nation-states and their members. Disparities of wealth would start to dissolve. Until then, the "underdevelopment" of nation-states, and their members, is a threat, and the security of the borders must be maintained to ensure the safety of its members.[10]

To open new understandings of this public debate, "neoliberalism" as a product of institutional sites, like think tanks, corporations, and political networks, must be abandoned. Instead, a concept of these institutional sites working in tandem with the loose trail of market-based meaning more broadly in society that works to cohere, and predispose public sensibilities, and which drives reasoning and decision-making, must be considered. Making the point that neoliberalism has become the

---

9. In 2002, shifts in the language applied to asylum seekers were apparent in Britain. They had "created a new social category of asylum seeker, increasingly portrayed as 'undeserving' in contrast to the 'deserving' refugee" (Sales 2002, 456). Twenty years later, Doğuş Şimşek (2021, 14) describes how Syrian refugees were subject to "[e]xpressions of racism and xenophobia [which] were once again inextricably linked with the economic status and security of the respondents. Statements such as, 'they' are not like 'us,' 'they' are taking 'our' jobs, 'they' are using 'our' resources have been most obviously deployed [. . .]."

10. In 2013, the conservative right-wing Coalition formed the government in Australia, with a strong mandate to secure its borders from asylum seekers. In the run-up, the Coalition accused the incumbent left Labor government of weakening border protection policies, which in turn led to a domestic law and order issue. Shadow Attorney-General George Brandis discusses the Coalition "plan" with media commentator Andrew Bolt, saying "there is a very direct link between the security of our border and the safety of our streets" (The Bolt Report, June 16, 2013).

prevailing logic in contemporary society, Aihwa Ong argues that this shift places emphasis on the assemblage of ideas:

> Like any global form, neoliberal rationality participates in shifting constellations of politics, cultures and actors. In contrast to popular accounts, neoliberalism is not conceptualized as a hegemonic order or unified set of policies. There is an urgent need to bypass broad assertions that common features of a neoliberal order are disseminated country by country, and evenly across a nation state. By specifying neoliberal mechanisms and their differential articulation with specific political configurations, I pinpoint mutations not in the space of the nation-state, but in the space of the assemblage.[11]

Thus for this project, it is the packaging of neoliberal logic in public language, as a conveyor of meaning "that migrates and is selectively taken up in diverse political contexts," that is of interest.[12] The impacts of this are global and profound. One effect is the rise of hate speech in public debate, with the focus on eliminating threats and problems and keeping people safe, rather than on the causes of economic disparities affecting them. Michael Pugh explains that "[p]overty, famine, conflict and refugee camps are featured in one set of news stories; boats arriving and detention centres in another. The first belongs to a context portrayed as a problem of failure, corruption and 'barbarism' in originating countries; the second as a threat to the identity and way of life of rich destination countries."[13] Illustrating how the neonarrative does its work, Pugh identifies this by explaining that "[s]ecuritization of the issue varnishes investment in controls and policing as enlightened rationality on the part of destination communities, contrasted with menacing, quasi-natural forces of migrants 'washing out' a homeland and national identity."[14]

11. Ong (2007, 7).
12. Ong (2007, 3).
13. Pugh (2004, 55).
14. Pugh (2004, 55).

Gloria Anzaldúa's work centers on borderlands as spaces where the contradictions of two systems and two constructed realities are laid bare. The antithetical subjectivities that spring from this collision of representations combine to rupture realities and build new identities.

> Faceless, nameless, invisible taunted with "hey cucaracho" (cockroach). Trembling with fear, yet filled with courage, a courage born of desperation. Barefoot and uneducated, Mexicans with hands like boot soles gather at night by the river where two worlds merge creating what Reagan calls a frontline, a war zone. The convergence has created a shock culture, a border culture, a third country, a closed country.[15]

Despite the pain and hardship, and because of it, these are powerful spaces where hegemony does not work, and which are a wellspring of new possibility and ideas. It is the potential of these third spaces to disrupt the logic of neoliberalism which is a crucial feature of this public debate. Political hegemony, emanating from the nation-state, is designed for those citizens within and part of that legal and geographical entity, not for those who dwell in its borderlands. Let me stress: the hegemonic messages do not necessarily work in border cultures.[16] The political imperative to control or imprison the subjectivities of those people, within those spaces, is a driver of communication and action. In controlling the disordering of neoliberal knowledge, nation-states like Australia invoke the language of public relations to smooth away any jarring dissonance that the public feels or associates with contemporary political activity on the borderlands. In relation to this, Keating reiterates that "the draining of complexity" of democracy and matters of social justice opens the door to "a form of

---

15. Anzaldúa (in Cantú, Hurtado, and Anzaldúa 2012, 33).

16. A Lowy Institute Poll finds: "there has been a sharp spike in anti-immigration sentiment. For the first time in Lowy Institute polling, a majority (54%, a 14-point rise from 2017) of Australians say the 'total number of migrants coming to Australia each year' is too high. Australians also appear to be questioning the impact of immigration on the national identity" (Lowy Institute 2018).

group-think harnessed to corporate greed."[17] But how precisely does this happen in a world that is a vast mosaic of differentiation, and in the historical context of an established, universal, human rights–based anchor to a democratic social ideal?

HUMAN RIGHTS AND THE "COSMOS OF THE MARKET"

On December 10, 1948, the United Nations adopted the *Universal Declaration of Human Rights* (UDHR).[18,19] Set out in its preamble and thirty articles was the statement of ideas on which to found "freedom, justice and peace in the world."[20] Joe Hoover explains that the signing marked a crossing point,[21] from a world of war and pain to a global commitment to human rights. Nonetheless, he points out that varied interpretations of the UDHR exist on a spectrum: at one end, as a "unique status as a symbol of moral consensus"; at the other end, as "a political imposition by the postwar liberal powers intent upon remaking the international order in their image."[22] Hoover explains:

> In the consensus narrative, the General Assembly's endorsement of the UDHR symbolized a break with a terrible era of world politics—based on narrow state interests, nationalism, colonialism and racist

---

17. Keating (2006, 14).

18. "Cosmos of the market"; Hayek (2012).

19. The *Universal Declaration of Human Rights* (1948) opens with the following statement: "Whereas the peoples of the United Nations have in the Charter reaffirmed their faith in fundamental human rights, in the dignity and worth of the human person and in the equal rights of men and women and have determined to promote social progress and better standards of life in larger freedom."

20. *Universal Declaration of Human Rights* (1948).

21. Hoover (2013, 5) writes that "[h]uman rights entail a particular logic, which shapes the politics that emerges. Human rights make use of the category of humanity to make a moral claim upon the legitimate organization of social life—these claims are formally universal in reference and global in scope, but the nature of these claims is not fixed."

22. Hoover (2013, 6).

ideologies—and provided a cornerstone of the foundation upon which a new international order could be built.[23]

However, a competing interpretation of the UDHR is as an "imperfect consensus,"[24] limited by its own language and lens.[25] Nonetheless, there is little disagreement that the signing of the historic document in the wake of the Second World War set in motion a powerful chain of ideas and action. Statements in the UDHR concerning dignity, equality, and freedom combined to form a powerful wellspring of ideas, providing the architecture for successive frameworks and documents. Today, those same ideas underpin the international human rights legal system.[26] Given the circulation and reach of ideas, it is noteworthy that the UDHR "has no legal force, [but] as the single most important statement of ethics, its authority is unparalleled."[27]

Sovereign states carefully scrutinized the drafting of the UDHR and the language of "human rights" for its legal and universally moralizing potential to influence a world order which had been based on colonialism and racism. Jessica Whyte explains that "[w]ith half of the world's population still living under colonial rule, colonial powers had no interest in allowing an international body to stipulate their responsibilities to their colonial subjects."[28] Her work points out examples of in the language of the UDHR masking the economic and social disparity in ways that render the idea of consensus illusionary.

---

23. Hoover (2013, 7).

24. Hoover (2013, 7) argues that the consensus in 1948 was subject to limitations, "which excluded colonized peoples and was opposed via abstention by six communist states, as well as Saudi Arabia and South Africa, this imperfect consensus is presented as a political failing, rather than a failure of the rights regime as such."

25. The vernacular implications of the UDHR are profound. Jessica Whyte (2017, 138) points out that "[t]o frame questions of justice in the language of human rights implies certain assumptions about what constitutes injustice—and how to vanquish it."

26. Thoms and Ron (2007, 684).

27. Antoon De Baets (2009, 20).

28. Whyte (2017, 145).

In 1948, the question of the form and limits of the responsibility of wealthy states to secure social and economic rights outside their own borders was inseparable from the question of the colonies (or "non-self governing territories," in the euphemistic language of the UDHR).[29]

Two tranches of human rights in the UDHR were given due consideration: civil and political, and social and economic. In time, it would be civil and political rights that were emphasized and given expression, while problematic social and economic rights were de-emphasized and sidelined. This point is perhaps best crystallized by Friedrich Hayek, who launched a "bracing attack on the UDHR," arguing "that to speak of *rights* in a socio-economic context "debases the word 'right,' the strict meaning of which it is very important to preserve if we are to maintain a free society."[30]

Arguably, while the idea of "universal rights" to social and economic rights was problematic, the idea of development was not. In this sense, "development," as pliable "double speak," could be applied to pave the way for economic subjugation. Hayek scaffolded this position and contended that "[t]he view that anyone has a right to a particular share of material resources is fundamentally incompatible with the idea of equality before the law; impersonal rules can never determine the allocation of property, and redistribution is therefore a threat to the rule of law."[31] In this sense, the language of human rights may have shifted to accommodate contingent neoliberalism because, as Charles R. Hale points out, civil society organizations "have gained a seat at the table, if they [are] well-connected and well-behaved."[32] In discussing human rights and neoliberalism, it may

29. Whyte (2017, 145).

30. Hayek, cited in Whyte (2017, 143).

31. Hayek, cited in Whyte (2017, 143).

32. Hale (2004, 18). According to Hale (2004, 19): "Neoliberal multiculturalism is more inclined to draw conflicting parties into dialogue and negotiation than to preemptively slam the door. Civil society organizations have gained a seat at the table, and if well-connected and well-behaved, they are invited to an endless flow of workshops, spaces of political participation, and training sessions on conflict resolution."

be as Jessica Whyte discusses, that "human rights law becomes a mode for converting people in this world, and neoliberal cost-benefit language defines freedom in quantitative terms."[33]

The dominance of plastic words like "development" in this discourse can be seen as part of the "language of human rights [which] emerges from a lineage for which the extension of European law was explicitly viewed as a project of cultural transformation or conversion."[34] The plasticity of "development" assists the conversion to neoliberalism. In this case, sovereign nations and NGOs may use the term "development," which has an aura of faith and universality,[35] as a form of neoliberalizing economic and social intervention, based on a model of corporate entrepreneurism. The following section discusses how neoliberalism animates concepts of asylum seekers, immigration, and statelessness in public debate in relation to this idea.

PLOTTING THE COURSE: PUBLIC RELATIONS CONCEPT FORMATION

To embed the discourse of neoliberalism, public relations language practices work to build a complex narrative structure, which embraces a range of contradictory positions and simplifies these into relatively dichotomous positions. It does this by establishing concepts, or "onomastically."[36] In turn, the concept constitutes, and pushes along, the neonarrative plot

---

33. Whyte (2017, 141) explains that "[t]oday, Arendt's recognition that one who lacks the protection of a nation-state is also deprived of human rights has become the justification for new forms of intervention like the 'responsibility to protect' that aim to extend the protection of human rights to the populations of states that are themselves 'unwilling or unable' to provide it. The recognition that human rights cannot be secured without an institutional order (or organized violence) to uphold them, has served to rationalize the projection of military might beyond the borders of sovereign territories."

34. Whyte, discussing the work of Talal Asad (2017, 138).

35. Poerksen (1995, 17).

36. Poerksen (1995, 28).

so that the public react "to this thrust with expectations concerning the outcome and culmination of the process."[37] To investigate how it does this, I apply the Foucauldian idea of concept formation,[38] specifically through the enunciative fields in presence, concomitance, and memory. This shows how "development," as a central element of the neonarrative, is working with related concepts of exclusion and inclusion, to reorder meaning and public receptivity to the seductive idea of embracing happiness or repelling fear.

UNSETTLING "DEVELOPMENT": REFUGEES AND ASYLUM SEEKERS

Benign sounding report titles, like "Strategies for development and transformation in the third world," show the in situ assemblage of neoliberal ideas to form concepts that plot the neonarrative.[39,40] In this example, the plastic words "strategy" and "development," used in episodic storied form and "by holding our attention,"[41] can mask sharp contradictions between human rights and neoliberal discourse, and build not just tolerance, but dependence, through the mapping of the limits of their distribution to encompass economic growth. Another example of this "guided

---

37. Ricoeur (2009, 277).

38. Foucault describes a three-part framework to analyze the formation of concepts, interested in the field of statements "where they appeared and circulated" (1972, 56). He says to look first at their forms of succession, by which he means the interplay of governing ideas that arrange reordering; second, to understand the forms of coexistence in the configuration of the enunciative field as presence, concomitance, and memory (I focus on in this in the analysis); and lastly, the procedure of intervention, which is "the way in which one transfers a style of statement from one field of application another" (Foucault 1972, 59).

39. Legal distinctions embed these terms: "An asylum seeker is someone who is seeking international protection but whose claim for refugee status has not yet been determined. In contrast, a refugee is someone who has been recognised under the *1951 Convention relating to the status of refugees* to be a refugee" (Australian Government 2021d).

40. World Economic Survey (2013).

41. Ricoeur (2009, 277).

movement of our expectations"[42] is a report titled "Investing in Refugees, Investing in Australia."[43] One section of the report discusses the role of the Commonwealth coordinator-general, who in turn reports to the prime minister, and that this "would increase the likelihood that government investments in refugee settlement are able to achieve maximum returns both for refugees and for the national economy."[44] The term "national development and identity" is used prominently in the document, and implies a level of consensus to the integration of other viewpoints and dispositions within a neoliberalization exchange. "Endowed with a plus sign,"[45] "development" has properties that are imprecise, yet scientifically authoritative. Toneless and colorless, its usage in vernacular bypasses notice or controversy but moves the reader toward predetermined expectations and outcomes. The reduction of meaning into a single descriptive word, such as "development," might appear far-fetched, but if contextualized within the neoliberal thesis, it explains how ideas can travel and become mobile, and the way this intersects with other fields to create concepts, which become intricate plots that bind people to neonarratives. This is no surprise, because according to Poerksen, "the nation state weeds out languages. It is the salesman of global unification."[46] For Poerksen, while "development" shifts and changes, it is embedded and parasitic: "an amoeba as big as a jellyfish, bobbing along in the wake of science."[47]

The retelling and repetition which push the plastic word "development" into different settings and contexts, and give it legitimacy to work *in concept*, are the fields of presence. Entwined with the notion of "development,"

---

42. Ricoeur (2009, 277).

43. Shergold, Benson, and Piper (2019).

44. See Shergold et al. (2019, 19), who illustrate the conscious importance of narrative as a powerful meaning-making tool in government: "a) Articulate publically [sic] a strong positive narrative by promoting Australia's proud record of accepting refugees and emphasising the contribution this has made to our national development and identity."

45. Poerksen (1995, 17).

46. Poerksen (1995, 3).

47. Poerksen (1995, 21).

over the last two decades, successive Australian governments[48] hardened their stance on asylum-seeker policy[49] in ways that can be characterized by an "appeal to nationalism and identity."[50] While highly contested in public debate, playing into this at various times has been a "political appeal to fear and segregation to scapegoat the other."[51] In the main however, the public's expectations have been firmly linked to a incontrovertible view that offshore detention facilities that impose mandatory detention are inevitable.[52]

Retelling to form concepts takes place in many forms and settings. For example, asylum seekers arriving by boat to Australia have been subject to dehumanizing patterns of language, with words and phrases labelling them such as "boat people," "queue jumpers," and "illegals."[53] Media commentators and political spokespeople legitimize such simplified

---

48. For Austin and Fozdar (2018, 3), in Australia, "there has been support across the major political parties for tougher border protection measures using a rhetoric focused on Australian identity."

49. Hence, in Australia policy, rhetoric and public opinion have aligned. Minns et al. (2018, 2) explain that "[o]ver the years, the arrival of asylum-seekers to Australia has been an issue of significant political contestation. Many sympathize with their plight and are spurred into pro-refugee support when the issue makes the front pages. However, since 1992, but especially from 2001 onwards, the Australian government has adopted strict policies to stop the flow of asylum-seekers, including detaining indefinitely in offshore detention centres all those who arrive by boat. Furthermore, they have had widespread public support for doing so."

50. Catherine Austin and Farida Fozdar discuss the contradictions and complexity around Australian national identity. They argue that nationalism was framed in two competing ways: first, as "traditional," where traits like having a "fair go" were emphasized, among other things; and second, where a "non-traditional" and more cosmopolitan frame was applied (Austin and Fozdar 2018, 15).

51. See also Minns et al. (2018, 2–3): "While the number of asylum-seekers Australia receives pale in comparison to those who arrived in Europe even before the current crisis, the Australian response has been far more drastic, with policies exorbitantly expensive and plagued with controversy."

52. López Zarzosa (2020, 3).

53. Writing in 2003, Michael Leach said that "[t]hroughout late 2001 and 2002, the Australian Government, seeking re-election, campaigned on a tough line against so-called 'illegal' immigrants. Represented as "queue jumpers," "boat people," and "illegals," most of these asylum seekers came from Middle Eastern countries, and, in the main, from Afghanistan and Iraq." See also O'Doherty and Lecouteur (2007).

messages through a collaborative process. This authorizes the neonarrative in ways that attach it to the new reality and elevate ideas of exclusion and threats to security, which serves to obscure the possibility of other humanitarian responses. A rich body of work has established the meaning-making by government in relationship to "cultures of fear" from "threat" through "other," to "illegality" and to "burden."[54] Acknowledging the patterns and forms of neoliberal language to emerge helps to understand what it seeks to mask, and how it (re)directs the communicative gaze.[55]

Boats immediately conjure an image: they are floating, in transit, carried by water and sometimes capsize. The imagery of asylum seekers metaphorically depicted as "boat people" was over time intended to be seamlessly woven into the Australian imagination, so that between the sphere of origin and application, "there is no tension; no spark jump [. . .]. The result: one takes the word for the thing."[56] This malleability in language is evidence of fields of presence: statements found elsewhere, and taken up by people more broadly. In the Australian context, public language referring to asylum seekers as "illegal," and "boat people,"[57] as if neutral, had a powerful ostracizing effect in the discursive space, shaping ideas

---

54. Natasha Klocker and Kevin M. Dunn discuss the tight rein government held on the media when representing asylum seekers and consequences for sidestepping: "There were occasions when the media deviated from the federal government's representation of asylum seekers. The media departed from the government line in instances where media workers' access to information was threatened, or in response to extreme events such as the drowning tragedy. Evidence of disruptions to a hierarchical exchange of meaning between government and media, although rare, highlight the possibility of establishing more balanced media representations of asylum seekers, even in the face of a government's unrelenting negativity" (2003, 89). See also Mckay et al. (2011).

55. "The White Australia Policy, in force from 1901 to 1973, restricted the entry of nonwhite, non-English speaking migrants, encouraging Australians to think of themselves as an outpost of Europe in the Pacific" (Austin and Fozdar 2018, 4).

56. Poerksen (1995, 76).

57. On June 16, 2013, media commentator Andrew Bolt used the term "boat people" repeatedly in the framing of his discussion with Shadow Attorney-General George Brandis (The Bolt Report 2013).

about their identity as trespassers.[58] This call to populism, according to Paul Gregoire, was not accidental, but the result of a ministerial directive:

> In fielding questions during a 19 November 2013 Senate estimates hearing, Pezzullo outlined that it was not his department that had started referring to asylum seekers arriving in Australian waters by boat as "illegal," but rather it was a directive from the new immigration minister Scott Morrison.[59]

Such a directive from the highest levels of government reveals how language is administered politically, and the power with which it is invested. Several years later, the mono-thinking around "illegal" "boat people" had become an opportune way of packaging the problem and tackling the subject within the logic of a binary. Politicians like Peter Dutton established the fear and threat of asylum seekers to Australian security by using terms such as "stopping the boats" and "turning back the boats," in relation to "Operation Sovereign Borders."[60] The reception of words and phrases like "boat people," within this government-sanctioned discursive and policy framework, needs to be considered in terms of the public relations idea of "publics"; in other words, a malleable social grouping that can be identified by shared characteristics, and who are connected to an "issue."[61] This idea is underpinned by the Foucauldian idea "that discourses control people by categorising them as normal or abnormal,"[62] and suggests that "publics" are not merely regarded by public relations practitioners as receivers or transmitters of messages; rather, they are targeted and

---

58. Kieran C. O'Doherty and Amanda Lecouteur (2007, 7) write that "'boat people' are thus portrayed as manipulating Australia into accepting them into the country."

59. Blogger Paul Gregoire (July 8, 2020) wrote: "The 1951 Refugee Convention sets out that asylum seekers fleeing persecution have not broken the law in entering a state party's border without a visa—this is by boat or otherwise—and therefore, these people should not be punished for having entered the country."

60. Kukuh Wardhani and Wardhani (2021, 588).

61. Jahansoozi (2006, 65).

62. Hughes and Demetrious (2006, 99).

constructed categories for social control. Deployed within a complex web of intrinsic and extrinsic public relations communicative practices, abstracted terms such as "boat people" rest on a series of decontextualized words, such as "solution," "problem," and "security," which blunt meaning and achieve numbing effects. No longer seen as extreme, these words displace complexity and "exert gravitational pull," as "publics" locked into the neonarrative warily turn their eyes toward a trouble-free future.[63] In the third wave of neoliberalism characterized by the rise of alt-right politics and fractured nationalism, these practices are particularly potent.[64] As Mavelli says, "in the neoliberal political economy of belonging, people with illnesses and disabilities will always be considered a burden and be excluded."[65]

Australia's borders are shown to be geographic, political, and discursive, and in each of these spheres they have become prohibited spaces, patrolled and policed. Patterns of language in Australian public debates in the last decades have worked to cover the "realities" of hardship and ruin in the lives of people seeking asylum. This renders it "hardly noticeable."[66] Thus, by changing the lens, "publics" begin to see how "illegal" "boat people" are the problem, and how a simplified administrative solution is to "stop the boats." This "call to action" not only deters any radical rethinking in this area, but secures "publics" to a controlling mindset that is an interplay of security and threat. The language of "fear versus comfort" has created the *semblance* of coherence linked to the language of

---

63. Poerksen (1995, 88).

64. Shedding light on the context, culture and effects of Australia's detention policy, Amy Nethery and Rosa Holman (2016, 1) explain that "[s]ince 2010, all asylum seekers who arrive in Australia's territory by boat are moved to immigration detention centres on the Pacific island nation of Nauru, or Manus Island in Papua New Guinea, where they remain until their applications for refugee status are assessed, and they are either returned to their country of origin or resettled in a safe third country. This offshore immigration detention regime is characterised by a high degree of secrecy, low levels of transparency and accountability, and few opportunities for external oversight. The result is the creation of a closed, controlled environment, in which individuals confined are routinely harmed." See also Rowe et al. (2019).

65. Mavelli (2018, 488).

66. Poerksen (1995, 69–70).

the marketplace and delivered through the instrument of public relations. And policy settings like those in Australia that sought to move asylum seekers to offshore detention centers, like Nauru and Papua New Guinea's Manus Island, demonstrate an endpoint.[67]

The fields of presence, which embed these ideas of threat and exclusion, are mobilized by public relations language practices, such as abstraction of meaning through simplification, the preparation for reception of messages by embedding exclusionary nationalistic neonarratives, and connoting certain words, woven into a plot that pushes meaning within set routes. This has worked to suspend progressive reform and policy development, and it has been remarkably successful from a political perspective.

THE COMMODIFICATION OF IMMIGRATION: USA EB5 INVESTOR VISA

> The EB-5 visa gives permanent U.S. residency to those investing into government-approved projects across the United States of America. The USA EB5 investment visa can be beneficial as it grants access to the U.S. education system, the right to live, retire, work and study in the USA, the ability to receive investment back upon the completion of the project and residency for the investor, any children (under 21) and their spouse.[68]

A swath of investment schemes for visa, residency, and citizenship give people access in nations such the United States, Canada, and Australia.[69] These transactional policy settings and programs are deeply entangled with both the logic and language of neoliberalism, and lay down meaning which in turn sets expectations of belonging and inclusion. However, citizenship and investor visa schemes go some way to develop a totalizing

67. Nethery and Holman (2016, 1).
68. La Vida Golden Visas (2021).
69. Government of Canada (2021).

definition of citizenship linked to economic objectives that promotes a uniformity and stifles diversity in societies, by failing to acknowledge the variety of situations and cultural contexts of different social groups. [70] These schemes, and their discursive dynamics within the public sphere, illustrate the idea of Foucauldian "concomitance" as the embedded reasoning which "serves as a model that can be transferred to other contents."[71] Again, the reductive idea of the market, of trade and exchange and investment, now frames decision-making and public debate as a political forum for legitimization. Its participating voices and questioners, challengers, and interventions are a complex interplay of shifting discursive elements, moving within this focus. The investor visa scheme in the following excerpt shows how statements that align with normative or allied fields of neoliberalism are active in discourse and the accepted premise for reasoning:

> The Australia investor visa scheme is developed for established business owners or investors to bring their funds and expertise to the country by being engaged in a new or already established Australian business. The visa is granted for 4 years and if you meet the Permanent Residency requirement, you can apply for permanent visa after 4 years. This is the first step towards business immigration to Australia.[72]

The commodification and framing of citizenship as form of investment is widespread.[73] Luca Mavelli discusses the "proliferation of citizenship-by-investment schemes primarily as a manifestation of the commodification of citizenship by states succumbing to the logic of the market," suggesting that such schemes are "part of a neoliberal political economy of belonging."[74] According to Roxana Barbulescu, "[c]itizenship-by-investment schemes

---

70. Hindess argues that citizenship is more accurately described as "one of the central organising features of Western political discourse" (Hindess, in Turner 1993, 19).

71. Foucault (1972, 58).

72. One Visa (n.d.).

73. Mavelli (2018, 483–486).

74. Mavelli (2018).

do not themselves produce injustice but they are unjust because they build on pre-existing large disparities in the world: If all countries were equal in living conditions would the scheme be objectionable? If the answer is no, as I think it is, then the source of injustice is global inequality rather than policies that do not themselves produce injustice."[75] Nonetheless, Barbulescu says that it is important to realize that such interventions, which promote the idea that citizenship is an investment or a market-based exchange, are not arbitrary, or accidental, or something that seeps out randomly, but rather are deliberate and calculated.[76] In this, I contend that the neonarrative is active in embedding meaning.

Using the Foucauldian understanding of neoliberalism as a concept, analyzed within fields of concomitance, ideas and language are embedded, not just in public debate, but in policy responses, which give them higher authority and become self-reinforcing, so that there is no other way to understand this topic. Conventional citizenship ideas focus on universal entitlement to resources, and on issues of exclusion and inclusion in participation. But for Bryan S. Turner, a cultural dimension is crucial and leads to empowerment, "namely the capacity to participate effectively, creatively and successfully within a national culture."[77] Examples of cultural citizenship are access to education and the capacity to acquire the language and heritage which form a cultural identity that can be exchanged intergenerationally.[78] However, the "ideals" of citizenship promoted by visa investment schemes are anchored to transaction, and extracting value for

---

75. Barbulescu (2014, 15).

76. For Barbulescu, "[n]eoliberalism does not spread like the flavour of a bag of tea in a cup of water: it needs promoters and legitimisation that will align support against other competing paradigms, especially in citizenship policies where there are strong path-dependency dynamics. These are important questions because citizenship-by-investment departs from citizenship traditions everywhere, because such policy revisions are largely unpopular and may have a high political cost and, not least, because they delegitimise the very existence of state bureaucracies administrating citizenship for the ultra-rich. With naturalisation becoming a transaction over-the-counter, the organisation that implemented it partly loses its purpose" (2014, 16).

77. Turner (1993, 12).

78. Turner (1993, 12).

the nation-state from the people in borderlands. Redefining the value of resources in cultural terms—knowledge, memory, and tradition—expands the notion of citizenship beyond the nation-state, as administrator of legal rights and responsibilities to facilitate a market-based society.

SUBMERGING MEMORY: STATELESSNESS

> A borderland is a vague and undetermined place created by the emotional reside of an unnatural boundary. It is in a constant state of transition. The prohibited and forbidden are its inhabitants.[79]

Without nationality, and excluded from political processes and rights such as health, education, and social security,[80] stateless people bear the brunt of the deep contradictions in political and economic systems of nation-states. For Lindsey N. Kingston, the term *statelessness* "failed to successfully emerge onto the international agenda," but the reason why has proven to be somewhat "elusive."[81] This may clarify the (relative) lack of mobilization of stakeholders, historically, to tackle the issue, as compared to other significant human rights challenges.[82] However, the nebulous *absence* of meaning in "statelessness" may be compounded when news gathering increasingly conforms to public relations practices by linking to the neonarrative, and in packaging and presenting an issue. Consequently, without clear links or defined relations, the idea of statelessness is an unformed idea, and its relationship to the nation-state is indistinct. As such, statelessness—not publicly discussed, and ill-defined—coheres to the idea of a "third space" in the borderlands, one on the extreme edges of dislocation. Megan Bradley explains that "the persistent and un-nuanced conflation of refugeehood and statelessness represents a potential disservice

---

79. Anzaldúa (in Cantú, Hurtado, and Anzaldúa 2012, 25).
80. Refugee Council of Australia (2021).
81. Kingston (2013, 80–81).
82. Kingston (2013, 80–81).

to the displaced, as it may perpetuate a mistaken impression of refugees as politically impotent victims, and inadvertently undermine refugees."[83] People are at the center of these policy matters and public debates, not categories on a spreadsheet. Margaret R. Somers argues that "[c]onflating the market with the laws of nature made cruelty and human suffering morally unimpeachable as hunger alone disciplined the poor to work."[84] But how do neoliberal language practices work to unmoor, submerge, and eviscerate the human struggle in this context?

This unmooring of people, hardship, and trauma from social justice enables the numbing category that sits within the liminal space of borderlands to emerge: the noncitizen.

> Noncitizens in Australia sit within the broad and diverse "middle" spectrum between the elite flexible citizen, often seen as the beneficiary of emerging "mutations" in sovereignty and citizenship, and the low skilled and often exploited contract or undocumented workers who are often constructed subject to "fragmented citizenship." Analysis of this heterogeneous "middle space" of Australian noncitizenship is instructive to citizenship studies more broadly, in that it shows how regimes shape and reshape the criteria that make a "desirable" migrant, and that nominal "skills" classification and visa categories can obscure a vast array of subjectivities, social practices and labour practices.[85]

A consideration is the way public relations language practices break the discursive ground, not only to prepare for the favorable reception of these divisive meanings, but to conceal the extent and nature of the human rights issues, affecting millions of people in the world who are not considered nationals in law by any state.[86] As such, the term *statelessness* is unmoored

---

83. Bradley (2014, 2).

84. Somers (2020, 229).

85. In this quote, Shanthi Robertson (2015, 946) cites Aihwa Ong (2007).

86. Hughes and Demetrious (2006).

to specific meaning, which denies people the right to belong. Working with a 10-year change agenda, the UNHCR writes:

> Statelessness is sometimes referred to as an invisible problem because stateless people often remain unseen and unheard. They often aren't allowed to go to school, see a doctor, get a job, open a bank account, buy a house or even get married. Denial of these rights impacts not only the individuals concerned but also society as a whole, in particular because excluding an entire sector of the population can lead to social tensions and significantly impair economic and social development.[87]

This is, in part, because government appears not to systemize or coordinate this dispersed cluster into a group or a public that can be understood, or "media packaged" in public debate. This is underpinned by the Foucauldian[88] idea that discourses control people by systems which divide, regroup, contrast, and classify in tangled repetitious cycles.[89] But perpetuating this works powerfully to erase an entire group. This self-referential activity buttresses rationality that supports the non-category of the non-citizen, and at the same time, reinforces and embeds its authority, legitimacy, and fields of memory, impoverished by assumptions and lack of relationship to truth over affiliations.[90] The true extent of statelessness is likely to be much higher than the public thinks. Tellingly, in

---

87. UNHCR (2021).

88. See Foucault's discussion of "girds of specification" (1972, 42).

89. Patrick Hughes and Kristin Demetrious explain this idea, showing how "economics creates us as rational or irrational; and scientific management creates us as compliant or troublesome elements of an organisation. Having thus been explained, we can then be controlled. In summary, discourses create new categories of normality, and either we fit those categories, or we deviate from them and take the consequences of our abnormality" (2006, 99).

90. Sara Dale and Katie Robertson argue that "[t]he second problem is more fundamental—we simply don't know how many stateless people there are in Australia. With no coordinated or consistent approach to collecting information regarding the extent of Australia's stateless population, meaningfully addressing statelessness—as Australia has committed to do—is impossible" (cited in Doherty, 2021).

a new report Katie Robinson and Sarah Dale state "in the most recent annual reporting to the United Nations High Commissioner for Refugees (UNHCR), Australia failed to record any data regarding the number of stateless persons in our territory. Yet even a rudimentary review of publicly available statistics on the Department of Home Affairs website for the same reporting period indicates there were more than 4,000 stateless persons known to immigration authorities."[91] As such, while statelessness may be cast into political and discursive exile from the nation-state, like the sea, the sun, and the air, it does not stop at the borders.

"TAKE CONTROL OF THE NARRATIVE BEFORE IT DOES REAL DAMAGE": AWAKENING DISINTEREST, DRAINING COMPLEXITY

> They don't talk about the wall anymore. See, we won. We got the wall. It's going to be up to 300 next week and it's going to be finished very soon. And as soon as we want, all of a sudden, they never talk about it. But you know where I talk about it? Numbers. The numbers are so good. The numbers are so low.[92]

The signing of the *Universal Declaration of Human Rights* in 1948 signified hope of a new world order, based on humanity and fundamental rights.[93] However, Donald Trump's words show that the public discussion of these human rights in the borderlands is a crucial concern for governments. Pugnacious public relations language practices not only embed meanings, but discourage alternative discourses that are present or may spring from third spaces: where people seeking asylum and refugee status, immigrants, and the stateless dwell. It is the potential of stories to rise from these third

---

91. Dale and Robertson (2021).
92. Donald Trump (2020).
93. Quotation in section title: Forbes (2021, n.p.).

spaces which is a constant preoccupation, precisely because they are capable of political and cultural intervention. As Anzaldúa says:

> My "stories" are acts encapsulated in time, "enacted" every time they are spoken aloud or read silently. I like to think of them as performances and not as inert and "dead" objects (as the aesthetics of Western culture think of art works). Instead, the work has an identity; it is a "who" or a "what" and contains the presences of persons, that is, incarnations of gods or ancestors or natural and cosmic powers. The work manifests the same needs as a person, it needs to be "fed."[94]

Stories emanating from third spaces are alive, spoken, and open; a point which highlights that the real purpose of the public relations strategy to "take control of the narrative" is to box in voices so they are not heard, and to neutralize ethical concerns. This point is powerfully illustrated in Francisco Cantú's (2018) *The Line Becomes a River: Dispatches from the Border*.

Written from his time as a United States border patrol guard on the troubled US–Mexican- border, Cantú's work adds to the literature that seeks to understand how power and language create realities, and what it means for the immigrants who fall outside the system. Of Mexican-American heritage, Cantú's journey is not just an account of his grisly experiences patrolling the border for illegal activity, but a search to understand what the border means culturally. Cantú is determined to do this in a visceral way that reaches beyond the four years of college education he spent studying international relations and learning about it "through policy and history."[95] Opposed by his mother, who thinks he should use his education to find a more suitable career—"you graduated with honors," she says[96]—Cantú determines that joining the border patrol

---

94. Anzaldúa (in Cantú, Hurtado, and Anzaldúa 2012, 89).

95. Cantú (2018, 22).

96. Cantú (2018, 24).

will help him experience, and thus know, the system and the border better. Arguments between them ensue—his mother points out that "the reality of the border is one of enforcement,"[97] but Cantú explains that he can help people, he can speak two languages, and that good people are needed in these roles. He reassures her that he will not lose sight of his humanity and compassion for Mexicans entering the United States. In closing, his mother reluctantly acquiesces: "Fine, my mother said, fine. But you must understand you are stepping into a system, an institution with little regard for people."[98] Cantú acknowledges this: "Maybe you're right, I replied, but stepping into a system doesn't mean the system becomes you. As I spoke, doubts flickered through my mind."[99]

Cantú's time as a federal law enforcer with a sworn duty to guard the borders of the United States is fraught. He participates in hunting down drug smugglers and their cargo, spotting groups of Mexicans entering US territory, scouting their trails, rounding them up, and processing them for deportation when they are caught. The work is confronting, brutal, and he sees firsthand the dehumanizing process whereby those who go missing crossing the border into the United States become invisible. The scale of this, perhaps, is not fully understood. Citing a newspaper article by Manny Fernandez, Cantú relates that in 2017 the Border Patrol had recorded over six thousand deaths between 2000 and 2016. Having seen the violent effects for people, Cantú writes: "All along the border, coroners, county medical examiners, and forensic anthropologists at state universities and nonprofit organizations struggled to identify thousands of remains. 'No one deserves to be just a number,' one forensic expert told Fernandez. 'The idea is to figure out who they are, and give them their name back.'"[100] Eventually Cantú leaves the border patrol, and toward the end of the book has another conversation with his mother in which they

---

97. Cantú (2018, 24).

98. Cantú (2018, 25).

99. Cantú (2018, 25).

100. Cantú (2018, 107).

both reflect on different stories of violence and pain that carry with them a lifelong sense of failure. His mother notes that "[w]hat I'm saying is that we learn violence by watching others, by seeing it enshrined in institutions. Then, even without choosing it, it becomes normal to us, it even becomes part of who we are."[101]

In the final section of the book, Cantú goes for a swim in the cool waters of the Rio Grande, where he observed that there are no cameras or sensors, no patrols or vehicles in the distance waiting to enforce American borders. In this untroubled reality he writes:

> As I swam toward a bend in the canyon the river became increasingly shallow. In a patch of sunlight, two longnose gars, relics of the Palaeozoic era, hovered in the silted waters. I stood to walk along the adjacent shorelines, crossing the river time and again as each bank came to an end, until finally, for one brief moment, I forgot in which country I stood. All around me the landscape trembled and breathed as one.[102]

This strangely poetic, honest, and imaginative book consistently elevates the idea that the borderlands are important places of power that open understanding of how constructed realities are built: what keeps us in check, why we obey, and what drives us to defy those expectations. Those borderlands have power, but it is power that manifests not only in the systems, like the freeways, the fences, cameras, and the processing centers, but in the place itself, the landscape (sky, river, grasslands, mountains), the people, and the language. And yet for all this, it is the system which prevails to shape reality. Cantú writes:

> The current state of crisis did not descend from nowhere. For as long as many of us can remember, the border has been depicted as a place out of control, overrun by criminality. In the narrative that

---

101. Cantú 2018, 230–231).
102. Cantú (2018, 247).

has dominated the national consciousness, violence and disorder are endemic to the region and those who are drawn to it. When words like *bord*er or *migrant* are uttered, they carry this narrative with them, along with a sense of obscure menace to people and places far from the country's frontier: loss of jobs, encroaching violence, the erosion of a familiar dominant culture. What we have long been made to look away from, however, are the places most affected by a militarized order, and migrants who are most impacted by the narrative that has so long excluded their experience.[103]

Shedding light on how public language can harness narrative styles to build a predestined reality or to marginalize identity, such as those described by Cantú on the US–Mexican border, Torill Moen[104] discusses how it involves, first, a dialogical collaboration where "one or more stories are written down and become fixed in a text." At this point, the text is disarticulated from a situated reality and becomes ahistorical. Second, and once detached from a specific context, it becomes "autonomized." Third, its importance grows and then colonizes other contexts into "new interpretive frames" from whence changed meanings flow. Lastly, "the narrative that is fixed in a text is thus considered an 'open work' where the meaning is addressed to those who read and hear about it. Looking on narrative as an open text makes it possible to engage in a wide range of interpretations."[105] The purposeful extraction of context and complexity in contemporary global debates concerning borderlands and the construction of problematized meanings and the resulting standardization of language have shaped recent closed political cultures.[106]

Unhurried, deliberate, the frequent dehumanization of immigrants and asylum seekers in public language has been a proven and effective

---

103. Cantú (2018, 252).

104. In this extract, Torill Moen (2006, 62) cites Paul Ricoeur's narrative theory.

105. Moen (2006, 62).

106. Anzaldua (in Cantú, Hurtado, and Anzaldúa 2012, 25).

political communication strategy to wash away the confronting human rights problems that affect people dwelling in the borderlands. Whirring in the background, market-based visa and citizenship schemes endorse a transactional relationship between people in borderlands and the nation-state, the place where they so desperately want to live, to work, and to contribute. Arguably, such schemes will generate passive forms of citizenships, which link to the notion of "thin community" and are associated with "liberal individualism," where freedom of choice and the pursuit of personal economic goals override the individual's responsibility to the collective common good.[107] While not the only reference point, this framework, underpinned by public relations working in "third spaces," categorizing, submerging realities, and sowing division, may map the extent of these citizens' sense of political inclusion and participation.

This chapter charts the assembly and embedding of neoliberal rationality through public relations language practices in relation to human rights. Opening a raft of seemingly unrelated material, it shows how this discourse has insinuated public debate to become a powerful driver in shaping realities, rendering some visible and desirable, while turning away from others. Voters are led toward an untroubled reassuring cul de sac of market-based ideas, free of friction. This not only obscures the clash of political ideas, which should rouse people to action, but prevents new ideas from breaking through and disrupting the semblance of coherence. As such, an alternative stance on these matters may be obfuscated. There may be no names or words to say it. Nonetheless, in the context of public debate in Australia, which elevated the dehumanizing idea of "boat people" amid the strict policy's indefinite and mandatory offshore detention, an oral history project in 2014 gave rise to a multitude of voices in refugee and immigration detention, specifically for younger people. Co-founder of the *Behind the Wire* project, André Dao, and Jamila Jafari, who shared her story of immigration detention, write:

---

107. Kane (2000, 224–225).

And there was hardly ever any detail about detention itself. We wanted to find a way to address that gap, because in our day jobs we were meeting people who had been in detention with the most incredible stories, and no platform for telling them. So our initial motivation was to find a way to make sure these voices—which should be the most important in this conversation—were part of the public discussion about immigration detention.[108]

Emerging voices from third spaces in public debate is heartening, but this is within a larger and more complex picture. If nothing else, this discussion shows that simplistic ideas, like "clear messaging" in public debate to instigate change, need to be abandoned. Using public relations as its instrument, neoliberalism in government, business, and society has achieved a high level of conceptual hegemony. In this, the featureless and bland plastic word "development" moves slowly, brushing up, boxing in ways to think about people in the borderlands. In turn, remote transactional expectations are set, which have implications for divergent, human-centred, and compassionate political spaces to open in public debates.

---

108. André Dao and Jamila Jafari discuss the rationale that underpinned the oral history project *Behind the Wire* (2021, 160).

6

Airborne

Public Relations, Plasticity, and Pandemic Politics

By mid-April 2020, the first full month of the pandemic, millions of people, rocked by the coronavirus health crisis, turned to the global media's unfolding reportage. From human isolation, lockdowns, food shortages, daily death and infection tallies, and government action and/or inaction to "doing" life differently (work, travel, community, recreation), nothing seemed unaffected.[1] The dystopian dynamic was compounded by a growing realization that the wealthiest nation on earth had become the new epicenter of the virus when "[t]he death toll in the US became the highest in the world."[2] At this historic moment, its healthcare system began to collapse, and the need for its state and federally elected representatives to govern for all people became critically apparent:

> April was a frantic blur, at hospitals, in makeshift wards in hallways and closets, in formless days as nurses tried to salve gasping patients. After 12 hours of tending to people for whom they had no answers, doctors stole a few moments to trade stories in their Facebook groups,

---

1. Winston (2020, 53).
2. Hills (2020).

telling what they had seen and what they had tried. Somehow, they hoped, their collective anecdotes might add up to something useful. "There's no consensus on what's the right thing to do," said Kathleen Kelly, an emergency room physician at Reston Hospital Center in Northern Virginia. "It's just like nothing anybody's seen."[3]

The rolling US national health crisis was compounded by the loss of trillions of dollars from the global markets and economic impacts.[4] The political implications of this were in turn intensified by President Donald J. Trump's seeming reluctance to show leadership.[5] Looking toward the November elections, concern in the Grand Old Party (GOP) turned to the impact this may have on the popular appeal of Republican candidates.[6]

On April 17, 2020, O'Donnell & Associates, Strategic Communications,[7] released the *Corona Big Book*[8] as a full-blown public relations tactical response to the political fallout from the pandemic. In the face of the

---

3. Fisher et al. (2020).

4. The impact of the coronavirus outbreak on the global economy was profound. Ben White (February 27, 2020) wrote: "It's an existential threat that has sewn panic across the globe and wiped out trillions in wealth. Equity markets were overvalued for many months and required only a clear threat to reprice. Now they have and the reckoning has been swift and harsh and is likely not over."

5. Early in the pandemic, Trump played down its severity and provided the American people with a wildly inaccurate scenario of its likely trajectory. Tanya Lewis (November 3, 2021) wrote: "Trump dismissed it as no worse than the flu and said the pandemic would be over by Easter."

6. In a rare insight into the process and planning stages of public relations, Alex Isenstadt (April 24, 2020) wrote: "The National Republican Senatorial Committee has sent campaigns a detailed, 57-page memo authored by a top Republican strategist advising GOP candidates to address the coronavirus crisis by aggressively attacking China."

7. O'Donnell & Associates (2020).

8. Alex Isenstadt (April 24, 2020) reported: "The memo includes advice on everything from how to tie Democratic candidates to the Chinese government to how to deal with accusations of racism. It stresses three main lines of assault: That China caused the virus 'by covering it up,' that Democrats are 'soft on China,' and that Republicans will 'push for sanctions on China for its role in spreading this pandemic.'"

fast-moving and apolitical virus, the fifty-seven-page strategy was designed to deflect attention away from the president and toward the idea of an America wronged and betrayed.[9] The "Main Messages"[10] focus on four "Hits": "China" (broken down into "China Release" and "China Coverup/Delay"); "WHO"; "Political Correctness Made this Crisis Worse"; "Dems Soft on China/Corona."[11] The animating ideas encouraged an isolationist and distrustful outlook as a form of patriotic freedom.[12] This excerpt demonstrates statements which were intended to be circulated widely, and amplified and monitored by a powerful, hypervigilant global media:

> The WHO sat back while china [sic] lied—and they knew it.
>
> We know communist China is lying about how many cases and deaths they have, what they knew and when they knew it—and the WHO never bothered to investigate further. Their inaction cost lives. As soon as Congress is back in session, there should be a hearing, along with a full investigation, to review whether American taxpayers should continue to spend millions of dollars every year to fund an organization that willfully [sic] parroted propaganda from the Chinese Communist Party.[13]

---

9. Note: at the time of writing the origin of the virus remains inconclusive. However, a *Scientific American* article into soon to be published studies "add[s] weight to original suspicions that the pandemic began at the Huanan Seafood Wholesale Market, which many of the people who were infected earliest with SARS-CoV-2 had visited," rather than an earlier hypothesis that it was intentionally released by the Wuhan Institute of Virology (Maxmen, February 28, 2022).

10. Includes a "Short Version" and "Expanded Version" (O'Donnell & Associates 2020, 3).

11. See "Table of Contents" (O'Donnell & Associates 2020, 2). Each "Hit" has "Key Points" and "Key Facts," along with graphics, hyperlinks, and prompts such as "timeline very important here" (O'Donnell & Associates 2020, 33–34).

12. If asked: "Isn't this Trump's fault? *Note—don't defend Trump, other than the China Travel Ban—attack China.* This is China's fault. The virus came from China and China covered it up. Because China lied about the extent of the virus, our public health officials acted late. I wish that everyone acted earlier—that includes our elected officials, the World Health Organization, and the CDC."

13. O'Donnell & Associates (2020, 45).

The *Corona Big Book* contains standard PR features and nomenclature, such as "Main Messages": "Short versions," "Expanded versions," "Timelines," "Hits," "Key Points," "Key Facts," and "Answers to Likely Arguments." In the processual retelling, media platforms like *Fox News* reported Senate Judiciary Committee Chairman, Lindsey Graham, repeating the *Corona Big Book* key messages. This moment, this retelling, reveals the full command of public relations, not just in disseminating, but in plotting and executing the neonarrative:

> I'm 100 percent convinced that without Chinese Communist Party deception the virus wouldn't be here in the United States, [. . .]. I'm 100 percent convinced they will never cooperate until they are made to do so. We can't let the Democratic Party give China a pass.[14]

A LIVING DOCUMENT: DISRUPTION AND IMPETUS

Deployed at an electoral tipping point—when the escalating pandemic threatened to shatter the Trump administration's utopian political and economic story of growth and prosperity—the public relations plan attempts to deflect public attention, and at the same time buttress the sagging neonarrative. The *Corona Big Book* speaks from the standpoint of privilege, safety, and impunity, perhaps from those who have benefited the most from neoliberalism, and as such, it raises ethical questions about the uncontrolled deployment of language and power, in relation to a pandemic that did not recognize boundaries or ideologically inflected meanings around "freedom." From a distance, the spreading stream of ideas from the public relations plan, channeled through multiple interlocutors, may appear to show the semblance of active debate, but I have argued that this is not the case; rather, the very notion of public debate has been debased

---

14. Lindsey Graham cited in an online article by Charles Creitz for *Fox News* (May 5, 2020).

and built on fears that had been purposefully stoked. In service of this, did the "Hits" provided to Republicans contribute to the "normalization," "mainstreaming," and "respectabilization" of the global far right in the forming of a closed and narrow view about these matters?[15] Moreover, the high-level messaging plan circulating among Republican Party candidates signals, not just that it is business as usual in public relations, but that it has the potential to be more potent and dangerous than ever.

Thus, the deep and ongoing entwinement between institutional public relations language practices and neoliberal knowledge formation in traditional modes, like public relations plans, remains a critical site to understand how today's and tomorrow's political debates are fashioned and energized. To dismiss public relations as an antiquated twentieth-century practice that has far less potency within digital conditions, and lacks relevance when the tools of communication are so readily available, is naïve, perhaps even irresponsible. The *Corona Big Book* shows that old-fashioned public relations is alive and well and working in seamless ways with the affordances of twenty-first-century digital conditions. But so too does other global public relations activity by multinational corporations. A good example occurred in 2014 when US coal producer Peabody Energy launched a public relations campaign to counter the view that fossil fuels need to be phased out, at the same time as reviving the discredited idea of "clean coal."

Building a bulwark against public criticism, the "Advanced Energy for Life" (AEFL), campaign objectives were to convince global leaders, multinational organizations, and "publics" more generally, that advanced coal technologies in turn would reduce emissions.[16] To peg the antithetical ideas, a clever, high-stakes public relations campaign was at play. Kate Sheppard

---

15. Ulrike M. Vieten (2020, 2) discusses the "new normal" in pandemic politics with "the blurring boundaries between legitimate democratic political protest and racist far-right populist positions challenging democracy, and the blurred boundaries between fact–knowledge and fiction–speculation...."

16. Sheppard (2014); for more about the intersection of Twitter users with the Advanced Energy for Life campaign, see also Demetrious (2017, 2019, and 2019a).

for *The Huffington Post* wrote that: "Burson-Marsteller, the world's largest PR firm, and its subsidiary, Proof Integrated Communications, [were] working behind the scenes on Peabody's PR effort."[17] According to Schneider et al., "The piece ricocheted around the climate and progressive blogosphere; soon after, the World Wildlife Fund Europe brought a complaint about the ad to the UK Advertising Standards Authority (ASA)."[18] Consequently, the ASA ruled that "clean coal," one of the main campaign tropes, which is the term designed to influence reader interpretation on a deeper connotative level, was untrue.[19]

Despite the ASA ruling, key AELF campaign tropes, "energy poverty" and "clean coal," were conspicuous in the Australian public sphere over 2014–2017, including on the social media site Twitter. Gaining social traction and hegemonic uptake at high political levels, as well as being amplified by other business voices in the media, the AEFL campaign was making considerable inroads to shape and, at the same time, stymie public debate.[20] But when in 2016 the US coal producer Peabody Energy filed for bankruptcy, a vast submerged network came to light that reveals another reality. Court documents in the legal process showed a thick and submerged network of financial relations to an extensive range of climate denial groups. Matt Kasper reported, "The breadth of the groups with financial ties to Peabody is extraordinary. Think tanks, litigation groups, climate scientists, political organizations, dozens of organizations blocking action on climate all receiving funding from the coal industry." The revelations contained in the court documents that Peabody Energy tabled provide rare evidence showing the extent to which this corporation funds climate denier groups. Among this list are the ethically controversial lobby group, the "American Coalition for Clean Coal Electricity" and the socially conservative free-market organization, the "American

---

17. Sheppard (2014).

18. Schneider et al. (2016, 137).

19. The ASA ruling took place on August 19, 2014; ASA (2014).

20. See Demetrious (2019a).

Legislative Exchange Council," as well as Berman and Company, "which is a public relations firm that is currently spreading disinformation about the Clean Power Plan."[21]

CHANGING CONTEXTS AND LANGUAGE PRACTICE: MOMENTS IN POLITICAL COMMUNICATION

Over many decades, market-based rationality flowing from public relations language practices has worked to generate an almost totalizing three-dimensional depiction of how to live, think, and act. Reproduced in so many sites, this "truth" appears to be the only plausible "solution" to the problems faced or the options available. Reconstructed time and time again, these ideas, and much of the thinking they form, is taken for granted. Nonetheless, there is movement in neoliberal meaning, breaks in the beliefs that constructed it in the first place, in the commitment to the cause, and in the oaths that were taken to bind individuals and institutions to constructing these new realities.

The communicative dynamics and rhythms emerging in 2020 within two US-based political and social movements, are intersecting with neoliberalism in contemporary contexts of the pandemic, in very different and ambiguous ways, which open the possibility of disruption and change. The first is an internal political critique within the Republican Party, focusing on a public website hosting Republican Voters Against Trump (RVAT). This internal party conflict specifically foregrounds ethics (or the lack of) in public language, and their effects. The second dynamic is a persuasive political campaign practice known as "deep canvassing," that was used by US activists within the same context of the upcoming presidential election. Neither of these examples represents a way forward to break the neoliberal nexus, but they do show that approaches are changing from all points of the spectrum. These examples show hesitation and anticipation

---

21. Kasper (2016, n.p.).

in social spaces that have been inscribed with deeply held positions. And for that reason, they are interesting.

REPUBLICAN VOTERS AGAINST TRUMP (RVAT)

In the run-up to the 2020 US presidential election, dissenting intraparty Republican activity saw a website called Republican Voters Against Trump (RVAT)[22] activate, and provide a forum that focused largely on President Donald J. Trump as a flawed individual who was not worthy of the office. Responding to feelings of embarrassment and shame, among others, generated by Trump's presidential communications and policy directions, the testimonials appear to provoke considerable reflection about public language and ethics. Overwhelmingly, the RVAT testimonials discuss Trump's divisive speaking style and the GOP's lack of restraint as points of departure. Trump's incivility was frequently cited. Also strongly condemned were presidential lying, obfuscating, manipulating, bragging, chicanery, cheating, deliberately creating confusion, petty fights, the repetition of misinformation, and the promotion of conspiracy theories that spawn division and extremism. Nonetheless, overlooked were the elite neoliberal forces that had propelled him into office.

For some, these tactics "preyed" on "Trump's base" and their ignorance and fear, in order to incite a clamor of hatred. That Trump has a childish penchant for yelling and calling names was frequently cited. The president's tweets were criticized many times, as well as his speeches and press conferences. The testimonials overwhelmingly show that some GOP members wanted to reclaim belief in the party's commitment to its traditional values and return a sense of decency associated with the past. This yearning was noticeable especially when Trump's personal incivility and the weakness of the GOP to uphold American democratic ideals were raised. Public websites like Republican Voters Against Trump and their

---

22. Republican Voters Against Trump is a project of umbrella group Defending Democracy Together (DDT). Note: this section draws on a fuller discussion in Demetrious (2020).

content—mainly short independent video testimonials—can be broadly interpreted as ventilating internal divisions. However, hopes that this dissenting activity within the GOP may translate more broadly into a change may not be well-founded, as issues raised, such as the increase of intolerance and populism, are greater than any individual candidate or Republican Party manager.

This steady drift toward the extreme right has occurred over several decades in the party. Skocpol and Hertel-Fernandez attribute this movement to the massive Koch political network, which "coordinates big money funders, idea producers, issue advocates, and innovative constituency-building efforts."[23] But in the Trump presidency, a range of other elements played a role in enabling his incivility and polarizing style, to be constantly redeployed, despite ridicule, public outcry, and admonishment. The toleration may be partly attributed to journalists, who underestimated the impacts of such styles in public culture by expecting voters to censure. Another factor muting press and public scrutiny may have been the presence of a presidential aura deflecting critique of, and leading to, an acceptance of Trump's dominance, and unwitting consent for his seemingly deliberate strategy to propagate and sow division. While it may seem counterintuitive, these "longstanding discursive rules of performance" underpin the relationship between the press and the president, and "help orient and constrain reporters' and editors' approaches to presidential figures, through hegemonic constructs."[24] Kathleen Bartzen Culver explains that, in the United States, the press is the central institution to protect equality, freedom, and democracy:

> This interaction certainly means consumption of content, including refusing to stay only in an echo chamber of alleged "news" that aligns only with your world view—be that on the left or the right. But it also means responsibly responding to content on social channels,

---

23. Skocpol and Hertel-Fernandez (2016, 681).

24. Parks (2020, 2–5).

creating content that adheres to principles of truth, and reacting to others in the digital and in-person public sphere with respect.[25]

Hence, polarization of voters may be aided from Trump's fractious relationship to the news journalists, as the presidential aura serves to obscure their analysis, despite this being a critically important site in which to uphold values. In the run-up to Trump's presidential election, journalists and political analysts overlooked the full significance of the slow-growing, far-right dynamic. Its presence was used to reach and grow Trump's base, especially in the social media platform Twitter. It is in these social media forums that Trump's deviation from statesmanlike, diplomatic norms is brought out in sharp relief. However, for Brian Ott, these communiques have significant contagious consequences: "Trump's simple, impulsive, and uncivil Tweets do more than merely reflect sexism, racism, homophobia, and xenophobia; they spread those ideologies like a social cancer."[26] Another dynamic that blunts critique and buttresses Republican Party extremism is the rise of right-leaning news media since the beginning of the twenty-first century.[27]

Hence, gaining wide circulation, Trump's vivid, simplistic messages appeal to angry and disaffected Americans with a call to identify as "patriots" and defend "liberty" and "freedom." In an address to the UN General Assembly denouncing "open-border activists" and globalism in 2019, as reported by *Fox News*, Trump said that " 'the future belongs to patriots" [. . . and] advised member states, 'If you want freedom, take pride in your country. If you want democracy, hold on to your sovereignty. If you want peace, love your nation.' "[28]

---

25. Culver (2018, 292).

26. Ott (2017, 64).

27. Skocpol and Hertel-Fernandez write that conservative politics "benefit greatly from openly-partisan commercial media outlets, including the Fox television network and right-wing talk radio" (2016, 683).

28. Adam Shaw (2019).

Shedding light on the interior language of politics, Virginia Held argues that ethical theories, such as those based on justice or on utility, have gendered predispositions and language "modeled on the experience of men in public life and in the marketplace."[29] On the other hand, the ethics of care "usually works with a conception of persons as relational, rather than as the self-sufficient independent individuals of the dominant moral theories."[30] Hence, the language of "men," glorifying patriotism, liberty, and freedom in political discourse, like the 2019 Trump example, reinforces the relations of power that serve to deny the "reality" of the marginal "other," and their relational experiences, and to devalue them further.

RVAT testimonials highlight the malaise in American political life, and to a greater or lesser extent, they each wrestle painfully with questions of ethics and public culture. Nonetheless, they are generally marked by an absence of focus on social systems, such as the influence of the Koch Network in the Republican Party, or any other large political donors or influence. For Rubenstein et al. (2018), the continuous onslaught of divisive words from the president is a precise, albeit unethical, political strategy, which underpins deep capitalist themes running through US society. Thus, Trump is merely the visible face of a much deeper and more complex set of power relations steering the Republican Party toward the ultra-free-market extremism which emerged long before the Obama presidential era and the idea of a voter backlash based on racial divides.[31]

This RVAT critique from conservative ranks is refreshing, but the importance of the media power structures, which spreads and holds these unethical cultures in place, is necessary for actual change. Despite the constant references in the RVAT testimonials to Trump's public performances of dishonesty and manipulation, the news media was seldom implicated.

---

29. Held (2005, 24).

30. Held (2005, 13).

31. Demetrious (2020); Gutsche (2018); Skocpol and Hertel-Fernandez (2016).

Nonetheless, *Fox News*,[32] as a GOP co-enabler, was singled out in the study, accused of promoting division, and not having American interests at heart. On the whole, the failure of the RVAT critiques to examine the Republican Party's relationship to *Fox News* more broadly suggests a lack of importance attributed to its critical historical and political role, which, in turn, fosters support for Trump's candidacy.[33] Hence, the media were rarely critiqued in the testimonials, and public relations was not mentioned at all, despite concerns that Trump's targeted media performances and far-right pandering have incendiary potential to incite his "base" into extremist action.

Overall, this suggests a reluctance, even among political ranks that are highly critical of the debasement of public language, to focus on the potential of communication, and of media industries to protect principles of truth. The public relations industry is thickly networked with the GOP, and its affiliations directly influence the tenor and approach of political communication.[34] Therefore, while the concerns raised circled the news media, and its part in shaping the "hateful" tenor of Trump's presidency in manipulating his "base," they stopped short of establishing a direct link between the two. On the whole, this suggests there is an acceptance of public relations' status and relationship to society. Nonetheless, perhaps the very discussion of public language, and its effects in the testimonials, may clarify how it positions minorities, immigrants, children in detention, and Muslims, and may provoke the reinterpretation of it as relational and ethical, rather than just as a tool for righteousness.

---

32. The Koch network has been the subject of much investigation as it wields colossal influence in US politics (Hertel-Fernandez, Tervo, and Skocpol 2018).

33. Bartlett (2015); Poletta and Callaghan (2017).

34. For example, Skocpol and Hertel-Fernandez point out that the "grassroots activation" group Americans for Prosperity states that directors typically move into a range of "top posts" in the conservative world, such as "ownerships of political consulting or public-relations firms that work especially for GOP clients" (2016, 691).

DEEP CANVASSING

Within the rise of populism, the far right, and the now entrenched neoliberal cultures, US activists are challenging market-based rationality in new and ambiguous ways. From 2016 to 2020, with the weight of presidential authority, Donald Trump dominated the global stage and used public language practices that inflamed tensions and gave rise to disinformation. From the announcement of his presidential candidacy to his run for re-election, a period of shifting terrain in political discourse took place, characterized by intensifying right-wing activism and associated extremism. Watching how the far-right rhetoric burned through the communicative landscape, these activists sought not just to fight the blaze, but also to understand how radical communication could be used to reach deep into pockets of inaccessible terrain. Deep canvassing[35] emerged in this setting as a persuasive political campaign practice used by activists and collectives for social change. Advocacy of social causes can take a variety of forms. In this interview, Dave Fleisher elaborates on deep canvassing's persuasive dialogical characteristics:

> There's no difference regarding who you can speak with in a deep canvass. Rather, the deep canvass is built on a different set of assumptions than a traditional canvass. In many campaigns, polling data and focus groups tell us that very few people are persuadable, so we ignore those voters and stick with talking to the voters who are already on our side. But many times this approach underestimates who's persuadable. In a deep canvass, we go to the turf where voters have voted against our causes in the past, and we find out why. Then we try to convince them to change their minds.[36]

---

35. In 2016, David Fleischer, a Los Angeles–based LGBT activist, described "deep canvassing" as a reciprocal persuasive community campaigning approach to promote marriage equality in the state, arising out of the disappointment and frustrations when the same-sex marriage bill was defeated in California. Note: this section draws on a fuller discussion in Demetrious (2021).

36. Fleisher interview with Fuld (2017).

In a competitive market-based democratic society, civil society in politicized action or activism is often seen as a counterpoint representing marginalized groups. In this, it has a unique intersubjective and deliberative role within communities that builds fairness. This point is illustrated by Jurgen Habermas, who argues that "civil society provides the social basis of autonomous public spheres that remain as distinct from the economic system as from the administration."[37] However, deep canvassing persuasively positions "voters" as central in the political decision-making process, and it is the significance of the tensions between persuasion and deliberation in democracy that is of interest.

Identifying how persuasive communication practices, like deep canvassing, are oriented in relation to neoliberalism is pivotal to understanding their ethical dimensions and contributions. While deep canvassing is a communication practice with a dominant market-based inflection, it also engages with a high level of intersubjectivity and, as such, does have deliberative components. Therefore, if deep canvassing constitutes a different dialogic approach, which bridges a path between deliberative-participatory civil society and capitalist market-based approaches, the question remains: Is this hybridization conceptually flawed, or does it open new ways to think about communication practice? Deep canvassing involves a constitutive process, and a focus on building cohesion and communicative bonds in community, and in this, it coordinates and builds cooperation, consensus, and agreement, rather than goal-oriented strategic action. Moreover, if deep canvassing is understood in the real-world contemporary US political context, riven with "norm breaking," as seen in the partisan divides that are reflected in "Trump's nativist and race-laden populism," then this question takes on a different complexion.[38] This norm-breaking populism not only degrades public culture, but threatens confidence in society's most trusted and important institutions. It requires a radical response.

37. Habermas (1994, 8).

38. Lieberman et al. (2019, 5).

In the run-up to the 2020 presidential elections, a context of authoritarianism and populism in the United States highlights the limitations in which deep canvassing is taking place, and the invidious choice of a black or white approach in respect to capitalist market-based or participative-deliberative approaches to advocacy. Hence, a bind exists where apathy or discrimination cannot be addressed, unless there is movement in getting people to vote and become part of a political community. While applying the lenses of capitalist market-based and deliberative-participatory approaches to democracy is useful in interpreting the chains of assumptions that underlie communication practices, Macpherson says it is not necessarily an "either or" situation, but a "vicious circle" because:

> We cannot achieve more democratic participation without a prior change in social inequality and in consciousness, but we cannot achieve the changes in social inequality and consciousness without a prior increase in democratic participation.[39]

This goes some way to providing a justification for deep canvassing and the blurring of the boundaries between deliberative-participatory and capitalist market-based approaches to democracy based on persuasion. But caution is needed in justifying hybrid communication practices within the neoliberal and authoritarian populist context from civil society sectors. Marnie Holborow argues that "[i]t is easy to see why these ideas about the weight of language in the global economy have some appeal: not only has communication between people changed beyond all recognition over the last two decades, but also those at the head of governments and corporations constantly promote the idea that we are living in a post-industrial 'information' age where spin, branding, and communication override everything else."[40] Of course, Peter F. Drucker in *The New Realities* (1989) forecast the rise of such communication-hungry,

---

39. Macpherson (1977, 100).

40. Holborow (2007, 56).

self-cannibalizing "knowledge societies," in which the economy is fueled and in turn shaped through its product, "the educated person," but the implications for democracy, especially in recent authoritarian and populist contexts, remain unclear.[41]

The RVAT platform for disaffected Republicans aims to awaken a values-based response to the polarizing presidential communications and policy directions over 2020, while the activist "deep canvassing" practice is a market-based persuasive approach to advocacy aimed at an elector. While it has some of the hallmarks of long-form dialogic or conversation, it is more accurately described as a hybrid form of "activist" public relations.[42] The RVAT and "deep canvassing" examples show that ranks are breaking, first, in both a powerful conservative political coalition, and second, in civil society, as activists approach intervention for social change reflexively. Both groups seek to do things differently in their realms, and through these ambivalences, puncture realities to build something new. In doing so, they are responding to the changing dynamics in the communicative space and showing both the intersection of hegemony and resistance to the neoliberal narrative. These factors prompt a reorientation to dynamics that are working within the discursive landscape, which may loosen the ties ever so slightly to enable real debate to slowly break away. Despite this, the dominant populist conditions in right-wing politics may not change significantly unless the structures that hold these cultures in place change.

---

41. Antonio Florida argues that "[t]o reduce the role of *citizens* [. . .] to that of *voters*, who limit themselves to a periodical evaluation of governors' performance, entails a dramatic impoverishment of democracy" (2013, 11). See Drucker (1989, 236).

42. According to Demetrious (2011, n.p.), "[a]ctivist public relations (PR) is a focused view of communication activity by politicized third sector groups such as social collectives, community action groups, and nongovernmental organizations (NGOs) to foster their public legitimacy as voices for social change. This aspect of PR describes practices that draw on principles, strategies, and tactics, such as promotion, to form public opinion and thus strengthen cases put to the state and business sectors as well as to the citizenry."

REFORMING PUBLIC RELATIONS AS PUBLIC INTEREST COMMUNICATION (PIC)

Public relations, or "PR," is an ambiguous term, in part because it is conceptually awkward. On the one hand, it is centrally linked to the legitimizing notion of the "public sphere" in democratic society where rational discussion, dialogue, and debate, separate from the state, take place in an open and civil way to clarify issues of importance in order to promote the good of its members.[43] On the other hand, public relations purposefully exploits and debases the public sphere in its role and instead works prodigiously to disperse discourse around its key value of an untethered market-based society, as a path to political "freedom." Wearing this mask, it produces meanings through the lens, and the language of, the market and industry, whether it is talking about home, family, friends, or politics. Its luster and appeal, in offering "solutions" to our "problems," enable it to greatly influence culture, which is in turn depoliticized.

The conceptual tension between the idea of the collective good and the pursuit of organizational self-interest is fairly clear—and not surprisingly, this has been an ongoing source of strain, friction, and ethical compromise for the occupational domain of public relations. This central flaw and the problems that flow from it have been at the heart of public relations' inability to establish credibility for its work and professional status. That public relations is part of a vast international neoliberal network of interacting institutional sites that buttress its work—for example, corporations, think tanks, business associations, political organizations, clubs, foundations, and the media—compounds these impacts so that the problems are entrenched and widespread.

Part of any professional project for an occupational domain is scoping and defining, not just its unique knowledge and expertise, but how it relates and benefits society more broadly. Ethics is therefore central to any professional project, so developing standards and codes of conduct and

---

43. Habermas (1995, 4).

providing for sanctions or disciplinary measures for those members who breach them are critical. In public relations advocacy, a claim to professionalism has often rested with its peak bodies.[44] However, associations like the Public Relations Society of America (PRSA) and the Public Relations Institute of Australia (PRIA) struggle in reconciling the gaps between "what public relations does" and "what it claims to do."[45] For example, Matilda Kolić Stanić's (2019) study of twenty national and international public relations association from Europe and the United States shows that the PRSA had a relatively poor track record in sanctioning wrongdoing.

> Namely, it has been shown that in the 50 years of the association's history, the Ethics Committee has investigated 231 cases of breaches of the code of ethics, and only 11 members have been sanctioned during this entire period.[46]

Kolić Stanić's study revealed that while every public relations association had an ethical code, the disciplinary committees did not have a high level of independence per se, and that sanctions for unethical professional conduct were infrequent. In other words, public relations' self-policing systems were either weak or ineffective, and were likely to have "lower coercive value . . . beyond the declarations of principle," raising the question of "how they really can benefit either the profession or the society."[47]

In this sense, public relations may be referred to as a "'mimic profession' which may have a code of ethics and other trappings of professions, but they have no power. They have taken on the coloration but not the substance of profession."[48] Moreover, Jacquie L'Etang and Magda Pieczka,[49]

---

44. L'Etang (1996, 1).

45. Briet and Demetrious (2010, 22).

46. Kolić Stanić (2019, 348).

47. Kolić Stanić (2019, 355–356).

48. Forsyth and Danisiewicz (1985, 64).

49. L'Etang and Pieczka (1996, 1–13).

argue that while professional status and the recognition and respectability it brings are important to public relations, the focus on achieving this largely rests on the conduct that individual practitioners exercise in making the right choices, rather than a critique of the occupation, its power disparities, lack of accountability, privileges, and social impacts.

Intimately interwoven with neoliberalism, public relations amplifies discourse that promotes new forms of social identity which are detached from the idea of the common good.[50] Rather, individuals are restless, divided social actors who are driven to achieve financial success, and within this frame ethical questions are narrowly conceived around the constructed notions of entitlement and self.

> From the point of view of this governmentality, there are no firms, producers, households, consumers, fathers, mothers, criminals, immigrants, natives, adults, children, or even citizens, but only entrepreneurs of the self, engaged in self-interested conduct as personal investment. The question of how to organize the conduct of these conducts requires techniques, practices, and above all, a way of knowing that deals with responsive subjects of "reality."[51]

This focus on individualism propagated through the neoliberal thought collective and public relations in turn obscures our interdependence with the planet and with ourselves. Thus, for Mary Wrenn:

> Neoliberal identity is isolating, disconnected from any larger community, and as such leaves the individual alienated. Alienation is a product of neoliberal capitalism that makes clear the connection between the market and the need for a constructed self-identification. As the division of labor intensifies and the individual becomes more

---

50. Chandler (2014).

51. Dilts (2010, 8).

removed from both process and product, the individual is less able to identify herself with any material contribution to society.[52]

Nonetheless, the character of public relations is influenced by changing social conditions and as such there are various inflections and approaches within the field. Therefore, it is not surprising that reform efforts within public relations ranks have focused on the interpretation of the "public" and how it might be reclaimed in a more theoretically rigorous way. Public interest communication (PIC) is an explicit attempt to align public relations to notions of the common good rather than organizational or individual self-interest.

Jane Johnston and Magda Pieczka argue that PIC offers a path through which public relations might achieve a higher level of respect in society, particularly in terms of its professional status:

> The treatment of public interest in the academic field of public relations reflects the development of the public relations professional project, including its claim to legitimacy made on the basis of serving the public interest, and the way in which it may be connected to and interrogated from positions articulated by communication theory. Public relations and professionalised communication have dealt with the notion of the public interest in both explicit and implicit ways.[53]

For Jasper Fessmann there is a recognizable difference between the two fields of public relations and PIC:

> PIC is emerging as a distinct field in part because of the maturity reached by PR as an academic discipline, which provides a powerful tool set to be applied to other communication areas. PIC takes the sophisticated techniques of the PR discipline and applies them to achieving social change. It is thus very similar to social marketing,

---

52. Wrenn (2014, 507).
53. Johnston and Pieczka (2018, 19).

which equally applies a sophisticated marketing tool set to achieving social change. PIC, however, is developing unique techniques of its own that will complement previous PR techniques. While strategic public relations has successfully been applied in social change campaigns in the past, specialized PIC expertise will further improve the effectiveness of these efforts.[54]

But the extent of the difference between PIC and PR is moot. Fessmann argues that a PIC campaign has "goals, measurable objectives, a limited time frame, and strategies and various tactics" but that its focus is social change rather than business or government goals.[55] This shows that, in a similar way to public relations, PIC is wedded to the idea of science and business framing, and thus it remains locked into the production of plastic words and neonarratives for knowledge formation. Moreover, it is likely to facilitate the colonization of civil society with neoliberal ideas and techniques, potentially undermining dialogue and deliberation. Nonetheless, openness to change in public relations is a necessary first step to address the ethical issues raised about the movement of neoliberal meaning through public relations discursive practices. But more than a gesture is required. Indeed, adopting a new name or an adjusted focus may just be another way of obscuring the ethical questions that are implicit in public relations practice and merely serve to prop up the industry.

Therefore, like deep canvassing, central to any critique or evaluation of PIC is whether the approach to the campaign aligns with an egalitarian, participatory, or a market-driven conception of democracy. As Wrenn has pointed out, dominant neoliberal identities are pitted in an aggressive contest to promote self-interest or to push government or other forms of power to bend to its will, whereas civil society[56] in pursuit of social change has a unique sharing role in distributing other people's experiences of the

---

54. Fessmann (2017, 17).

55. Fessmann (2017, 17).

56. In understanding the interrelations of civil society with government and business, Jem Bendell (2000, 17) writes that a "three-part model that draws on the work of Antonio

world, and bridging the isolation that hardens dispositions in communities. PIC's orientation toward these competing democratic models is crucial in understanding if its advocacy and the "deliberative" dynamics it creates is undoing "PR," or if it is simply embedding neoliberalism more deeply in the pockets that, until recently, have been relatively uncontrolled by market-based cultures.[57]

As I have argued, communicative action of any kind can determine what sort of political complexion dominates in society. The hybrid practice of PIC offers a grounding in core democratic values, but it remains in the family of public relations, which I have argued is problematic. Therefore, a stronger critique and a deeper understanding of how public relations works discursively, and from there dynamically intersects in cultural and communicative contexts, and scoping impacts like the emergence of PIC, indeed questioning this very "new reality," may be a useful basis for any discussion of advocacy and reform.

NEUTRALITY, PURPOSE, POWER, AND PUBLIC LANGUAGE

Writ large within the conditions of the pandemic is dissatisfaction with "public" language: its instrumental malleability, its debasement, and its thwarted potential in opening possibility. As we have seen, contemporary

---

Gramsci to differentiate between civil society, the state and the economy is helpful. In this way organisations can be classified as either belonging to the state (government), market (business) or civil society (NGO) sectors—or a hybrid of them."

57. In the late 1990s and early in the following decade, I investigated cases of grassroots activism in civil society that had characteristics, distinct from public relations, which I described in "Public Relations, Activism and Social Change: Speaking Up" (2013). I used the term "public communication" to denote this approach which broadly had these traits: openness to the permeation of ideas which can lead to different knowledge formations; receptivity to creating new subject positions with politically diverse participants and to creating a long-term commitment to issues and groups; commitment to ethics and upholding values like truth-telling, peacefulness, and respect of existing normative social systems; pursuit of an ideal that it is possible to dilute the antagonism between social groups to produce rational debate and critical public opinion; commitment to the explanation of choices to the public as people and citizens,

communicative conditions are given impetus by the coronavirus, and public relations–inflected language practices continue to hold sway; but they may be challenged and changed within unexpected, new, and emerging political contexts. Digital technologies, together with news and social media platforms, provide powerful new ways to seed and propagate unfounded fear, bias, and ignorance as naturalized "truth." In its wake, an increasing cacophony of incivility, confusion, dogmatism, and simplification has proliferated since the global health crisis. And many times, it is the focus on the controversy—the jeers and jibes, the point scoring, the next episode in an ongoing feud, as well as the querulous champions—that subjugates the public's gaze. Such an incursion in the public sphere merely resembles debate and serves to deaden public response to political action based on critical public opinion.

This book has argued that, over many decades, public relations wordwork has stimulated the reshaping of public debate to gut political struggle and replace it with totalizing acquiescence on the one hand, and oppression on the other. Jodi Dean describes these political formations as "neodemocracies," which "are configured through contestation and conflict. They reject the fantasy of a public and instead work from the antagonisms that animate political life."[58] The establishment of this acrimonious relationship is not arbitrary. Rather, public relations language practices are "living" and a crucial dynamic in the sphere of public debate. Popular, academic, and political analysis pigeonholes this as "spin," and from this position, there appears to be no more to say about it. In this, its provenance, discursive form, and potential, has been vastly underestimated. Public relations language practices are working as conveyors of knowledge formation within digitized third-wave neoliberalism—conditions that support populism, authoritarianism, and the rise of alt-right politics.[59] Primed to

---

not market-based "publics" or consumers; and an emphasis on the interdependence between people, nature, and the future to achieve social cohesiveness and personal fulfillment.

58. Dean (2003, 108).

59. Rowe et al. (2019).

support mono-thinking, these are cultures on which exaggeration, fear mongering, smear, and discredit are enabled, in part because a shorthand of plastic words have quietly installed the "tram tracks," over many decades, to bypass critique, and to bypass ethics. Today, public relations language practices are no longer articulated exclusively to the industry's confrontation of the intrinsic and extrinsic contradictions besetting its activities. Rather, such language practices widely proliferate, and are increasingly becoming the default mode of communicating across a range of social settings and domains, reducing and totalizing ideas within a market-based reality.

The fragmentation of ideas in pandemic society is exacerbated by digital disinformation and technology, which fracture the shared understandings that previously had been united by memory and tradition.[60] However, dead language does not mean it is without power. Quite the contrary, this is when it serves as a platform to be revived for another purpose. Jodi Dean argues that "the notion of communicative capitalism conceptualizes the commonplace idea that the market, today, is the site of democratic aspirations, indeed, the mechanism by which the will of the demos manifests itself."[61] Within these networked and digital conditions which revolve around the market, the notions of civil society, "democracy," and political debate are upended, as rancor and antagonism prevail as the normative mode. This may create communicative conditions which paradoxically tolerate and/or promote a greater predisposition in the subject toward public relations–inflected language practices. The words the public think, speak, and hear simply can never be understood or regarded as at a distance from ethical consideration. And as Uwe Poerksen shows: no matter how bland, how formless, how numb this plastic language may sound—it is not.

Public language is the means to social formation and is always a dynamic interplay of history and fiction. In this case, public language

---

60. Christians, in Christians and Traber (1997, 5).

61. Dean (2008, 104).

emanating from government, business, activists, or individuals can never be simply exempted as "neutral" in the neoliberal sense: a logic which underpins much thinking of the communicative space.[62] This orientation to neutrality serves not only to embed a cavalier disregard for the power of public language, but also to obscure the responsibilities of media commentators, networks, and platforms from the consequences of the words they publish. The control of ideas and actions through public relations language practices has profound impacts and interrelationships with society and politics, which in turn shape public opinion, imagination, ethical culture, and individual agency. But bounded and closed cultures and systems mean that it is not always clear how this happens.

The studies of public debate in climate change (Chapter 4) and borderlands (Chapter 5) show that neoliberalists do not necessarily champion or promote the crude idea of laissez-faire. Rather, their approach often relies on maintaining *the conditions* that support the role of the state in the construction and maintenance of market-based economies. According to Mirowski, taking this position means that "[t]he state must be stripped of obligations to society and used instead to insulate the market from democracy."[63] So, while it is accepted that democracy exists, the neoliberalist view is that this reality is subordinate to the greater reality: that of the market, because the market knows best, in a godlike way. However, this can only be accomplished if the market is allowed to manifest itself in its full complexity. The slow insinuation of neoliberal language structures and ideas in public debate is critical to this end, and this is carefully strategized in a multitude of sometimes counterintuitive ways. And in this, I have argued that public relations is far more important than previously credited and is working in a range of ways that are far from unremarkable.

---

62. Konings (2018, 61).
63. Mirowski (2013, 84).

UNTANGLING PUBLIC RELATIONS AND NEOLIBERALISM

Over the last seven decades, hawkish public relations institutions and practitioners wielding hidden influence and power within media hierarchies, business networks, political sites, and administrative systems have reinforced neoliberal stories and interpretive positions through a multitude of textual material and reference points. Ever distrustful of the media, public relations has worked from a range of positions to keep a tight rein on the circulation of ideas and language. From the production of media releases, to "op-ed" pieces, to policy statements, reports, dossiers and profiles, and public commentary, to lobbying and monitoring "enemies," its many tactical responses are routinely put to work. Perhaps a growing sense of familiarity with public relations, especially as "spin," is part of the reason it does not occupy a more central place in the neoliberal critique.

In untangling public relations and neoliberalism today, the framework of intrinsic and extrinsic public relations practices provides broad categories to understand ethical questions about communicative practices and their implications in shaping public imagination and public opinion. These are new ways to think about language. But we need new ways. These ideas are accessible and make sense of the many disparate, seemingly competing phenomena in society. And they are urgently required, because the disciplinary boundaries of public relations have failed. But as I have argued, they have failed because they have been set up to fail; the historical relationship between public relations and neoliberalism has been purposefully suppressed—a strategy that has enabled its pervasive language structures to work in public debates and the (re)ordering of ideas to take place from many reference points. In this, the generative interrelationship set in motion by the Mont Pèlerin Society, in 1947, offers a hugely fruitful way to make sense of the somewhat shifting, highly nuanced, and historically long application of neoliberal thought, and its entwinement with public relations.

The insinuation and embedding of discourses of public relations in key domains—health, education, government, business, and culture—have bolstered and extended the grip of neoliberalism to be naturalized in everyday life. To move beyond simple critique, or despair, there is a need to understand communicative modes in ways that more comprehensively consider how the loss of knowledge and the totalization of ideas occur. From that, it might just be possible to find better ways to think about public language and culture. And if individuals and groups can find a way to accept and respect each other, a room may open that sets new expectations.

REFERENCES

Abbey, Edward. 1975. *The Monkey Wrench Gang*. Philadelphia and New York: J. B. Lippincott.

Advertising Standards Authority. 2014. "ASA Ruling on Peabody Energy Corporation." August 8, 2014. https://www.asa.org.uk/rulings/adjudications/2014/8/peabody-energy-corporation/shp_adj_266168.aspx#.WIfPEHpRonI. Accessed September 27, 2021.

Agence France-Presse. 2019. "Climate Crisis Is Greatest Ever Threat to Human Rights, UN Warns." *The Guardian*. September 19, 2019. https://www.theguardian.com/law/2019/sep/09/climate-crisis-human-rights-un-michelle-bachelet-united-nations. Accessed September 8, 2021.

Almiron, Núria. 2019. "Rethinking the Ethical Challenge in Climate Change Lobbying: A Discussion of Ideological Denial." In *Climate Change Denial and Public Relations: Strategic Communication and Interest Groups in Climate Inaction*, edited by Núria Almiron and Jordi Xifra, pp. 9–25. Abingdon, Oxon, and New York: Routledge.

Andersen, Stephen O., Nancy J. Sherman, Suely Carvalho, and Marco Gonzalez. 2018. "The Global Search and Commercialization of Alternatives and Substitutes for Ozone-Depleting Substances." *Comptes Rendus Geoscience*, 350, 410–424.

Anzaldúa, Gloria. 2012. "Breaking borders/constructing bridges: Twenty-five years of Borderlands/la frontera." In Cantú, Norma E., Aída Hurtado, and G. Anzaldúa, 3–13. Borderlands/La Frontera: The New Mestiza.

Araujo, Luis, and Geoff Easton. 2012. "Temporality in Business Networks: The Role of Narratives and Management Technologies." *Industrial Marketing Management*, 41(2), 312–318.

Arnold, Andrew B. 2014. *Fueling the Gilded Age: Railroads, Miners, and Disorder in Pennsylvania Coal Country*. New York and London: New York University Press.

Aronczyk, Melissa. 2018. "Public Relations, Issue Management, and the Transformation of American Environmentalism, 1948–1992." *Enterprise & Society*, 19(4), 836–863.

Austin, Catherine, and Farida Fozdar. 2018. "Framing Asylum Seekers: The Uses of National and Cosmopolitan Identity Frames in Arguments about Asylum Seekers." *Identities: Global Studies in Culture and Power*, 25(3), 245–265.

Australian Dictionary of Biography. 2021. "White, Eric (1915–1989)." https://adb.anu.edu.au/biography/white-eric-15809. Accessed September 7, 2021.

Australian Government. 2021. "Ozone Depleting Substances." https://www.environment.gov.au/protection/ozone/ozone-science/ozone-depleting-substance. Accessed September 6, 2021.

Australian Government. 2021a. "Australian Antarctic Program: Mining in Antarctica." https://www.antarctica.gov.au/about-antarctica/geography-and-geology/geology/mining/. Accessed September 6, 2021.

Australian Government. 2021b. "Australian Antarctic Program: Protocol on Environmental Protection to the Antarctic Treaty (The Madrid Protocol)." https://www.antarctica.gov.au/about-antarctica/law-and-treaty/the-madrid-protocol/. Accessed September 6, 2021.

Australian Government. 2021c. "Coal Resources." Geoscience Australia. https://www.ga.gov.au/scientific-topics/energy/resources/coal-resources. Accessed September 8, 2021.

Phillips, Janet. (2015). Asylum seekers and refugees: What are the facts? Parliament of Australia, Department of Parliamentary Services. Research paper series, 2014–15. Retrieved from https://www.aph.gov.au/about_parliament/parliamentary_departments/parliamentary_library/pubs/rp/rp1415/asylumfacts. 1-15. Accessed 12 July 2022.

Australian Greens. 2020. "Climate Change and Energy." The Greens. https://greens.org.au/policies/climate-change-and-energy Accessed September 8, 2021.

Ball, Stephen J. 2016. "Neoliberal Education? Confronting the Slouching Beast." *Policy Futures in Education*, 14(8), 1046–1059.

Brandt, Allan M. 2012. "Inventing Conflicts of Interest: A History of Tobacco Industry tactics." *American journal of public health* 102(1), 63–71.

Bancroft, Corinne. 2018. "The Braided Narrative." *Narrative*, 26(3), 262–281.

Barbulescu, Roxana. 2014. "Global Mobility Corridors for the Ultra-Rich: The Neoliberal Transformation of Citizenship." RSCAS 2014/01. Should Citizenship Be for Sale? Robert Schuman Centre for Advanced Studies, EUDO Citizenship Observatory.

Bartlett, Bruce. 2015. "How Fox News Changed American Media and Political Dynamics." *SSRN Electronic Journal*, 10.2139/ssrn.2604679. 1-21. https://papers.ssrn.com/sol3/papers.cfm?abstract_id=2604679

Bartzen Culver, Kathleen. 2018. "Trump, Democracy, and the Extension of Journalism Ethics." In *The Trump Presidency, Journalism, and Democracy*, edited by Robert E. Gutsche Jr., pp. 282–298. New York and London: Routledge.

Basiago, Andrew D. 1995. "Methods of Defining Sustainability." *Sustainable Development*, 3(3), 109–119.

Beck, Ulrich. 1992. *Risk Society towards a New Modernity*. London: Sage Publications.

Beck, Ulrich. 2009. "Ulrich Beck on the Need for a United Europe in the Face of the Economic Crisis." Speakers Corner. April 13, 2009. https://www.speakerscorner.co.uk/blog/ulrich-beck-on-the-need-for-a-united-europe-in-the-face-of-the-economic-crisis. Accessed September 6, 2021.

Beck, Ulrich. 2010. "Climate for Change, or How to Create a Green Modernity?" *Theory, Culture and Society*, 2(2–3), 254–266.

Beck, Ulrich, Anthony Giddens, and Scott Lash, eds. 2000. *Reflexive Modernization: Politics, Tradition and Aesthetics in the Modern Social Order*. Oxford: Polity Press.

Beder, Sharon. 2006. *Free Market Missionaries: The Corporate Manipulation of Community Values*. London and New York: Earthscan.

Bell, Allan. 1994. "Climate of Opinion: Public and Media Discourse on the Global Environment." *Discourse & Society*, 5(1), 33–64.

Bendell, Jem. 2000. *Terms for Endearment: Business, NGOs and Sustainable Development*. Sheffield: Routledge.

Benford, Robert D., and David A. Snow. 2000. "Framing Processes and Social Movements: An Overview and Assessment." *Annual Review of Sociology*, 26(1), 611–639.

Bernays, Edward. 1928. *Propaganda*. New York: Horace Liveright.

Bloom, Peter. 2017. *The Ethics of Neoliberalism: The Business of Making Capitalism Moral*. Abingdon, Oxon, and New York: Routledge.

Bonchek, Mark. 2016. "How to Build a Strategic Narrative." *Organizational Culture*. March 25, 2016. https://hbr.org/2016/03/how-to-build-a-strategic-narrative. Accessed September 8, 2021.

Booker, Christopher. 2009. "Climate Change: This Is the Worst Scientific Scandal of Our Generation." *The Telegraph*, November 28, 2009. https://www.telegraph.co.uk/comment/columnists/christopherbooker/6679082/Climate-change-this-is-the-worst-scientific-scandal-of-our-generation.html Accessed 8 Sept. 2021.

Boucher, Geoff. 2011. "The Politics of Aesthetic Affect—A Reconstruction of Habermas' Art Theory." *Parrhesia*, 13, 62–78.

Boylan, Kelly. 2014. "The Philosophy of Freedom." *Madison Historical Review*. 11, no.1 (2014): 3. https://commons.lib.jmu.edu/cgi/viewcontent.cgi?article=1002&context=mhr&httpsredir=1&referer= 1-10.

Bradley, Megan. 2014. "Rethinking Refugeehood: Statelessness, Repatriation, and Refugee Agency." *Review of International Studies*, 40(1), 101–123.

Brenner, Neil, Jamie Peck, and Nik Theodore. 2010. "Variegated Neoliberalization: Geographies, Modalities, Pathways." *Global Networks* 10(2), 182–222.

Bricker, Brett Jacob. 2013. "Climategate: A Case Study in the Intersection of Facticity and Conspiracy Theory." *Communication Studies*, 64(2), 218–239.

Breit, Rhonda, and Kristin Demetrious. 2010. "Professionalisation and Public Relations: An Ethical Mismatch." *Ethical Space: The International Journal of Communication Ethics*, 7(4), 20–29.

Brooks, Cleanth, and Robert Penn Warren. 1979. *Modern Rhetoric*. 4th edition. New York, San Diego, Chicago, San Francisco, and Atlanta: Harcourt Brace Jovanovich.

Brown, Wendy. 2003. "Neo-liberalism and the End of Liberal Democracy." *Theory & Event* 7(1). https://muse.jhu.edu/article/48659.

Brown, Wendy. 2015. *Undoing the Demos: Neoliberalism's Stealth Revolution*. New York: Zone Books.

Brown, Wendy. 2018. "Neoliberalism's Frankenstein: Authoritarian Freedom in Twenty-First Century 'Democracies.'" *Critical Times*, 1(1), 60–79.

Brown, Wendy. 2019. *In the Ruins of Neoliberalism: The Rise of Antidemocratic Politics in the West*. Wellek Library Lectures. New York: Columbia University Press. https://

search.ebscohost.com/login.aspx?direct=true&db=nlebk&AN=2088020&authtype=sso&custid=deakin&site=eds-live&scope=site.

Brulle, Robert J. 2014. "Institutionalizing Delay: Foundation Funding and the Creation of US Climate Change Counter-Movement Organizations." *Climatic Change*, 122(4), 681–694.

Brulle, Robert J., and Carter Werthman. 2021. "The Role of Public Relations Firms in Climate Change Politics." *Climatic Change*, 169(1), 1–21.

Burgin, Angus. 2012. *The Great Persuasion: Reinventing Free Markets since the Depression*. Cambridge, MA: Harvard University Press.

Butler, Eamonn. n.d. *A Short History of the Mont Pelerin Society Based on a History of the Mont Pelerin Society by Max Hartwell*. https://buriedtruth.com/files/Mont_Pelerin_Society-History_of_MPS-2014.pdf.

Cantú, Francisco. 2018. *The Line Becomes a River: Dispatches from the Border*. London: Penguin.

Cantú, Norma E., Aída Hurtado, and G. Anzaldúa. 2012. "Breaking Borders/Constructing Bridges: Twenty-Five Years of Borderlands/la Frontera." *Borderlands/La Frontera: The New Mestiza*, 3–13.

Carbon Brief. 2011. "'Climategate' Used by US Republicans to End IPCC Funding." Carbon Brief: Science. February 21, 2011. https://www.carbonbrief.org/climategate-used-by-us-republicans-to-end-ipcc-funding Accessed September 8, 2021.

Carson, Rachel. 1962. *Silent Spring*. Boston, MA: Houghton, Mifflin.

Cawley, Clare J., and Amber Morgan Freeland. 2012. *A Comparative Study: The Effect Culture Has on Australian Public Relations and How It Differs from American Public Relations Practices*. 1–9.

Champ, Michael A. 2011. "Etymology and Use of the Term 'Pollution.'" *Canadian Journal of Fisheries and Aquatic Sciences*, 40, s2.

Chandler, David. 2014. Beyond Neoliberalism: Resilience, the New Art of Governing Complexity. *Resilience*, 2:1, 47–63, DOI: 10.1080/21693293.2013.878544

Christiano, Thomas. 1997. "The Significance of Public Deliberation." In *Deliberative Democracy: Essays on Reason and Politics*, edited by James Bohman and William Rehg, pp. 243–278. Cambridge, MA: MIT Press.

Christians, Clifford, and Michael Traber, eds. 1997. *Communication Ethics and Universal Values*. London: Sage Publications.

CIC. 2020. "Patrick Michaels: Decades of Denial: Perpetuating Climate Change Disinformation." https://climateinvestigations.org/patrick-michaels/. Accessed September 20, 2021.

Cowie, Jefferson, and Nick Salvatore. 2008. "The Long Exception: Rethinking the Place of the New Deal in American History." *International Labor and Working-Class History*, 74(Fall 2008), 1–32.

Crafts, Nicholas, and Peter Fearon. 2010. "Lessons from the 1930s Great Depression." *Oxford Review of Economic Policy*, 26(3), 285–317.

Crane, Jasper E. 1949. "Mr Leonard E. Read, Foundation for Economic Education Inc Irvington-On-Hudson NY." Exhibit D-6. Hearings before the House Select Committee on Lobbying, Direct and Indirect, Volume 3, Parts 7–10. June 28, 1949. https://books.google.com.au/books?id=eaeU2iVbweEC&pg=RA1-PA67&lpg=

References

RA1-PA67&dq=Leonard+E+Read+Hill+and+Knowlton&source=bl&ots=e-vtsik WyJ&sig=ACfU3U0qSM0AzQ1Hfs7PJe2VdgRsZDslbg&hl=en&sa=X&ved=2ah UKE. wj7vLqW95PoAhX383MBHck3DLkQ6AEwAXoECA4QAQ#v=snippet&q=intellectual%20peak&f=false. Accessed September 7, 2021.

Cawley, Clare J., and Amber Morgan Freeland. 2012. "A Comparative Study: The Effect Culture has on Australian Public Relations and How It Differs from American Public Relations Practices."

Creitz, Charles. 2020. "Graham Claims Democrats Want to 'give China a Pass' over Coronavirus out of Spite toward Trump." May 5, 2020. *Fox News*. https://www.foxnews.com/media/lindsey-graham-democrats-give-china-pass-coronavirus. Accessed September 9, 2021.

Cronin, Anne M. 2018. *Public Relations Capitalism: Promotional Culture, Publics and Commercial Democracy*. Cham, Switzerland: Palgrave Macmillan.

Cronin, Anne M. 2020. "The Secrecy–Transparency Dynamic: A Sociological Reframing of Secrecy and Transparency for Public Relations Research." *Public Relations Inquiry*, 9(3), 219–236.

CSIRO. 2020. "The 2019-2020 Bushfires: A CSIRO Explainer." February 18, 2020. https://www.csiro.au/en/Research/Environment/Extreme-Events/Bushfire/preparing-for-climate-change/2019-20-bushfires-explainer.

CSIRO and Bureau of Meteorology. 2020. *State of the Climate 2020*. https://www.csiro.au/en/research/environmental-impacts/climate-change/state-of-the-climate. Accessed September 8, 2021.

Cunningham, Michelle, Luke Van Uffelen and Mark Chambers. 2019. "The Changing Global Market for Australian Coal." *Reserve Bank of Australia*. https://www.rba.gov.au/publications/bulletin/2019 /sep/the-changing-global-market-for-australian-coal.html. Accessed September 8, 2021.

Cunningham, Paul A., Edward H. Huijbens, and Stephen L. Wearing. 2012. "From Whaling to Whale Watching: Examining Sustainability and Cultural Rhetoric." *Journal of Sustainable Tourism*, 20(1), 143–161.

Curry Jansen, Sue. 2009. "Phantom Conflict: Lippmann, Dewey, and the Fate of the Public in Modern Society." *Communication and Critical/Cultural Studies*, 6(3), 221–245.

Curry Jansen, Sue. 2013. "Semantic Tyranny: How Edward L. Bernays Stole Walter Lippmann's Mojo and Got Away with It and Why It Still Matters." *International Journal of Communication*, 7, 1094–1111.

Curry Jansen, Sue. 2017. *Stealth Communications: The Spectacular Rise of Public Relations*, Polity Press. ProQuest Ebook Central. http://ebookcentral.proquest.com/lib/deakin/detail.action?docID=4773600.

Curtin, Patricia A. 2012. "Public Relations and Philosophy: Parsing Paradigms." *Public Relations Inquiry*, 1(1), 31–47.

Cutlip, Scott M. 1961. "Journalism Teaching—A Forum for AEJ Members: History of Public Relations Education in the United States." *Journalism Quarterly*, 38(3), 363–370.

Cutlip, Scott M. 1994. *The Unseen Public Relations: A History*. Hillside, NJ: Lawrence Erlbaum Associates.

Cutlip, Scott M. 1995. *Public Relations History: From the 17th to the 20th Century: The Antecedents*. Mahwah, NJ: Taylor & Francis Group.

Dale, Sarah. and Katie Robertson. 2021. "We Need to Do More to Help Stateless Children Realise Their Right to Australian Citizenship." *SBS News*. March 25, 2021. https://www.sbs.com.au/news/we-need-to-do-more-to-help-stateless-children-realise-their-right-to-australian-citizenship/33935673-b52e-4b1e-8233-78bb554ca5e2 Accessed September 20, 2021.

Dao, André, and Jamila Jafari. 2021. "Behind the Wire: An Oral History Project about Immigration Detention." In *Refugee Journeys: Histories of Resettlement, Representation and Resistance*. Edited by Jordana Silverstein and Rachel Stevens, ANU Press, The Australian National University, Canberra, Australia. doi: 10.22459/RJ.2021.07.

Davies, William. 2014. *The Limits of Neoliberalism: Authority, Sovereignty and the Logic of Competition*. London: Sage Publications.

Davies, William. 2017. "Essay: Populism & the Limits of Neoliberalism." April 30, 2017. https://williamdavies.blog/2017/04/18/populism-the-limits-of-neoliberalism/. Accessed August 6, 2021.

D'Cruz, Glenn, and Niranjala Weerakkody. 2015. "Will the Real Waleed Aly Please Stand up? Media, Celebrity and the Making of an Australian Public Intellectual." *Media International Australia*, 156(1), 142–151.

De Baets, Antoon. 2009. "The Impact of the Universal Declaration of Human Rights on the Study of History." *History and Theory*, 48(February 2009), 20–43.

Dean, Jodi. 2003. "Why the Net Is Not a Public Sphere." *Constellations*, 10(1), 95–112.

Dean, Jodi. 2008. "Communicative Capitalism: Circulation and the Foreclosure of Politics." In *Digital Media and Democracy Tactics in Hard Times*, edited by Megan Boler, pp. 101–122. Cambridge, MA: MIT Press.

Dean, Jodi. 2009. *Democracy and Other Neoliberal Fantasies: Communicative Capitalism and Left Politics*. Durham, NC: Duke University Press.

Debord, Guy, and Donald Nicholson-Smith. 1994. *The Society of the Spectacle*. New York: Zone Books.

Delingpole, James. 2009. "Watching the Climategate Scandal Explode Makes Me Feel Like a Proud Parent." *The Spectator* 12. December 12, 2009. https://www.spectator.co.uk/article/watching-the-climategate-scandal-explode-makes-me-feel-like-a-proud-parent. Accessed September 8, 2021.

Demetrious, Kristin. 2008. "The Object of Public Relations and Its Ethical Implications for Late Modern Society: A Foucauldian Analysis." *Ethical Space: The International Journal of Communication Ethics*, 5(4), 22–31.

Demetrious, Kristin. 2011. "Activist Public Relations." *Wiley Online Library*. January 28. https://onlinelibrary.wiley.com/doi/10.1002/9781405186407.wbieca076. Accessed September 9, 2021.

Demetrious, Kristin. 2013. *Public Relations, Activism, and Social Change: Speaking Up*. New York and Abingdon, Oxon: Routledge.

Demetrious, Kristin. 2016. "Stoking Expectations: Public Relations and the Politics of 'Bogans.'" In *Contemporary Publics: Shifting Boundaries in New Media, Technology and Culture*, edited by P. David Marshall, Glenn D'Cruz, Sharyn McDonald, and Katja Lee, pp. 181–197. London: Palgrave Macmillan.

References

Demetrious, Kristin. 2016a. "Sanitising or Reforming PR? Exploring 'Trust' and the Emergence of Critical Public Relations." In *The Routledge Handbook of Critical Public Relations*, edited by Jacquie L'Etang, David McKie, Nancy Snow, and Jordi Xifra, pp. 101–116. Abingdon: Routledge.

Demetrious, Kristin. 2017. "Contemporary Publics, Twitter and the Story of PR: Exploring Corporate Interventions to Promote 'Clean Coal' in Australia." *Journal of Public Interest Communications*, 1(1), 94–113.

Demetrious, Kristin. 2019. "Twitter and the Struggle to Transform the Object: A Study of Clean Coal in the 2017 Australian Energy Policy Public debate." *Journal of Public Interest Communications*, 3(1), 49–65.

Demetrious, Kristin. 2019a. "'Energy Wars': Global PR and Public Debate in the 21st Century." *Public Relations Inquiry*, 8(1) (January 2019), 7–22. https://doi.org/10.1177/2046147X18804283.

Demetrious, Kristin. 2020. "Loss, Awakening and American Exceptionalism: A Moment in Contemporary US Political Communication." *Ethical Space: The International Journal of Communication Ethics*, 17(2), 15–23.

Demetrious, Kristin. 2021. "Deep Canvassing: Persuasion, Ethics, Democracy and Activist Public Relations." *Public Relations Inquiry*, 1–17, (July 2021). https://doi.org/10.1177/2046147X211033838.

Demetrious, Kristin, and Anne Surma. 2019. "In Ordinary Places: The Intersections between Public Relations and Neoliberalism." *Public Relations Inquiry*, 8(2), 105–108.

Denord, Francois. 2009. "French Neoliberalism and Its Divisions: From the Colloque Walter Lippmann to the Fifth Republic." In *The Road from Mont Pèlerin: The Making of the Neoliberal Thought Collective*, edited by Philip Mirowski and Dieter Plehwe, pp. 45-67. Cambridge, MA, and London: Harvard University Press.

Derrida, Jacques. 1983. "The Principle of Reason: The University in the Eyes of Its Pupils." *Diacritics*, 13(3), 2–20.

Deuze, Mark. 2009. "Media Industries, Work and Life." *European Journal of Communication*, 24(4), 1–14.

Dilts, Andrew. 2010. "From 'Entrepreneur of the Self' to 'Care of the Self': Neoliberal Governmentality and Foucault's Ethics." In *Western Political Science Association 2010 Annual Meeting Paper*. 1-16. https://papers.ssrn.com/sol3/papers.cfm?abstract_id=1580709

Doherty, Ben 2018. "Stateless in Australia: New Centre to Shine Light on Those Incarcerated without Hope." *SBS World News*. https://www.theguardian.com/australia-news/2018/mar/27/stateless-in-australia-new-centre-to-shine-light-on-those-incarcerated-without-hope Accessed September 9, 2021.

Doherty Ben. "'Somewhere to Call Home': Helping Stateless Children Realise Their Right to Australian Citizenship." *The Guardian*. March 24, 2021. https://www.theguardian.com/australia-news/2021/mar/25/somewhere-to-call-home-helping-stateless-children-realise-their-right-to-australian-citizenship. Accessed September 8, 2021.

Donahue, Shannon. 2004. "How Clean Are Green Ads: Evaluating Environmental Advertising in Contemporary Media." *Program in Writing and Rhetoric*. https://pdfs.semanticscholar.org/3427/8e25d7775d194a52bfb3d7069203b51d840b.pdf

Drucker, Peter, F. 1989. *The New Realities*. Oxford: Heinemann Professional Publishing.

Dunlap, Riley E., and Aaron McCright. 2015. "Challenging Climate Change: The Denial Countermovement." In *Climate Change and Society: Sociological Perspectives*, edited by Riley E. Dunlap and Robert J. Brulle, pp. 300–332. New York: Oxford University Press.

Dunlap, Riley E., and Peter J. Jacques. 2013. "Climate Change Denial Books and Conservative Think Tanks: Exploring the Connection." *The American Behavioural Scientist* 57(6): 699–731.

Dwyer, Thomas J., ed. 1961. *The Australian Public Relations Handbook*. North Melbourne, Victoria: Ruskin Business Management.

Eagleton-Pierce, Matthew. 2016. *Neoliberalism: The Key Concepts*. New York: Routledge.

Effron, Malcah, Margarida McMurry, and Virginia Pignagnoli. 2019. "Narrative Co-Construction: A Rhetorical Approach." *Narrative*, Volume 27 (3) (October), 332–352.

Eley, Geoff. 1990. "Is All the World a Text? From Social History to the History of Society Two Decades Later." *CSST Working Paper #55; CRSO Working Paper #445*. October, 1990. https://deepblue.lib.umich.edu/bitstream/handle/2027.42/51212/445.pdf?sequence=1 Accessed September 8, 2021.

Environmental Justice Foundation. 2017. *Beyond Borders: Our Changing Climate—Its Role on Conflict and Displacement*. London, United Kingdom. https://ejfoundation.org/reports/beyond-borders Accessed September 20, 2021.

Epstein, Kayla. 2019. "Climate Change Isn't an Intangible Future Risk. It's Here Now, and It's Killing Us." *Washington Post*. August 10, 2019. https://www.washingtonpost.com/science/2019/08/09/climate-change-isnt-an-intangible-future-risk-its-here-now-its-killing-us/. Accessed September 8, 2021.

Ewen, Stuart. 1996. *PR! A Social History of Spin*. New York: Basic Books.

Fairclough, Norman. 1989. *Language and Power*. London: Longman.

Fairclough, Norman. 1992. "Linguistic and Intertextual Analysis within Discourse Analysis." *Discourse and Society*, 3, 193–217.

Fairclough, Norman. 2003. *Analysing Discourse: Textual Analysis for Social Research*. London and New York: Routledge.

Fairclough, Norman. 2005. "Neo-Liberalism: A Discourse-Analytical Perspective." *Polifonia*, 10(10), 21–52.

Fenton Communicaitons. 2009. *Now Hear This The 9 Laws of Successful Advocacy Communications*. 1–12. http://www.sabrizain.org/traffic/library/ninelaws.pdf

Fenster, Marl. 1999. *Conspiracy theories: Secrecy and power in American culture*. Minneapolis, MN: University of Minnesota Press.

Fessmann, Jasper. 2017. "Conceptual Foundations of Public Interest Communications." *The Journal of Public Interest Communications*, 1(1), 16.

Fessmann. Jasper. 2019. An Unlevel Playing Field: A Primer on the Problems of Climate Change Communications." In *Strategic Climate Science Communications: Effective Approaches to Fighting Global Warming Denial*, edited by J. Fessmann, pp. 1–11. Wilmington, DE: Vernon Press.

Finley, Laura, and Luigi Esposito. 2019. "The Immigrant as Bogeyman: Examining Donald Trump and the Right's Anti-immigrant, Anti-PC Rhetoric." *Humanity & Society*, 44(2): 178-197.

Fishback, Price. 2007, "The New Deal." In *Government and the American Economy: A New History*, edited by P. Fishback, pp. 384–430. Chicago: University of Chicago Press.

Fisher, Marc, Abigail Hauslohner, Hannah Natanson, and Lori Rozsa. 2020. "This Year, April Was . . . Hope." *Washington Post*. May 2, 2020. https://www.washingtonpost.com/graphics/2020/national/coronavirus-april-deadly-month/ Accessed September 9, 2021.

Florida, Antonio. 2013. "Participatory Democracy versus Deliberative Democracy: Elements for a Possible Theoretical Genealogy. Two Histories, Some Intersection." *7th ECPR General Conference*. Sciences Po, Bordeaux, September, 2013. 4 -7.

Forbes. 2021. "15 Ways To Gain Control of the Narrative during a PR Crisis." https://www.forbes.com/sites/forbesagencycouncil/2021/05/20/15-ways-to-gain-control-of-the-narrative-during-a-pr-crisis/?sh=72b822db61c6. Accessed September 8, 2021.

Forsyth, Patrick B., and Thomas J. Danisiewicz. 1985. "Toward a Theory of Professionalization." *Work and Occupations*, 12(1), 59–76.

Foucault, Michel. 1972. *The Archaeology of Knowledge and the Discourse on Language*. Translated by A. M. Sheridan Smith. New York: Pantheon Books.

Franczak, Liz. 2019. "The Century of Spin." *The Baffler*, 44. March 2019. https://thebaffler.com/salvos/the-century-of-spin-franczak. Accessed September 20, 2021. 92–104.

Franta, Benjamin. 2018. "Global Warming's Paper Trail." *Project Syndicate*. September 12, 2018. https://www.project-syndicate.org/commentary/secret-energy-industry-research-on-global-warming-by-benjamin-franta-2018-09?barrier=accesspaylog. Accessed September 8, 2021.

Freeman, Edward R. 1984. *Strategic Management: A Stakeholder Approach*. Boston: Pitman.

Friedman, Milton. 1976. "Afterword" in Read, Leonard. [1958] 2008. *I, Pencil*. New York: Foundation for Economic Education Inc. https://history.fee.org/media/3736/84-i-pencil.pdf.

Fuld, Joe. 2017. "7 Questions with Dave Fleischer on Deep Canvassing." *The Campaign Workshop*. February 2. https://www.thecampaignworkshop.com/7-questions-dave-fleischer-deep-canvassing. Accessed September 9, 2021.

Gregoire, Paul. 2020. "When It Comes to Punishing Refugees, Dutton Is the New Morrison." https://www.sydneycriminallawyers.com.au/blog/when-it-comes-to-punishing-refugees-dutton-is-the-new-morrison/. Accessed September 8, 2021.

Giroux, Henry A. 2004. *Terror of Neoliberalism: Authoritarianism and the Eclipse of Democracy*. Taylor & Francis Group.

Government of Canada. 2021. "Immigrate with a Start-Up Visa: Who Can Apply." https://www.canada.ca/en/immigration-refugees-citizenship/services/immigrate-canada/start-visa/eligibility.html#money. Accessed September 8, 2021.

Groves, J. Randall. 2012. "Canon and Grand Narrative in the Philosophy of History." *Journal of East-West Thought* 1(2), 39–52.

Grunig, James E. 1977. "Review of Research on Environmental Public Relations." *Public Relations Review*, 3(3), 36–58.

Grunig, James E., and Todd Hunt. 1984. *Managing Public Relations*. New York: Holt, Rinehart and Winston.

Gutsche, Robert E., Jr. 2018. "Introduction: Translating Trump: How to Discuss the Complications of Covering New Presidential Politics." In *The Trump Presidency,*

Journalism, and Democracy, edited by Robert E. Gutsche Jr., pp. 1–15. New York and London: Routledge.

Habermas, Jurgen. 1984. *The Theory of Communicative Action Reason and the Rationalization of Society*, Vol. 1. Boston: Beacon Press.

Habermas, Jurgen. 1989. *The Theory of Communicative Action the Critique of Functionalist Reason*, Vol. 2. Cambridge: Polity Press.

Habermas, Jurgen. 1995. *The Structural Transformation of the Public Sphere: An Inquiry into the Category of Bourgeois Society*. Cambridge, MA: MIT Press.

Habermas, Jurgen. 1994. "Three Normative Models of Democracy". Democratic and Constitutional Theory Today. *Constellations* Volume I, No I. ww.sze.hu/~smuk/Nyilvanossag_torvenyek_CEE/Szakirodalom/Deliberat%C3%ADv%20demokrácia/habermas_3_normative_models_of_democracy.pdf

Hager, Nicky, and Bob Burton. 1999. *Secrets and Lies: The Anatomy of an Anti-Environmental PR Campaign*. Munroe, ME: Common Courage.

Hale, Charles R. 2004. "Rethinking Indigenous Politics in the Era of the 'Indio Permitido.'" *NACLA Report on the Americas*, 38(2), 16–21.

Harper, Donald. 2011. "Structural Functionalism: University of Leicester: School of Management." *Management Journal*, 25(6), 101–115.

Harrison, Bruce E. 1992. *Environmental Communication and Public Relations Handbook*. 2nd edition. Rockville, MD: Government Institutes.

Harvey, David. 2005. *A Brief History of Neoliberalism*. Oxford. Oxford University Press.

Hass, Bruce, and Michael Kleine. 2003. "The Rhetoric of Junk Science." *Technical Communication Quarterly*, 12(3), 267–284.

Hayek, Friedrich. 1949. "The Intellectuals and Socialism." *University of Chicago Law Review*, 16(3), 417–433.

Hays, Samuel P. 1981. "The Environmental Movement." *Journal of Forest History*, 25(4), 219–221.

Hazlitt, Henry. 1978. *Economics in One Lesson*. Three Rivers Press. New York.

Hazlitt, Henry. 2006. "The Early History of FEE." FEE Timely Classic, originally published in *The Freeman*, 1984. Foundation for Economic Education, Inc. Irvington-On-Hudson, New York. https://fee.org/media/4183/0605hazlitt.pdf.

Hecht, David K. 2012. "How to Make a Villain: Rachel Carson and the Politics of Anti-Environmentalism." *Endeavour*, 36(4), 149–155.

Held, Virginia. 2005. *The Ethics of Care: Personal, Political, and Global*. Oxford: Oxford University Press.

Herring, Horace. 2001. "The Conservation Society: Harbinger of the 1970s Environment Movement in the UK." *Environment and History*, 7(4), 381–401. http://www.environmentandsociety.org/sites/default/files/key_docs/herring-7-4.pdf.

Herrnstein Smith, Barbara. 1980. "Afterthoughts on Narrative." *Critical Inquiry*, 7(1), 213–236.

Hertel-Fernandez, Alexander, Caroline Tervo, and Theda Skocpol. 2018. "How the Koch Brothers Built the Most Powerful Rightwing Group You've Never Heard Of." *Guardian*. September 26, 2018. https://www.theguardian.com/us-news/2018/sep/26/koch-brothers-americans-for-prosperity-rightwing-political-group Accessed September 9, 2021.

Higgs, Robert. 1997. "The Dream of the Mont Pèlerin Society." *The Independent Review*. Mises Institute. May 31, 1997. https://mises.org/library/dream-mont-pelerin-society.

Hills, Mike. 2020. "Coronavirus: How the Pandemic in US Compares with Rest of World." *BBC News*. May 27, 2020. https://www.bbc.com/news/world-us-canada-52771783. Accessed September 9, 2021.

Hindess, Barry. 1993. "Class Inequality and Resentment." In *Citizenship and Social Theory*, edited by Bryan S. Turner, pp. 33–50. London: Sage Publications.

Holborow, Marnie. 2007. Dublin City University. *Journal of Language and Politics*, 6(1), 51-73.

Holborow, Marnie. 2015. *Language and Neoliberalism*. Taylor & Francis Group.

Holcomb, John M. 2005. "Public Affairs in North America: US Origins and Development." In *The Handbook of Public Affairs*, edited by Phil Harris and Craig S. Fleisher, pp. 31–49. London: Sage Publications.

Holmgren, Lindsay. 2021. "Narrative in the Economic Sphere: The International Monetary Fund and the Scripting of a Global Economy." *Narrative*, 29(2), 192–209. https://doi.org/10.1353/nar.2021.0011.

hooks, bell. 2006. "Postmodern Blackness." In *Cultural Theory and Popular Culture: A Reader*, edited by John Storey, pp. 454–460. 3rd edition. Essex: Pearson Prentice Hall.

Hoover, Joe. 2013. "Rereading the Universal Declaration of Human Rights: Plurality and Contestation, Not Consensus." *Journal of Human Rights*, 12(2), 217–241.

House Select Committee on Lobbying Activities. 1950. Part 8 of Hearings before the House Select Committee on Lobbying Activities, House of Representatives, Eighty-First Congress, Second Session, Created Pursuant to H. Res. 298. July 18, 1950. Foundation for Economic Education. https://www.google.com.au/books/edition/Hearings_Before_the_House_Select_Committ/sM9FAQAAMAAJ?hl=en&gbpv=1&dq=inauthor:%22United+States.+Congress.+House.+Select+Committee+on+Lobbying+Activities%22&printsec=frontcover. Accessed September 7, 2021.

Hubbard, Bethany. 2012. "The Ecologist January 1972: A Blueprint for Survival." *Ecologist Informed by Nature*. https://theecologist.org/2012/jan/27/ecologist-january-1972-blueprint-survival. Accessed September 8, 2021.

Hudson, Marc. 2019. "'A Form of Madness': Australian Climate and Energy Policies 2009-2018. *Environmental Politics*, 28(3), 583–589.

Hudson, Marc and Christopher Wright. 2015. "Recycling Rules: Carnival of Coal is a Blast from the PR Past." *The Conversation*, 10 August, 2015. https://theconversation.com/recycling-rules-carnival-of-coal-is-a-blast-from-the-pr-past-45819

Hughes, Patrick, and Kristin Demetrious. 2006. "Engaging with Stakeholders or Constructing Them? Attitudes and Assumptions in Stakeholder Software." *Journal of Corporate Citizenship*, 23, 93–101.

Humphrys, Elizabeth. 2019. *How Labour Built Neoliberalism: Australia's Accord, The Labour Movement and The Neoliberal Project*. Chicago, IL: Haymarket Books.

IPCC, 2021: Summary for Policymakers. In: *Climate Change 2021: The Physical Science Basis. Contribution of Working Group I to the Sixth Assessment Report of the Intergovernmental Panel on Climate Change* [Masson-Delmotte, V., P. Zhai, A. Pirani, S.L. Connors, C. Péan, S. Berger, N. Caud, Y. Chen, L. Goldfarb, M.I. Gomis, M. Huang, K. Leitzell, E. Lonnoy, J.B.R. Matthews, T.K. Maycock, T. Waterfield, O. Yelekçi, R. Yu, and B. Zhou (eds.)]. Cambridge University Press, Cambridge, United Kingdom and New York, NY, USA, pp. 3–32, doi:10.1017/9781009157896.001.

Isenstadt, Alex. 2020. "GOP Memo Urges Anti-China Assault over Coronavirus." *Politico*. April 24, 2020. https://www.politico.com/news/2020/04/24/gop-memo-anti-china-coronavirus-207244 Accessed September 9, 2021.

Jahansoozi, Julia. 2006. "Relationships, Transparency, and Evaluation." In *Public Relations Critical Debates and Contemporary Practice*, edited by J. L'Etang and M. Pieczka, pp. 61-92. Mahwah, NJ: Lawrence Erlbaum and Associates.

Jayaraj, Vijay. 2016). "Hero or Villain: The Myth of Harmful CO2." *Master Resource: A Free-Market Energy Blog*, December 22, 2016. https://www.masterresource.org/carbon-dioxide/myth-harmful-co2/ Accessed 8 Sept. 2021.

Jin, Dal Yong. 2008. "Neoliberal Restructuring of the Global Communication System: Mergers and Acquisitions." *Media, Culture & Society*, 30(3), 357–373.

Joffe, Josef. 2019. "The Religion of Climatism: A New Faith Emerges." *Commentary*. November 2019. https://www.commentarymagazine.com/articles/josef-joffe/the-religion-of-climatism/ Accessed September 8, 2021.

Johnston, Jane, and Magda Pieczka, eds. 2018. *Public Interest Communication: Critical Debates and Global Contexts*. Taylor & Francis Group. New York.

Jones, Alfred Haworth. 1971. 'The Search for a Usable American Past in the New Deal Era." *American Quarterly*, 23, 5.

Jones, Andrew. 2017. "The Alt-Right Revolution in the Early 21st Century." *Geopolitical Economy Research Group*. https://geopoliticaleconomy.org/wpcontent/uploads/2017/09/Jones-Paper.pdf.

Kane, John. 2000. "Communitarianism and Citizenship." In *Rethinking Australian Citizenship*, edited by Wayne Hudson and John Kane, pp. 215–230. Cambridge: Cambridge University Press.

Kasper, Matt. 2016. "Peabody Energy Funding Climate Change Denial and Anti-Renewable Campaigns." *Energy and Policy Institute*, July 11, 2016. https://www.energyandpolicy.org/peabody-energy-funding-climate-denial-anti-renewable-energy/ Accessed September 28, 2021.

Keating, AnaLouise. 2006. "From Borderlands and New Mestizas to Nepantlas and Nepantleras: Anzaldúan Theories for Social Change." *Human Architecture: Journal of the Sociology of Self-Knowledge*, 4(3), Article 3. http://scholarworks.umb.edu/humanarchitecture/vol4/iss3/3.

Kelsey, Darren, Frank Mueller, Andrea Whittle, and Majid KhosraviNik. 2016. "Financial Crisis and Austerity: Interdisciplinary Concerns in Critical Discourse Studies." *Critical Discourse Studies*, 13(1), 1–19.

Kingston, Lindsey N. 2013. "A Forgotten Human Rights Crisis: Statelessness and Issue (Non)Emergence." *Human Rights Review*, 14, 73–87. https://doi.org/10.1007/s12142-013-0264-4.

Klocker, Natascha, and Kevin M. Dunn. 2003. "Who's Driving the Asylum Debate? Newspaper and Government Representations of Asylum Seekers." *Media International Australia*, 109, 71–93.

Koether, George. 1981. *The Freeman*, 31(6) (September). 515 – 576.

Kolić Stanić, Matilda. 2019. "What Can Happen to Public Relations Who Behave Unethically?" In *Proceedings of the ENTRENOVA-ENTerprise REsearch InNOVAtion Conference (Online)*, 5(1), 347–358.

Konings, Martijn. 2018. "From Hayek to Trump: The Logic of Neoliberal Democracy." *Socialist Register*, 54, 48–73.

Krašovec, Primož. 2013. "Neoliberal Epistemology: From the Impossibility of Knowing to Human Capital." *Filozofija I društvo* XXIV(4), 63–83.

Lamme, Margot Opdycke, and Karen Miller Russell. 2009. "Removing the Spin: Toward a New Theory of Public Relations History." *Journalism & Communication Monographs*, 11(4), 280–362.

La Vida Golden Visas. 2021. "USA EB5 Investor Visa." https://www.goldenvisas.com/usa. Accessed September 8, 2021.

Leach, Michael. 2003. "Disturbing Practices: Dehumanizing Asylum Seekers in the Refugee 'Crisis' in Australia, 2001–2002." *Refuge*, 21, 25–33.

Leary, John Patrick. 2018. *Keywords: The New Language of Capitalism*. Chicago: Haymarket Books.

Le Bon, Gustave. [1895] 1960. *The Crowd: A Study of the Popular Mind*. New York: Viking Press.

L'Etang, Jacquie, and Magda Pieczka. 1996. *Critical Perspectives in Public Relations*. Routledge.

L'Etang, Jacquie. 2009. "Radical PR: Catalyst for Change or an Aporia?" *International Journal of Communication Ethics*, 6(2), 13–18.

Lewis, Tanya. 2021. "How the U.S. Pandemic Response Went Wrong—and What Went Right—during a Year of COVID." *Scientific American*. November 3, 2021. https://www.scientificamerican.com/article/how-the-u-s-pandemic-response-went-wrong-and-what-went-right-during-a-year-of-covid/. Accessed September 9, 2021.

Liberaal, Archief vzw. 2004. "Inventory of The General Meeting Files (1947–1998)." Inventories of the Liberaal Archief—New Series No. 1, 1–108.

Lieberman, Robert C., Suzanne Mettler, Thomas B. Pepinsky, Kenneth M. Roberts, and Richard Valelly. 2019. "The Trump Presidency and American Democracy: A Historical and Comparative Analysis." *Perspectives on Politics*, 17(2): 470–479.

Lindlof, Thomas R., and Bryan C. Taylor. 2002. *Qualitative Communication Research Methods*. London: Sage Publications.

Lippmann, Walter. [1922] 1921. *Public Opinion*. New Brunswick, NJ, and London: Transaction.

Lippmann, Walter. [1937] 2017. *The Good Society*. London and New York: Routledge.

Lockwood, Alex. 2008. "Seeding Doubt: How Sceptics Use New Media to Delay Action on Climate Change." Paper delivered to the Association for Journalism Education Annual Conference: New Media, New Democracy. Sheffield University.

Lott, John R. 2009. "Why You Should Be Hot and Bothered about 'Climate-gate.'" *Fox News*. November 24, 2009. https://www.foxnews.com/opinion/why-you-should-be-hot-and-bothered-about-climate-gate . Accessed September 8, 2021.

Lowy Institute. 2018. "2018 Lowy Institute Poll." https://www.lowyinstitute.org/publications/2018-lowy-institute-poll. Accessed September 8, 2021.

Lytle, Mark Hamilton. 2017. "Rachel Carson: Saint or Sinner?" *Human Ecology Review*, 23(2), 55–64. published 2017 by ANU Press, The Australian National University, Canberra, Australia. dx.doi.org/10.22459/HER.23.02.2017.06

Macfarlane, Robert. 2009. "Rereading: Robert Macfarlane on The Monkey Wrench Gang." *The Guardian*. September 26, 2009. https://www.theguardian.com/books/2009/sep/26/robert-macfarlane-monkey-wrench-gang. Accessed September 8, 2021.

Macnamara, Jim, and Robert Crawford. 2010. "Reconceptualising Public Relations in Australia: A Historical and Social Re-analysis." *Asia Pacific Public Relations Journal*, 11(2), 1–15.

Macpherson, Crawford Brough. 1977. *The Life and Times of Liberal Democracy*. Oxford and New York: Oxford University Press.

Mäkelä, Maria, Samuli Björninen, Laura Karttunen, Matias Nurminen, Juha Raipola and Tytti Rantanen. 2021. "Dangers of Narrative: A Critical Approach to Narratives of Personal Experience in Contemporary Story Economy." *Narrative*. 29(2), 139–159. doi:10.1353/nar.2021.0009.

Mangan, Lucy. 2019. "Climategate: Science of a Scandal Review—The Hack That Cursed Our Planet." *The Guardian*. November 15, 2019. https://www.theguardian.com/tv-and-radio/2019/nov/14/climategate-science-of-a-scandal-review-the-hack-that-cursed-our-planet . Accessed September 8, 2021.

Martín Rojo, Luisa, and Alfonso Del Percio, eds. 2019. *Language and Neoliberal Governmentality*. Milton: Taylor & Francis Group.

Maslin, Mark. 2019. "Five Climate Change Science Misconceptions—Debunked." *The Conversation*. September 15, 2019. https://theconversation.com/five-climate-change-science-misconceptions-debunked-122570.

Mavelli, Luca. 2018. "Citizenship for Sale and the Neoliberal Political Economy of Belonging." *International Studies Quarterly*, 62, 482–493.

Maxmen, Amy. 2022. "New Studies Support Wuhan Market as Pandemic's Origin Point: Nature Epidemiology." *Scientific American*. February 28, 2022. https://www.scientificamerican.com/article/new-studies-support-wuhan-market-as-pandemics-origin-point/. Accessed March 20, 2022.

Mckay, Fiona. H., Samantha L. Thomas, and Susan Kneebone. 2011. "It Would Be Okay if They Came through Proper Channels": Thomas Community Perceptions and attitudes toward Asylum Seekers in Australia. *Journal of Refugee Studies*. doi:10.1093/jrs/fer010

McKenna, Bernard J., and Philip. Graham. 2000. "Technocratic Discourse: A primer." *Journal of Technical Writing and Communication*, 30(3), 219–247.

McKenna, Mark. 2019. "Scott Morrison's Quiet Australians." *The Monthly*. July 2019. https://www.themonthly.com.au/issue/2019/july/1561989600/mark-mckenna/scott-morrison-s-quiet-australians. Accessed September 6, 2021.

McKie, David, and Debashish Munshi. 2007. *Reconfiguring Public Relations: Ecology, Equity, and Enterprise*. Abingdon, Oxon, and New York: Routledge.

Meadows, Donella H., Dennis L. Meadows, Jorgen Randers, and William W. Behrens. 1972. *The Limits to Growth: A Report for the Club of Rome's Project on the Predicament of Mankind*. London: Potomac Associates.

Means, Alexander J., and Graham B. Slater. 2019. "The Dark Mirror of Capital: On Post-Neoliberal Formations and the Future of Education." *Discourse: Studies in the Cultural Politics of Education*, 1 – 15. doi:10.1080/01596306.2019.1569876.

Meretoja, Hanna. 2018. *The Ethics of Storytelling: Narrative Hermeneutics, History and the Possible*. Oxford and New York: Oxford University Press.

Miller, David, and William Dinan. 2008. *A Century of Spin: How Public Relations Became the Cutting Edge of Corporate Power*. London: Pluto Press.

Miller, Karen S. 1999. *Voice of Business: Hill & Knowlton and Postwar Public Relations*. Chapel Hill and London: University of North Carolina Press.

Miller Russell, Karen 2014. "Arthur Page and The Professionalization of Public Relations." In *Pathways to Public Relations: Histories of Practice and Profession* edited by St. John III, Burton, Opdycke Lamme, Margot, and Jacquie L'Etang, pp. 306–320. London: Taylor & Francis Group.

Minerals Council of Australia. n.d. "Policy." https://minerals.org.au/policy Accessed September 8, 2021.

Minns, John, Kieran Beadley, and Fabricio H. Chagas-Bastos. 2018. "Australia's Refugee Policy: Not a Model for the World." *International Studies*, 55(1), 1–21.

Mirowski, Philip, Jeremy Walker, and Antoinette Abboud. 2013. "Beyond Denial." *Overland* 210, 80–86.

Mirowski, Philip. 2015. "Postface: Defining Neoliberalism." In *The Road from Mont Pèlerin: The Making of the Neoliberal Thought Collective*, edited by Philip Mirowski and Dieter Plehwe, pp. 417–455. Cambridge, MA, and London: Harvard University Press.

Mirowski, Philip. 2016. "This Is Water (Or Is It Neoliberalism?)." *Institute for New Economic Thinking*. May 25, 2016. https://www.ineteconomics.org/perspectives/blog/this-is-water-or-is-it-neoliberalism Accessed September 6, 2021.

Mirowski, Philip. 2018. "The Movement That Dare Not Speak Its Name." *American Affairs*, 2(1). 118 – 141. https://americanaffairsjournal.org/2018/02/neoliberalism-movement-dare-not-speak-name/

Mirowski, Philip. 2019. "Hell Is Truth Seen Too Late." *boundary 2*, 46(1), 1–53. doi: https://doi.org/10.1215/01903659-7271327. Accessed September 6, 2021.

Mirowski, Philip, and Dieter Plehwe, eds. 2015. *The Road from Mont Pèlerin: The Making of the Neoliberal Thought Collective*. Cambridge, MA and London, Harvard University Press.

Mirowski, Philip, and Dieter Plehwe, eds. 2009. *The Road from Mont Pèlerin: The Making of the Neoliberal Thought Collective*. Cambridge, MA, and London: Harvard University Press.

Moen, Torill. 2006. "Reflections on the Narrative Research Approach." *International Journal of Qualitative Methodology*, 5(4), 56–69.

Moloney, Kevin. 2006. *Rethinking Public Relations*. London and New York: Routledge.

Mont Pelerin Society. 2021. "About the Mont Pelerin Society." https://www.montpelerin.org/about-mps/. Accessed September 7, 2021.

Nethery, Amy, and Rosa Holman. 2016. "Secrecy and Human Rights Abuse in Australia's Offshore Immigration Detention Centres." *International Journal of Human Rights*, 20(7), 1018–1038.

Nikiforuk, Andrew. 2019. "Against 'Sustainability' and Other Plastic Words." *The Tyee* 2. May 2019. https://thetyee.ca/Opinion/2019/05/02/Sustainability-Plastic/.

Nuccitelli, Dana. 2016. "Russian Email Hackers Keep Playing Us for Fools: The 2016 US Presidential Election Wasn't the First Case of a Successful Email Hacking Faux Scandal." *The Guardian*. December 22, 2016. https://www.theguardian.com/environment/climate-consensus-97-per-cent/2016/dec/22/russian-email-hackers-keep-playing-us-for-fools. Accessed September 8, 2021.

O'Doherty, Keiran, and Amanda Lecouteur. 2007. "'Asylum Seekers,' 'Boat People' and 'Illegal Immigrants': Social Categorisation in the Media." *Australian Journal of Psychology*, 59(1), 1–12. doi:10.1080/00049530600941685.

O'Donnell & Associates. 2020. *Corona Big Book*. O'Donnell & Associates Strategic Communications. April 17, 2020. https://static.politico.com/80/54/2f3219384e018 33b0a0ddf95181c/corona-virus-big-book-4.17.20.pdf.

One Visa. n.d. "Australia Investor Visa Guide." https://www.one-visa.com/australia-visa-resources/investor-visas-australia. Accessed September 20, 2021.

Ong, Aihwa. 2007. "Neoliberalism as a mobile technology." *Transactions of the Institute of British Geographers*. 32(1): 3–7. DOI: 10.1111/j.1475-5661.2007.00234.x

Opdycke Lamme, Margot. 2014. *Public Relations and Religion in American History: Evangelism, Temperance, and Business*. London: Taylor & Francis Group.

Opitz, Edmund A. 1998. *Leonard A. Read: A Portrait, The Advancement of Human Liberty Is a Learning Process*. Foundation for Economic Education Inc., Irvington-On-Hudson NY. https://fee.org/articles/leonard-e-read-a-portrait/ Accessed August 14, 2021.

Oreskes, Naomi, and Erik M. Conway. 2012. *Merchants of Doubt: How a Handful of Scientists Obscured the Truth on Issues from Tobacco Smoke to Global Warming*. London: Bloomsbury.

Oreskes, Naomi, Erik M. Conway, and Charlie Tyson. 2020. "How American Businessmen Made Us Believe That Free Enterprise Was Indivisible from American Democracy: The National Association of Manufacturers' Propaganda Campaign 1935–1940." https://www.cambridge.org/core/services/aop-cambridge-core/content/view/39EF97CA5DF92FBA60588364D38FA76E/9781108843058c4_95-119.pdf.

Ott, Brian L. 2017. "The Age of Twitter: Donald J. Trump and the Politics of Debasement." *Critical Studies in Media Communication, National Communication Association*, 34(1), 59–68.

Parks, Perry. 2020. "The Ultimate News Value: Journalism Textbooks, the US Presidency, and the Normalization of Donald Trump." *Journalism Studies*, 21(4), 512–529.

Peacock, Matt. 2012. *Killer Company: James Hardie Exposed*. Sydney: ABC Books/HarperCollins.

Pearce, Fred. 2010 "'Climategate' Was PR Disaster That Could Bring Healthy Reform of Peer Review." *The Guardian*. February 10, 2010. https://www.theguardian.com/environment/2010/feb/09/climate-emails-pr-disaster-peer-review . Accessed September 8, 2021.

Peck, Jamie. 2010. *Constructions of Neoliberal Reason*. Oxford: Oxford University Press.

Peck, Jamie, and Nik Theodore. 2019. "Still Neoliberalism?" *The South Atlantic Quarterly*, 118(2) 245–265.

Peetz, David. 2018. "The Labour Share, Power and Financialisation." *Journal of Australian Political Economy*, 81, 33–51.

Peters, Chris. 2010. "No-Spin Zones: The Rise of the American Cable News Magazine and Bill O'Reilly." *Journalism Studies*, 1(6), 832–851.

Phelan, James. 2008. Narratives in Contest; or, Another Twist in the Narrative Turn. *PMLA/Publications of the Modern Language Association of America*, 123(1), 166–175. doi:10.1632/pmla.2008.123.1.166.

Phelan, Sean. 2014. *Neoliberalism, Media and the Political*. Basingstoke, Hants: Palgrave Macmillan.

Phelan. 2018. "Neoliberalism and Media." In *The SAGE Handbook of Neoliberalism*, edited by Damien Cahill, Melinda Cooper, Martijn Konings, and David Primrose, pp. 539–552. London, Thousand Oaks, CA, New Delhi and Singapore: SAGE Publications Ltd.

Phillips-Fein, Kim. 2009. "Business Conservatives and the Mont Pèlerin Society." In *The Road from Mont Pèlerin: The Making of the Neoliberal Thought Collective*, edited by Philip Mirowski and Dieter Plehwe, pp. 280–301. Cambridge, MA, and London: Harvard University Press.

Pieczka, Magda. 1996. "Paradigms, Sytmes Theory and Public Relations." In *Critical Perspectives in Public Relations*, edited by Jacquie L'Etang and Magda Pieczka, pp. 124–156. London: International Thomson Business Press.

Pieczka, Magda. 2019. "Looking Back and Going Forward: The Concept of the Public in Public Relations Theory." *Public Relations Inquiry*, 8(3), 225–244.

Piotr, Zuk, and Jan Toporowski. 2020. "Capitalism after Communism: The Triumph of Neoliberalism, Nationalist Reaction and Waiting for the Leftist Wave." *Economic and Labour Relations Review*, 31(2): 21–24.

Plehwe, Dieter. 2009. "Introduction." In *The Road from Mont Pèlerin: The Making of the Neoliberal Thought Collective*. edited by Philip Mirowski and Dieter Plehwe, pp. 1-26. Cambridge, MA, and London: Harvard University Press.

Plehwe, Dieter. 2019. "Think Tank Networks and The Knowledge-Interest Nexus. The Case of Climate Change." In *Climate Change Denial and Public Relations. Strategic Communication and Interest Groups in Climate Inaction*, 140–156. London, New York, NY: Routledge.

Plitzko, Dominik. 2018. "The Rise of Right-Wing Media"—How Breitbart and Fox News Won the 2016 US Election." *North American Cultural Studies*, 1–3.

Poerksen, Uwe. 1995. *Plastic Words: The Tyranny of a Modular Language*. University Park: Pennsylvania State University Press.

Poletta, Francesca, and Jessica Callaghan. 2017. "Deep Stories, Nostalgia Narratives, and Fake News: Storytelling in the Trump Era." *American Journal of Cultural Sociology*, 5(3), 392–408.

PR Watch. 2021. "PR Watch Archives." The Center for Media and Democracy. https://www.prwatch.org/content/pr-watch-archives. Accessed September 16, 2021.

Prather, Michael, Pauline Midley, F. Sherwood Rowland, and Richard Stolarski. 1996. "The Ozone Layer: The Road Not Taken." *Nature*, 381, 551–554.

Pugh, Michael. 2004. "Drowning Not Waving: Boat People and Humanitarianism at Sea." *Journal of Refugee Studies*, 17(1), 50–69.

Rea, Jeannie. 2016. "Critiquing Neoliberalism in Australian Universities." *Australian Universities' Review*, 58(2), 9–14.
Read, Leonard E. 1946. "Mr C M White, President, Republic Steel Corp. Republic Buidling, Clevand 1, Ohio." October 7, 1946. Exhibit B-9. Hearings Before the House Select Committee on Lobbying, Direct and Indirect, Volume 3, Parts 7–10. https://books.google.com.au/books?id=eaeU2iVbweEC&pg=RA1-PA67&dq=Leonard+E+Read+Hill+and+Knowlton&hl=en&sa=X&ved=0ahUKEwjg94Shp9DoAhUJzDgGHfzCDHYQ6AEIJzAA#v=onepage&q=Leonard%20E%20Read%20Hill%20and%20Knowlton&f=false.
Read, Leonard E. [1958] 2008. *I, Pencil*. New York: Foundation for Economic Education. https://history.fee.org/media/3736/84-i-pencil.pdf.
Reference for Business. 2021. "History of Manning Selvage & Lee (MS&L)." https://www.referenceforbusiness.com/history2/71/Manning-Selvage-Lee-MS-L.html. Accessed September 7, 2021.
Refugee Council of Australia. 2021. https://www.refugeecouncil.org.au/stop-the-boats/. Accessed September 8, 2021.
Refugee Council of Australia. 2021a. https://www.refugeecouncil.org.au/statelessness-australia/2/. Accessed September 8, 2021.
Reicher, Stephen. 2001. "The Psychology of Crowd Dynamics." In *Blackwell Handbook of Social Psychology: Group Processes*, edited by Michal A. Hogg and R. Scott Tindale, pp. 182–208. Malden, MA. and Oxford: Blackwell Publishers.
Republican Voters Against Trump. 2020. https://rvat.org/. Accessed September 9, 2021.
Rettberg, Jill Walker. 2014. *Seeing Ourselves through Technology: How We Use Selfies, Blogs and Wearable Devices to See and Shape Ourselves*. London: Palgrave Macmillian. doi: 10.1057/9781137476661.
Reuters. 2021. "Fact Check: NASA Did Not 'Admit Man-Made Climate Change Is a Hoax." NASA. February 2, 2021. https://www.reuters.com/article/uk-factcheck-nasa-climate-change-idUSKBN2AI2KX Accessed August 19, 2021.
Ricoeur, Paul. 2009. *Hermeneutics and the Human Sciences*. Paris: Cambridge University Press.
Rienstra, Byron, and Derek Hook. 2006. "Weakening Habermas: The Undoing of Communicative Rationality." *Politikon: South African Journal of Political Studies*, 33(3), 313–339. doi: 10.1080/02589340601122950.
Ritchie, Donald A. 1998. "Investigating the Watergate Scandal." *OAH Magazine of History*, 12(4), 49–53.
Robertson, Shanthi. 2015. "Contractualization, depoliticization and the limits of solidarity: noncitizens in contemporary Australia." *Citizenship Studies* 19(8), 936–950.
Robinson, Fiona. 2011. "Stop Talking and Listen: Discourse Ethics and Feminist Care Ethics in International Political Theory." *Millennium: Journal of International Studies*, 39(3), 845–860.
Maia, Rousiley CM. 2018. "Politicisation and Depoliticisation within the Deliberative System: assessing interactions and tensions of political communication." *Les Enjeux de l'information et de la communication*, 183(S1), 149–160.
Rowe, Emma, Christopher Lubienski, Andrew Skourdoumbis, Jessica Gerrard, and David Hursh. 2019. "Templates, Typologies and Typifications: Neoliberalism as

Keyword." *Discourse: Studies in the Cultural Politics of Education*, 40(2), 150–161. https://doi.org/10.1080/01596306.2019.1569875.

Rubin, Charles T. 1994. *The Green Crusade: Rethinking the Roots of Environmentalism*. New York: Free Press.

Rubin, David M., and David P Sachs. 1973. *Mass Media and the Environment: Water Resources, Land Use and Atomic Energy in California*. New York: Praeger.

Rubenstein, Jennifer, Dovi, Suzanne, Pineda, Erin R., Woodly, Deva, Kirshner, Alexander S., El Amine, Loubna, and Muirhead, Russell. 2018. "Political and Ethical Action in The Age of Trump." *Contemporary Political Theory*, (17), 331–362.

Sales, Rosemary. 2002. "The Deserving and the Undeserving? Refugees, Asylum Seekers and Welfare in Britain." *Critical Social Policy*, 22(3), 456–478.

Sandman, Peter M. 1993. *Responding to Community Outrage: Strategies for Effective Risk Communication*. American Industrial Hygiene Association. http://petersandman.com/media/RespondingtoCommunityOutrage.pdf.

Scanlon Foundation Research Institute. 2018. "A Changing Australia: How Migration Is Shaping the Nation." https://scanloninstitute.org.au/sites/default/files/2020-01/Sept2018_Scanlon-Institute_Narrative-1.pdf.

Schneider, Nathan. 2007. *Neoliberal Political Economy and the Religious Revival*. Department of Religious Studies University of California, Santa Barbara. http://citeseerx.ist.psu.edu/viewdoc/download?doi=10.1.1.538.8215&rep=rep1&type=pdf Accessed August 6, 2021.

Schneiider, Jen, Steve Schwarze, Peter K. Bsumek, and Jennifer Peeples. 2016. *Under Pressure: Coal Industry Rhetoric and Neoliberalism*. Palgrave Studies in Media and Environmental Communication. London: Palgrave Macmillan.

Selvage, James P. 1942. "A Look Ahead at Public Relations." New York, November 4, Box 104, Folder 8, George E. Sokolsky Papers, Hoover Institution Archives.

Shabecoff, Philip. 1988 "Global Warming Has Begun, Expert Tells Senate." *New York Times*. June 24, 1988. https://www.nytimes.com/1988/06/24/us/global-warming-has-begun-expert-tells-senate.html. Accessed September 98, 2021.

Shaw, Adam. 2019. "Trump Slams Open-Border Activists for 'Evil' Agenda, Decries Iran 'Bloodlust' in Fiery UN Speech." *Fox News*. September 24, 2019. https://www.foxnews.com/politics/trump-to-tout-nationalism-un-general-assembly Accessed September 23, 2021.

Sheppard, Kate. 2014. "World's Biggest Coal Company, World's Biggest PR Firm Pair Up to Promote Coal for Poor People." *The Huffington Post*. March 29, 2014. http://www.huffingtonpost.com.au/entry/peabody-burson-marstellar-coal_n_5044962 Accessed January 25, 2017.

Shergold, Peter, Kerrin Benson, and Margaret Piper. February 2019. "Investing in Refugees, Investing in Australia: The Findings of a Review into Integration, Employment and Settlement Outcomes for Refugees and Humanitarian Entrants in Australia." Commonwealth of Australia, Department of the Prime Minister and Cabinet. https://www.homeaffairs.gov.au/reports-and-pubs/files/review-integration-employment-settlement-outcomes-refugees-humanitarian-entrants.pdf.

Shevory, Thomas. 2007. *Toxic Burn: The Grassroots Struggle against the WTI Incinerator*. Minneapolis: University of Minnesota Press.

Şimşek, Doğuş. 2021. "Winners and losers of neoliberalism": the intersection of class and race in the case of Syrian refugees in Turkey." *Ethnic and Racial Studies*, 44(15), 2816–2835. https://doi.org/10.1080/01419870.2020.1854812.

Skocpol, Theda, and Alexander Hertel-Fernandez. 2016. "The Koch Network and Republican Party Extremism." *American Political Science Association*, 14(3), 681–699.

Skrdlik, Josef, and Maya Beney. 2021. "Alexander Betts: Human Displacement Will Be One of Our Defining Challenges This Century." *Varsity*. April 9, 2021. https://www.varsity.co.uk/interviews/21180. Accessed September 20, 2021.

Somers, Margaret. 2020. "The Moral Economy of the Capitalist Crowd: Utopianism, the Reality of Society, and the Market as a Morally Instituted Process in Karl Polanyi's The Great Transformation." *Humanity: An International Journal of Human Rights, Humanitarianism, and Development*, 11, 227–234. 10.1353/hum.2020.0017.

Smith, David N. 2019. "Authoritarianism Reimagined: The Riddle of Trump's Base." *The Sociological Quarterly*, 60(2), 210–223.

Snow, Nancy, and Philip M. Taylor. 2006. "The Revival of the Propaganda State US Propaganda at Home and Abroad since 9/11." *The International Communication Gazette*, 68(5–6), 389–407. doi: 10.1177/1748048506068718.

Stedman Jones, Daniel. 2012. *Masters of the Universe: Hayek, Friedman and the Birth of Neoliberal Politics*. Princeton, NJ, and Oxford: Princeton University Press.

Steger, Manfred B., and Ravi K. Roy. 2010. *Neoliberalism: A Very Short Introduction*. Oxford: Oxford University Press.

Surma, Anne, and Demetrious, Kristin. 2018. "Plastic Words, Public Relations and the Neoliberal Transformation of Twentieth Century Discourse." *Ethical Space: The International Journal of Communication Ethics*, 15(1–2), 92–107.

Tamboukou, Maria. 2013. "A Foucauldian Approach to Narratives." In *Doing Narrative Research*, edited by M. Andrews, C Squire, & M. Tamboukou, pp. 88–107. London: Sage Publications. https://www-doi-org.ezproxy-b.deakin.edu.au/10.4135/9781526402271

Tarrow, Sidney. 1988. "National Politics and Collective Action: Recent Theory and Research in Western Europe and the United States." *Annual Review of Sociology* 14, 421–440.

Tchilingirian, Jordan Soukias. 2018. "Producing Knowledge, Producing Credibility: British Think-Tank Researchers and the Construction of Policy Reports." *International Journal of Politics, Culture, and Society*, 31, 161–178.

Tedlow, Richard S. 1976. "The National Association of Manufactures and Public Relations During the New Deal." *The Business History Review*, 50(1), 25–45.

The Bolt Report. 2013. "Transcript of Interview with Andrew Bolt: The Bolt Report: 16 June 2013: Asylum Seekers." https://parlinfo.aph.gov.au/parlInfo/search/display/display.w3p;query=Id%3A%22media%2Fpressrel%2F2527534%22. Accessed September 8, 2021.

The Corporation. 2003. Mark Achbar, Jennifer Abbott, and Joel Bakan. Big Picture Media Corporation. Zeitgeist Films.

The Museum of Public Relations. 2021. https://m.facebook.com/PRMuseum/posts/948487048581802.

Thoms, Oskar N. T., and Ron James. 2007. "Do Human Rights Violations Cause Internal Conflict?" *Human Rights Quarterly*, 29, 674–705.

Tucker, Jeffery A. 2009. "Hazlitt and the Great Depression." *Mises Institute*. https://mises.org/library/hazlitt-and-great-depression Accessed September 7, 2021.

Tumarkin, Maria. 2018. *Axiomatic*. Melbourne: Brow Books.

Turner, Bryan S., ed. 1993. *Citizenship and Social Theory*. Vol. 24. Sage.

Turner, Graeme. 2021. "First Contact: Reading Raymond Williams." *European Journal of Cultural Studies*, 24(4), 1030–34. https://doi.org/10.1177/13675494211026335.

Trump, Donald. 2020. "Donald Trump Immigration Speech Transcript, August 18: Yuma, Arizona." https://www.rev.com/blog/transcripts/donald-trump-immigration-speech-transcript-august-18-yuma-arizona. Accessed September 8, 2021.

UNHCR. 2021. "What Is Statelessness." https://www.unhcr.org/ibelong/wp-content/uploads/UNHCR-Statelessness-2pager-ENG.pdf. Accessed September 8, 2021.

Union of Concerned Scientists. 2009. "Debunking Misinformation about Stolen Climate Emails in the 'Climategate' Manufactured Controversy." Reports and Multimedia: Explainer. December 8, 2009; updated August 25, 2011. https://www.ucsusa.org/resources/debunking-misinformation-about-stolen-climate-emails. Accessed September 8, 2021.

United Nations. 2019. *Report of the Secretary-General on the 2019 Climate Action Summit and the Way Forward in 2020*. December 11, 2019. https://www.un.org/en/climatechange/assets/pdf/cas_report_11_dec.pdf.

Universal Declaration of Human Rights. 1948. https://www.un.org/en/about-us/universal-declaration-of-human-rights.

University of Pittsburgh. 2016. *Keywords Project*. https://keywords.pitt.edu.

Vidal, John. 2013. "Margaret Thatcher: An Unlikely Green Hero?" *The Guardian*. September 4, 2013. https://www.theguardian.com/environment/blog/2013/apr/09/margaret-thatcher-green-hero. Accessed September 8, 2021.

Vieten, Ulrike M. 2020. "The 'New Normal' and 'Pandemic Populism': The COVID-19 Crisis and Anti-Hygienic Mobilisation of the Far-Right." *Social Sciences*, 9(9), 165. https://doi.org/10.3390/socsci9090165.

von Mises, Margit. 1976. *My Years with Ludwig von Mises*. New Rochelle, NY: Arlington House. https://cdn.mises.org/My%20Years%20with%20Ludwig%20von%20Mises_2.pdf

Wardhani, Tara, Kukuh and Baiq Wardhani. 2021. "Domestic Politics Analysis on Australia Turning Back Boat Policy." *Proceedings of Airlangga Conference on International Relations (ACIR 2018)—Politics, Economy, and Security in Changing Indo-Pacific Region*, 588–594. doi: 10.5220/0010280705880594.

Warf, Barney. 2021. "The Coronavirus Pandemic and American Neoliberalism." *Geographical Review*, 111(4), 496–509, doi: 10.1080/00167428.2021.1884981. https://doi.org/10.1080/00167428.2021.1884981

Watts, Anthony. 2009. "Breaking News Story: CRU Has Apparently Been Hacked: Hundreds of Files Released." *WUWT: Watts Up With That*. November 19, 2009. https://wattsupwiththat.com/2009/11/19/breaking-news-story-hadley-cru-has-apparently-been-hacked-hundreds-of-files-released/. Accessed September 8, 2021.

White, Ben. 2020. "Virus Panic Update." *Politico*. February 27, 2020. https://www.politico.com/newsletters/morning-money/2020/02/27/virus-panic-update-785714. Accessed September 9, 2021.

White, Charles M. 1946. "Mr. Leonard E. Read, President, Foundation for Economic Education Inc New York." Exhibit B-11. Hearings Before the House Select Committee on Lobbying, Direct and Indirect, Volume 3, Parts 7–10. https://books.google.com.au/books?id=eaeU2iVbweEC&pg=RA1-PA67&lpg=RA1-PA67&dq=Leonard+E+Read+Hill+and+Knowlton&source=bl&ots=e-vtsikWyJ&sig=ACfU3U0qSM0AzQ1Hfs7PJe2VdgRsZDslbg&hl=en&sa=X&ved=2ahUKEwj7vLqW95PoAhX383MBHck3DLkQ6AEwAXoECA4QAQ#v=onepage&q=%20Hill%20and%20Knowlton&f=false. Accessed September 7, 2021.

White, Damian Finbar, Alan P. Rudy, and Chris Wilbert. 2007. "Anti-Environmentalism: Prometheans, Contrarians and Beyond." In The Sage Handbook of Environment and Society, edited by Jules Pretty, Andy Ball, Ted Benton, Julia Guivant, David R. Lee, David Orr, Max Pheffer, and Hugh Ward, pp. 124–141. London: Sage Publications.

Whyte, Jessica. 2017. "Human Rights and the Collateral Damage of Neoliberalism." *Theory & Event*, 20(1), 137–151.

Wilcox, Denis L., and Glen T. Cameron. 2012. *Public Relations Strategies and Tactics*, 10th edition. Glenview, IL: Pearson Education.

Winston, Brian. 2020. "Find Me a Four-Year-Old Child': Journalistic Ethics in a Time of Plague." *Ethical Space: The International Journal of Communication Ethics*, 17(3–4), 52–60.

Wisconsin Historical Society. 2021. "The Great Forces Shaping Our Future." https://www.wisconsinhistory.org/Records/Image/IM77586 . Accessed September 7, 2021.

World Economic Survey. 2013. "Chapter II Strategies for Development and Transformation." https://www.un.org/development/desa/dpad/wp-content/uploads/sites/45/Chapter2.pdf. Accessed September 8, 2021.

Wrenn, Mary. 2014. "Identity, Identity Politics, and Neoliberalism." *Panoeconomicus*, 61(4), 503–515.

Wrenn, Mary V. 2016. "Immanent Critique, Enabling Myths, and the Neoliberal Narrative." *Review of Radical Political Economics*, 48(3), 452–466.

Wrenn, Mary V., and William R. Waller. 2017. "Care and the Neoliberal Individual." *Journal of Economic Issues*, 52(2), 495–502. doi: 10.1080/00213624.2017.1321438.

Wright, Handly J., and Byron H. Christian. 1949. *Public Relations in Management*. New York, London, and Toronto: McGraw-Hill.

Zarzosa, Helia López. 2020. "Immigration Detention Through Time." http://www.against-inhumanity.org/wp-content/uploads/2020/05/Lopez-Immigration-Detention-Through-Time-UAI-UK.pdf.

INDEX

For the benefit of digital users, indexed terms that span two pages (e.g., 52–53) may, on occasion, appear on only one of those pages.

Advanced Energy for Life (AEFL) campaign, 181–83
Advertising Standards Authority (ASA), 181–83
alt-right politics, 20–21, 162–63
American Coalition for Clean Coal Energy, 182–83
American Enterprise Institute, 129–30
"The American Family Robinson" (radio program), 55–56
American Legislative Exchange Council, 182–83
Anzaldúa, Gloria, 148–51, 153, 167, 170–71
Australia
  alt-right politics in, 20–21
  climate change denial in, 112–13
  immigration policy in, 151n.10, 158–65, 168
  mining in, 93–94
  neoliberal governments in, 19–20
  offshore immigration detention facilities and, 159–60, 163–64
  public relations industry in, 72–73
Australian Greens, 93–94

Ball, Stephen, 13–14n.10, 23–24
Bancroft, Corinne, 85–86
Barbulescu, Roxana, 165–66
Bartzen Culver, Kathleen, 185–86
Beck, Ulrich, 122n.36, 141–43
Bell, Allan, 121–22
Berman and Company, 182–83
Bernays, Edward L., 25–28
A Blueprint for Survival (Goldsmith), 120n.30
Bonchek, Mark, 85–86
"boat people," 161–62
borderlands
  as conceptual space, 9–10
  free enterprise and, 151
  hegemony and, 153–54
  human rights and, 170–71
  neoliberalism and, 9–10, 148–51, 153–54, 201
  noncitizens and, 168
  public relations language and, 148–50, 153–54, 170–71
  statelessness and, 167–70
  US–Mexico border and, 148–51, 153, 171–74
boundary riders, 28–29
Bradley, Megan, 167–68
braided narratives, 85–87, 96–97, 98, 105
Brant, Karl, 68

Bricker, Brett Jacob, 135–36
Brown, Wendy, 22–23, 36n.90, 41–42, 106
Brulle, Robert, 145–46
Burson-Marsteller, 181–82

Cantú, Francisco, 149n.6, 171–74
Carson, Rachel, 111n.6, 117–18
Cato Institute, 129–30
Champ, Michael A., 116–17
Chemical Manufacturers Association, 117
China, 178–80
chlorofluorocarbons (CFCs), 11n.3
citizenship by investment schemes, 164–66
Clean Air Act, 122–23
clean coal, 124–25, 181–83
Clean Water Act, 122–23
climate change. *See also* climate change denial; Climategate
  agricultural practices and, 113–14
  anthropogenic theories regarding, 9, 111–14, 122–23, 126–27, 132–35, 136–37
  extreme weather events and, 113–14, 127–28
  fossil fuels and, 113–14
  global risks posed by, 146–47
  Intergovernmental Panel on Climate Change (IPCC) report and, 111–12, 113–14, 133–35
  mitigation policies regarding, 112–13, 121–22
  refugees created by, 31, 148n.1
climate change denial
  conservative media and, 130–32
  conservative think tanks and, 129–30
  corporate profits and, 145–46
  definition of, 109n.1
  free enterprise and, 112–13, 126–27, 133–35
  "game of telling" and, 129–32
  neoliberalism and, 9, 109–11, 112–15, 117, 126–31, 133–35, 144, 201
  nostalgia and, 144–45
  oil companies and, 110n.4
  plastic words and, 9, 115–16
  policy time and energy absorbed by, 112–13, 129
  public relations industry and, 9, 114–15, 121–22, 128, 144–46
  scientists' motives questioned in, 127–28
  separation of "human" and "nature" as component of, 114, 126–27, 143
Climategate
  anti-elitism and, 135–36
  Climate Research Unit and, 133–35, 140–41
  criminal act leading to disclosure of, 133
  Delingpole on, 133–39
  exoneration of scientists involved in, 138–39
  leaked emails and, 133–35
  media coverage of, 137–39, 141
  misrepresentation at heart of, 141
  neonarrative and, 136–37, 140–41
  plastic words and, 138–39
  United Nations Climate Change Conference (2009) and, 133–35
Colloque Walter Lippmann (1938), 51–52
Competitive Enterprises Institute (CEI), 129–30
coronavirus pandemic
  China and, 178–80
  Corona Big Book and, 178–81
  disinformation and, 200
  limitations of public language during, 10, 198–99
  Republican Party and, 178, 180–81
  US healthcare system and, 177–78
  US societal division and, 86n.42
  World Health Organization and, 178–79
Cronin, Anne, 43–44
Curry Jansen, Sue, 36–37, 40–41

Dale, Sarah, 169–70
Dao, André, 175–76
Davies, William, 100n.92
Davis, Will, 38
Dean, Jodi, 14n.11, 14n.12, 44–45, 91n.57, 106n.108, 199–200
Debord, Guy, 75–76

Index

deep canvassing, 183–84, 189–92, 197–98
Delingpole, James, 132, 136–41, 144–45
democracy
  digital communication and, 1–2, 200
  free enterprise and, 45
  mass communication societies and, 25–28
  neodemocracy and, 199–200
  neoliberalism and, 22–23, 41–42, 56–57, 106
  public language and, 7–8, 12–13
  social inequality and, 191, 197–98
  transparency and, 41
Denord, François, 51–52
Dilts, Andrew, 195
Dinan, William, 53–54
Drucker, Peter F., 17–18, 23–24, 38, 44–45, 191–92
Dunlap, Riley E., 129–30
Dutton, Peter, 162–63
Dwyer, Thomas James, 72–73

Eagleton-Pierce, Matthew, 141–42
EB-5 immigration visa (United States), 164
"ecological PR," 118–22, 124–25
Edelman, Richard, 40
Effron, Malcah, 86–87
Endangered Species Act, 122–23
Eric White and Associates, 72
ethical neutrality, 200–1

Fessmann, Jasper, 196–97
First Amendment, 43–44
Fleisher, Dave, 189
Foucault, Michel
  concept formation and, 157–58
  concomitance and, 164–67
  discourse analysis and, 5, 12n.5, 101–2, 162–63, 169–70
  knowledge production and, 81–82
  positivism and, 89n.51
Foundation for Economic Education (FEE)
  establishment (1946) of, 66n.72
  Hill and Knolton and, 66–67

  Mont Pèlerin Society and, 54–55
  publications by, 48, 65–66, 68–69
  Read and, 62–64, 65–66, 68–69, 71–72
  Republic Steel Corporation and, 66–67
Fox News, 32–33, 34–35n.86, 180, 187–88
Franczak, Liz, 25–28
freedom
  climate change denial and, 127–28
  consumer goods and, 89–90
  neoliberalism and, 114
  as neonarrative, 90–92
  as "plastic word," 89–96
free enterprise
  climate change denial and, 112–13, 126–27, 133–35
  democracy and, 45
  Mont Pèlerin Society's role in promoting, 5–6, 47–48, 51–52
  neoliberalism and, 6–7, 18–19, 22–23, 47–48, 76–77
  neonarratives and, 90–92
  public relations industry and, 45, 59
  Selvage on, 58–59
Freeman, R. Edward, 121–22
free society, 60, 61–62, 64, 128, 156
Friedman, Milton, 54–55, 64–65, 70–71

Giroux, Henry A., 78
Global Climate Coalition, 122–23
Global Financial Crisis (2007-8), 20–21
Global War on Terror, 43–44
Graham, Lindsey, 180
Grand Old Party (GOP). *See* Republican Party
Great Depression (1929-41), 18–19, 49–50
greenwashing, 124–25
Gregoire, Paul, 161–62
Grunig, James E., 118–19

Habermas, Jürgen
  civil society and, 190
  communicative action and, 33–34, 42–43, 44–45
  knowledge formation and, 43–44
  public sphere and, 16, 38–39, 78–79

Hale, Charles R., 156–57
Hansen, James E., 122–23
Harrison, E. Bruce, 121n.34, 124–25
Hawke, Bob, 19–20
Hayek, Friedrich August von
   Colloque Walter Lippmann and, 51–52
   free enterprise promoted by, 60–61, 71
   free society promoted by, 60, 62
   on intellectuals and neoliberalism and, 60–62
   Mont Pèlerin Society and, 5–6, 8–9, 18–19, 47–48, 51–52, 60–61
   on prices and communication, 65
   public relations industry and, 71–72, 80n.17
   Read and, 67–68
   socialism opposed by, 61–62, 69
   Universal Declaration of Human Rights and, 156
Hazlitt, Henry, 53–54, 56–57, 65–66, 67–68
Heartland Institute, 129–30
Held, Virginia, 187
Herrnstein Smith, Barbara, 97–98
Higgs, Robert, 57–58
Hill, John W., 49–50, 55–56. *See also* Hill and Knowlton
Hill and Knowlton, 50n.13, 51, 54–55, 66–67, 72
Holborow, Marnie, 191–92
Holmgren, Lindsay, 82–83
Hook, Derek, 33–34
Hoover, Joe, 154–55
Hudson, Marc, 112–13

"I, Pencil" (Read), 48, 63–65
Institute of Economic Affairs, 129–30
Institute of Public Affairs, 129–30
"The Intellectuals and Socialism" (Hayek), 48, 60–63
Intergovernmental Panel on Climate Change (IPCC), 111–12, 113–14, 133–35
Iraq War (2003-12), 44–45

Jacques, Peter J., 129–30
Jafari, Jamila, 175–76

Johnston, Jane, 196
Jones, Andrew, 21n.36
Jones, Phil, 140–41

Kasper, Matt, 182–83
Keating, AnaLouise, 153–54
Keating, Paul, 19–20
Kelly, Kathleen, 177–78
Keynes, John Maynard, 19–20, 49–50, 68–69
Kingston, Lindsey N., 167–68
Koch Network, 34–35n.86, 185, 187
Koether, George, 90n.53
Kolić Stanić, Matilda, 193–94

Lamme, Margot Opdycke, 4–5
Le Bon, Gustave, 27n.63
Lee Jr., Morris M., 55–56
L'Etang, Jacquie, 2–3, 194–95
The Limits to Growth (Club of Rome report), 120–21
Lippmann, Walter, 25–28, 65n.71
"A Look Ahead at Public Relations" (Selvage), 48, 58–60
Lytle, Mark Hamilton, 117

MacPherson, Crawford Brough, 191
Mäkelä, Maria, 83–84, 87
Manus Island detention center, 163–64
Marshall Institute, 129–30
Mavelli, Luca, 162–63, 165–66
Michaels, Patrick, 131n.68
Miller, David, 53–54
Minerals Council of Australia, 93–94
Mirowski, Philip, 62–63, 129, 201
Moen, Torill, 174
The Monkey Wrench Gang (Abbey), 120–21
Mont Pèlerin Society (MPS)
   Colloque Lippmann and, 67–68
   first American meeting (1958) of, 54–55
   founding (1947) of, 47–48, 202
   free enterprise promoted by, 5–6, 47–48, 51–52
   Hayek as founder and president of, 5–6, 8–9, 18–19, 47–48, 51–52, 60–61
   Hazlitt and, 53–54

Index

limited government promoted by, 51–52
neoliberalism promoted by, 5–6, 18–19, 47–48, 52–53, 79–81
personal liberty promoted by, 51–52
public relations industry and, 8–9, 18–19
US participants in, 51–52, 54–55, 69–70
Morrison, Scott, 162

National Association of Manufacturers (NAM), 50–53, 54–56
Nauru detention center, 163–64
neoliberalism. *See also* neonarratives
alienation and, 195–96
alt-right politics and, 162–63
borderlands and, 9–10, 148–51, 153–54, 201
climate change denial and, 9, 112–13, 129–30, 133–35, 144, 201
as "common sense," 6–7, 22–23, 77–78
communicative role of language undermined by, 13–14, 35, 43–44
democracy and, 22–23, 41–42, 56–57, 106
digital communication and, 199–200
freedom and, 114
free enterprise and, 6–7, 18–19, 22–23, 47–48, 76–77
Global Financial Crisis and, 20–21
globalization and, 36–37
Great Depression and, 18–19, 46–47
hegemony and, 14–15, 40, 79–81, 84, 175–76
human rights and, 156–57
immigration policy and, 164–65
limited government and, 76–77
media voices promoting, 115
Mont Pèlerin Society and, 5–6, 18–19, 47–48, 52–53, 79–81
plastic words and, 56–57, 76–78, 141–42
political leaders promoting, 19–20
publics and, 14–15, 71, 139–40
tensions within, 69–71
think tanks promoting, 19–20
transnational nature of, 6–7, 47–48
university education and, 23–24

neonarratives
climate change denial and, 109–11, 113–15, 117, 126–28, 130–31, 135
communication restricted by, 78, 109–10
freedom and, 90–92
free enterprise and, 90–92
goal-oriented nature of, 103
hegemony and, 98–99
nationalism and, 164
nation state, prosperity, and exclusion, 151, 160–61
nostalgia and, 128
plastic words and, 8–9, 92–93, 96–103
public relations industry and, 79–81, 110, 114–15
public sphere and, 86–87
New Deal, 48–50, 53–54
The New Realities (Drucker), 17–18, 191–92
Nuccitelli, Dana, 141

O'Donnell & Associates, Strategic Communications, 178–79
Ong, Aihwa, 151–52
O'Reilly, Bill, 131–32, 144–45
Ott, Brian, 186
ozone layer, 11n.3, 121–22

Peabody Energy, 126n.54, 181–83
Peck, Jamie, 22, 99–100
Peters, Chris, 131–32, 139–40
Phelan, James, 25n.55, 82, 96–97, 132, 136–37
Phillips-Fein, Kim, 52–53, 67–68
Pieczka, Magda, 196
plastic words
brutality masked by, 92–93, 143
climate change denial and, 9, 115–16
communication thwarted by, 6–7, 95–96, 101–2
"development" and, 158–60
"environment" and, 115–16
ethical elision and, 100–1, 106–7
"freedom" and, 89–96
as "master key to every day," 90–92
modular character of, 93, 106–7, 140–41

plastic words (*cont.*)
   neoliberalism and, 56–57, 76–78, 141–42
   neonarratives and, 8–9, 92–93, 96–103
   occupation of higher spheres by, 6–7
   proliferation of, 6–7, 38–39, 92–93
   public relations industry and, 35, 39–40, 88–89
   publics and, 43–44
   technocratic framing and, 101–2
   temporality and, 99–100
   utopian tenor of, 99–100
Poerksen, Uwe, 6–7, 39–40, 88–89, 93–95, 99, 140–41, 158–59, 200
pollution
   chemicals industry and, 117
   "ecological PR" and, 118–22
   emergence of the word, 115–16
   human activity and, 116–17, 120–21
   impetus for changing humans' relations with nature and, 121–22, 126–27
   legislation to address, 122–24
   media coverage of, 116–17
populism
   immigration policy and, 161–62
   market-based distortions and the rise of, 33–34
   public debate and, 6–7
   Trump and, 13n.9, 190
positivism, 89–90
Proof Integrated Communications, 181–82
public interest communication (PIC), 196–98
public relations
   academic legitimization of, 30
   borderlands and, 148–50, 153–54, 170–71
   boundary riders and, 28–29
   civil society and, 123–25
   communicative role of language undermined by, 35, 38
   coronavirus communications and, 178–81
   corporate interests advanced via, 25–28, 31, 40, 117
   digital communication and, 181
   "ecological PR" and, 118–22, 124–25

   ethics and, 4, 193–95, 197, 199–200
   extrinsic and intrinsic practices in, 4–6, 103–7, 115, 202
   free enterprise advocacy and, 45, 59
   globalization and, 36–37
   hegemony and, 4, 15–16, 29
   human rights and, 9–10
   neonarratives and, 79–81, 110, 114–15
   plastic words and, 35, 39–40, 88–89
   publics created by, 82–83, 144
   risk communication and, 125–26
   secrecy and, 43–44
Public Relations, Activism and Social Change: Speaking Up (Demetrious), 4
publics
   elite overtures to, 25–28
   immigration policy and, 162–64
   neoliberalism and the establishment of, 14–15, 71, 139–40
   plastic words and, 43–44
   public relations and the creation of, 82–83, 144
   Selvage on, 55–56
Pugh, Michael, 152

Rea, Jeannie, 23–24
Read, Leonard E.
   Foundation for Economic Education and, 62–64, 65–66, 68–69, 71–72
   free enterprise promoted by, 63–65, 69
   Hayek and, 67–68
   on "Invisible Hand" of the market, 63–65
   limited government promoted by, 65
   Mont Pèlerin Society and, 71–72
   socialism opposed by, 69
   von Mises and, 68
   White and, 70–71
Reagan, Ronald, 19–20
Republican Party
   anti-environmental movement and, 122–23
   coronavirus and, 178, 180–81
   Koch network and, 185, 187
   public relations industry and, 188

Republican Voters Against Trump (RVAT) and, 183–88, 192
Republic Steel, 66–67
Ricoeur, Paul, 81, 82n.26, 115n.15, 127–28, 138
Rienstra, Byron, 33–34
risk communication, 125–26
Robinson, Fiona, 78–79
Robinson, Katie, 169–70
Roofs and Ceilings (Friedman and Stigler), 70–71
Roosevelt, Franklin D., 48–50
Rousiley, C. M. Maia, 39n.99
Rubin, Charles T., 118–19
Russell, Karen Miller, 4–5

Sandman, Peter M., 125–26
Selvage, James P., 48, 55–57, 58–60
Shabecoff, Philip, 122–23
Sheppard, Kate, 181–82
Silent Spring (Carson), 117–18
Smith, Adam, 65
Snow, Nancy, 43–44
The Society of Spectacle (Debord), 75–76
Somers, Margaret R., 167–68
spin, 25, 199–200, 202
statelessness, 167–70
Stigler, George, 70–71
strategic narratives, 85–86

Tamboukou, Maria, 81–82
Taylor, Philip, 43–44
Thatcher, Margaret, 19–20, 145n.122
Theodore, Nik, 22, 99–100
think tanks, 19–20, 48, 54–55, 63–64, 106–7, 129–31, 151–52, 182–83, 193
Trump, Donald
  base of voters supporting, 32, 184–85, 187–88
  coronavirus pandemic and, 178, 180–81
  immigration policy and, 170–71, 186
  partisan media sources supporting, 32, 187–88
  political polarization and, 186
  populist communication style of, 13n.9, 190
  presidential election (2020) and, 184–86, 189
  Republican Voters Against Trump and, 183–88, 192
  Twitter and, 186
Tumarkin, Maria, 100n.91
Turner, Bryan S., 166–67
Turner, Graeme, 1–2, 6–7

United Kingdom, 20–21
United Nations Climate Change Conference (Copenhagen, 2009), 133–35
United Nations High Commissioner for Refugees (UNHCR), 168–70
Universal Declaration of Human Rights (UDHR), 154–56, 170–71
US–Mexico border, 148–51, 153, 171–74

von Mises, Ludwig, 8–9, 51–52, 54–55, 62–63, 68, 90n.53

Watts, Anthony, 140–41
Werthman, Carter, 145–46
White, Charles, 66–67, 70–71
Whyte, Jessica, 155, 156–57
Williams Jr., A. D., 65–66
Wise Men association, 55–56
World Health Organization (WHO), 178–79
Wrenn, Mary, 195–96, 197–98